"Shakespeare and Swedenborg are both Titans. In the presence of such giants, small men seem to wither and blow away . . . "   —ELBERT HUBBARD.

EMANUEL·SWEDENBORG

SWEDENBORG

LIFE AND TEACHING

by

GEORGE TROBRIDGE

The present edition is a sixth reprint of the 1935 (Fourth) Edition of the Swedenborg Society of London. The courtesy of the Swedenborg Society is hereby acknowledged in permitting the publication of the book in this country.

1968

SWEDENBORG FOUNDATION

INCORPORATED

NEW YORK

The portrait of Swedenborg is from a crayon drawing by Torsten Schonberg, one of a series of Sweden's great men commissioned by the Swedish authorities on the occasion of Stockholm's World Fair 1930.

Manufactured in U. S. A. by
Kingsport Press, Inc., Kingsport, Tennessee

PREFACE TO FOURTH EDITION

GEORGE TROBRIDGE's *Life of Emanuel Swedenborg* was first published, under the auspices of the Swedenborg Society, in 1907. A second edition, enlarged and supplied with illustrations, was issued in 1920. A third edition, abridged, in paper covers, appeared in 1930.

In preparing this, the fourth edition, for the press, it was found that the last twenty-five years have produced such vital changes in general outlook, that such a book, written as it was for a pre-war world, would ill serve its author's purpose to-day unless it were brought up to date. The intervening years have seen not only scientific discoveries that have revolutionized our conceptions of the universe, not only economic and social changes that have given religious thought a new focus and a new direction, but also a subtle, yet pervasive modification in the methods of writing, and even in the associations of words themselves.

To give the book a more modern "manner" has been therefore, the revisor's aim, in addition to making such corrections as most revisions necessitate, and these latter proved more numerous than usual in such cases. It has not been easy. It has entailed an unexpected amount of emendation, pruning and re-phrasing. Here and there the changes had to be drastic. Yet, the book is still Trobridge's *Life of Swedenborg,* in plan, in substance, and in execution.

What has been done by the revisor has been no more, in his opinion, than the author himself, if he were still in this world, would approve as being necessary in order that the book may, at this day, serve the purpose for which it was written.

A large number of passages in inverted commas throughout the book bear no reference to their source. In practically every case they are taken from Dr. R. L. Tafel's *Documents Concerning Swedenborg,* a collection embracing every item of authentic information procurable by its compiler in Sweden, England, Germany, America, etc.

The few remaining cases refer to scattered items of information which came to light after Dr. Tafel's collection was published.   E. C. M.

September, 1935.

CONTENTS

SWEDENBORG

CHAPTER I

SWEDENBORG'S ANCESTRY AND EARLY LIFE

WONDER has been expressed at Swedenborg's turning from natural science to theology in middle life; heredity might have had something to do with his interest in both subjects. His father was an eminent Lutheran bishop, and so he was reared in a theological atmosphere; while his grandfathers on both sides of the family were connected with the great mining industry of Sweden. Daniel Isaacsson, the father of Bishop Swedberg was a miner and mineowner at Fahlun, who rose from comparative poverty to affluence by a successful mining venture. Albrecht Behm, Swedenborg's maternal grandfather, had occupied a similar position at the Board of Mines to that which he himself held later.

The variety of names in the same family is explained by the custom of adopting new surnames, sometimes from the family seat, in place of the usual patronymic, and from the change of title brought about by the ennoblement of the Swedberg family. The sons of Daniel Isaacsson called themselves Swedberg from the name of their homestead, "Sweden"; while Swedberg was again changed, to Swedenborg, when the bishop's family was ennobled by Queen Ulrica Eleonora in 1719.

Jesper Swedberg was the second son of Daniel Isaacsson, and was born in 1653. His parents, who were pious people, devoted him to the Church, and he was ordained in 1682. He was appointed Chaplain of the Horse Guards in that year, Court Chaplain in 1686, Dean and Pastor of Vingåker in 1690, Professor in Upsala University in 1692, Dean of Upsala in 1694, and Bishop of Skara in 1702, which last office he held for thirty-three years. He was a man of upright and pious life, an indefatigable worker, and an enthusiastic reformer; one, in fact, whose exemplary conduct and untiring zeal made him conspicuous among his less earnest and more careless brethren. "If he had lived a few hundred years earlier," wrote one of his contemporaries, "he might have increased the number of Swedish saints . . . his learning, industry, exemplary life, good intentions, and zeal for God's glory deserve to be venerated even by a more enlightened century." He was active in the cause of education, whether as army chaplain, when he offered a premium to every soldier who learned to read, or later as professor of theology, and afterwards rector, in Upsala University. He endeavoured to reform the teaching in the public schools, composing and editing many textbooks himself; and in every way exerted himself to promote the advancement of learning.

Although Sweden was a Protestant country, the study of the Bible had fallen into desuetude in those lax times. Bibles, indeed, were somewhat expensive luxuries, a high price being charged for them by the privileged publishers. Swedberg set himself to remedy this, and to provide a cheap edition that all might possess; but, although he obtained the royal sanction, and expended a considerable sum of money himself in preparing such an edition, the power of vested interests was too strong, and the project fell through. His labours in connection with the revision of the Swedish translation of the Bible also came to naught; while his attempted improvement of the Swedish hymn and psalm book only brought upon him a charge of heresy, and led to the suppression of the work. In every direction he seems to have been thwarted by the jealousy, apathy, and stolid conservativeness of those who should have been his supporters and helpers in good works. Nevertheless, he persevered in his laudable efforts to the end of his long life.

Swedberg's religion was of an eminently practical character. In the Lutheran Church, as in other Protestant bodies, faith had been elevated to such pre-eminence that good works were disparaged, and morality suffered in consequence; Swedberg held that true faith could not be dissociated from a life of charity and active usefulness. He complained that "many contented themselves with the first and second paragraphs of the 'great faith' (*stor-tron*), but that they would have nothing to do with the third paragraph, with 'sanctification and a holy life.'" "'Faith of the head' (*hjärne tron—i.e.* brain faith) and 'devil's faith' with him were synonymous." He was a fearless preacher, denouncing the shortcomings of those in high places, as well as the backslidings of humbler sinners; being especially severe against the neglect of religious duties by the former, and the scandalous abuse of their rights of Church patronage.

His catholicity was remarkable, considering the age in which he lived; he was willing to see what was good in all the churches, and, during a visit to England, eagerly discussed the question of Christian unity with Bishop Fell of Oxford. In Roman Catholic countries he admired the care given to the poor, and the devotion of high-born persons to the sick and destitute; in his own land he gave a word of approval to the earnestness of the Pietists, although he did not agree with all their tenets and practices. He was described by Counsellor Sandels as "a man full of zeal but without bigotry."

His personal tastes were simple and easily satisfied. He had a fair share of this world's goods, but died poor, as he had expended large sums in printing and publishing and other disinterested efforts.

11

His books for the most part were unsuccessful, and he complained that he had rooms full of unsold copies; remarking, with realistic humour, that after his death, they would probably be used by the women for their cakes.

It is not surprising that, to an earnest and devout man like Bishop Swedberg, the spiritual world should have seemed very real and near at hand. He had an assured faith in the presence of angels among men, and of the helpful offices they fulfil as "ministering spirits, sent forth to minister unto them who shall be heirs of salvation" (Heb. i. 14). He lived in the society of his "guardian angel," with whom, he declared, he was able to converse at times. He believed that he had other spiritual intimations on different occasions, and seems to have been possessed of powers of hypnotic healing. Not long after his ordination, he tells us that loud voices were heard by him and all in the village, singing toward evening in the church, which convinced him of the presence of angelic visitors, and caused him to feel more strongly than ever before the sacredness of the calling to which he had devoted himself. All these matters have a bearing on the still more extraordinary experiences of his son, Emanuel; the idea of the intimate relations that subsist between the physical and the spiritual worlds was no doubt familiar to the latter from his father's teaching.

Such was the father of the subject of this biography. Of his mother we do not hear much; she was doubtless quite fully occupied with household cares, having borne nine children during her twelve years of married life. She died at thirty years of age, when Emanuel was only eight.

Strangely little is known of Swedenborg's childhood. He was born at Stockholm on January 29, 1688, and was the second son, and third child, of his parents. Beyond these meagre facts, all that we can learn of this period of his life is from a letter addressed by him, in 1769, to his friend, Dr. Beyer, Professor of Greek in Gothenburg University. In this he says: "From my fourth to my tenth year I was constantly engaged in thought upon God, salvation, and the spiritual experiences of men; and several times I revealed things at which my father and mother wondered, saying that angels must be speaking through me. From my sixth to my twelfth year I used to delight in conversing with clergymen about faith, saying that the life of faith is love, and that the love which imparts life is love to the neighbour; also that God gives faith to every one, but that those only receive it who practise that love. I knew of no other faith at that time than that God is the Creator and Preserver of nature, that He imparts understanding and a good disposition to men, and several other things that follow thence. I knew nothing at that time of that learned faith which teaches that God the Father imputes the righteousness of His Son to whomsoever, and at such times as, He chooses, even to those who have not repented and have not reformed their lives. And had I heard of such a faith, it would have been then, as it is now, above my comprehension."

If direct information is wanting as to the childhood of Swedenborg, we may fill up the blank to some extent from our imagination, building upon a knowledge of the family circumstances at different periods. At the time of his birth his father was exercising the functions of Court chaplain at Stockholm. In the Swedish capital, then, the first three or four years of the child's life were spent, and he doubtless carried away impressions of the busy city,—with its lofty buildings, its rushing flood of deep green waters coming down from Lake Mälaren, its shipping, its military displays, and the coming and going of royalty and nobility in their summer carriages or winter sleighs,—to the quiet rural home at Vingåker, to which the family removed in 1692. Here, for a few brief months, he revelled, as all children do, in the flowery fields and delightful farmyards, and was petted by the good people of the parish, who were also overwhelmingly kind to his father.

The next ten years of his life were passed in Upsala, his parents residing in the cathedral square; and here his early education was received. His tutor was Johannes Moraeus, afterwards Dr. Moraeus, a cousin on his mother's side, but we hear little of his studies. Counsellor Sandels speaks of "the thoughtful care which was bestowed on his education," and that he speaks truly we cannot doubt, knowing what we do of the father.

Upsala, where the free, happy days of his boyhood were passed, was at that time a city of some five thousand inhabitants, and its cathedral was reckoned the finest Gothic building in the north of Europe. Within its walls many monarchs had been crowned in days of yore, and many also lay buried. We can fancy the lad wandering through the aisles, and meditating upon vanished greatness; or listening with the other members of the family to the daily service, in which the father often took part. This service was not so cold and lifeless as Protestant services were, at this period, in some other countries, for the Lutheran Church retained many of the less objectionable usages of Rome. A portrait of Jesper Swedberg shows him sitting at a table with a folio Bible before him opened at a doubtless favourite text, 1 Cor. xvi. 22, "If any man love not the Lord Jesus Christ, let him be Anathema Maran-atha"; while above the precious Book hangs the crucifix. Through an open door, over which stands a cross, we have a vista of a church interior terminating in an altar with lights burning before it, and an altar-piece above.

We can imagine the interest with which Emanuel would watch the building of his father's "large new stone house" in the square; and the impression made upon his youthful mind by the terrible fire which, shortly after it was finished, destroyed not only the new house, but many other buildings, including the grand cathedral itself.

14

The account of the building of this house given in the Swedish *Biographiskt Lexicon* throws a very pleasing light upon the character of Swedenborg's father. "It is interesting," says the writer, "to hear him speak about the building of this new house. 'I know, and I can testify—for I was always present—that not the least work was done, that not a stone was raised, with sighs or a troubled mind, but all was done cheerfully and gladly. No complaint, no hard or disagreeable word was heard, no scoldings and no oaths were uttered.' When the house was finished, in the autumn of 1698, he inaugurated it by inviting and entertaining all the poor of the town. He and his wife and children waited upon them. Everything was done in an orderly manner, and this feast of charity was concluded with singing, prayer, thanksgiving, and mutual blessing." We may assume that Swedenborg, who was then ten years of age, took his share in this kindly entertainment.

Another circumstance that must have left its mark upon his memory was the death of his mother in 1696; and this sad event was followed by the loss of his elder brother a few weeks later. Of the remaining children (seven besides himself), his sister Anna, sixteen months his senior, seems to have been his favourite. Before she had completed her seventeenth year, she was married to Dr. Ericus Benzelius, Librarian to the University of Upsala; but she was not lost to her fond brother. It was about this time that he entered upon his college course, and the probability is, though direct evidence is wanting, that he resided with her until he left the University in 1709; for his father removed to Brunsbo in 1702, on his appointment to the bishopric of Skara. We know practically nothing of his doings during these years. He certainly did not waste his time; but there is no record of his having gained any important distinction. Counsellor Sandels says that he made "the best use of advantages enjoyed, comparatively, by but few," and describes the academical disputation which he published,

15

with the permission of the authorities, on leaving his *alma mater* as "a clever work for a youth." After leaving the University he published some of his efforts at composing Latin verse, which manifested, says Sandels, "a remarkable readiness of wit, and showed that he had made a good use of his time in youth." He continued to exercise this faculty for some years, and was looked upon in his family circle as something of a poet.

Having done with tutors, lectures and classbooks, he retired for a time to Brunsbo, the episcopal residence near Skara, where he began to make plans for an extended foreign tour. The difficulty seems to have been how to raise the means, his father having little wealth and many responsibilities, and being withal somewhat "near." Under date of July 13, 1709, he wrote to his brother-in-law Benzelius, begging his assistance in carrying out his project. He also desired his recommendation to some English college where he might improve himself in mathematics, physics, and natural history. He proposed to prepare for his own use a summary of the principal discoveries in mathematics during the recent centuries, to which he would add anything new he might learn in his travels.

In this same letter he tells his brother-in-law that he has acquired the art of book-binding, from a man who had been working for his father. I mention this as characteristic of his industrious and practical nature. Wherever he went in his later travels he endeavoured to gain a knowledge of useful trades. Writing from London in 1711, he says: "I also turn my lodgings to some use, and change them often; at first I was at a watchmaker's, afterwards at a cabinet-maker's, and now I am at a mathematical instrument maker's; from them I pick up their trades, which some day will be of use to me." He learnt to make brass instruments; and at Leyden, later, to grind glass for lenses, etc., that he might furnish himself with appliances that he could not afford to buy. His brother-in-law had commissioned him, when in England, to procure some globes for the University Library at Upsala, but these proving too expensive, and difficult to convey safely, he was asked to obtain the printed sheets that they might be mounted in Sweden. The makers, however, refused to supply them; so young Swedberg applied himself to learn engraving, and prepared the sheets himself.

But to return. It was a full year after his application to Benzelius for assistance that he was enabled to start upon his travels; a year of disappointment and impatient waiting for something to turn up. Not a happy time for one of Emanuel's active disposition; especially when he met with discouragement in his favourite studies at home. The busy, practical bishop was probably as little appreciative of mathematics as he was of metaphysics; and certainly he would look with disapproval on a life of idleness, or of no definite occupation, in a young man of twenty-two. There can be no doubt the son was unhappy. On March 6, 1710 he writes to Benzelius, the one great friend of his early life:

"I have little desire to remain here much longer; for I am wasting almost my whole time. Still, I have made such progress in music, that I have been able several times to take the place of our organist; but for all my other studies this place affords me very little opportunity; and they are not at all appreciated by those who ought to encourage me in them."

Some relief from this unsatisfactory mode of life was found in a short visit to the great Swedish engineer and inventor, Christopher Polhammar (afterwards known by his title of nobility, Polhem). With him the youth was in his element, and Polhammar appreciated his capacity. He wrote to Benzelius: "We were pleased and satisfied with one another . . . ; especially when I found him able to assist me in the mechanical undertaking which I have in hand, and in making the necessary experiments; in this

17

matter I am more indebted to him than he is to me. Moreover, I value more highly a quick and intelligent person, with whom I can enjoy the discussion of subjects on which I possess some little knowledge, than I do a few weeks' board and lodging."

The autumn of 1710 finds young Swedberg in London; and, from this date, his occasional letters to Dr. Benzelius give us a brief but interesting account of his doings for the five years of his absence from Sweden.

His journey to London was not without perils, his life having been in danger four different times. The vessel in which he sailed was nearly wrecked on approaching the English coast; then they were boarded by pirates; the next evening were fired into by a British guardship, being mistaken for the same pirates; and, finally, after arriving safely in the Thames, Swedberg narrowly escaped hanging for breaking the strict quarantine regulations, established on account of the existence of the plague in Sweden.

His first letter to Benzelius from London is of great interest, and reveals not only his "immoderate desire" (to borrow his own expression from a later letter) for study, but the remarkable breadth of his sympathies.

"I study Newton daily," he says, "and am very anxious to see and hear him. I have provided myself with a small stock of books for the study of mathematics, and also with a certain number of instruments, which are both a help and an ornament in the study of science; such as, an astronomical tube, quadrants of several kinds, prisms, microscopes, artificial scales, and *camera obscuræ,* by William Hunt and Thomas Everard, which I admire and which you, too, will admire. I hope that after settling my accounts, I may have sufficient money left to purchase an air-pump."

It does not appear that this desire to meet Newton was ever gratified, though he made the acquaintance in England of many notabilities, including Flamsteed, Halley, and

Woodward, by the last-named of whom he was introduced to various members of the Royal Society, and other learned men.

Among other items of information in this letter, dated October 13, 1710, is that "the magnificent St. Paul's Cathedral was finished a few days ago in all its parts." In its virginal purity, before the smoke of the great city had had time to obscure the beauty of its details, it doubtless impressed him mightily. But he was more impressed at Westminster; not by the architecture, however, upon which he does not remark. "In examining the royal monuments in Westminster Abbey," he says, "I happened to see the tomb of Casaubon; when I was inspired with such a love for this literary hero, that I kissed his tomb, and dedicated to his *manes,* under the marble"—some Latin verses, which it is not necessary to quote.

Of his studies in England, mathematics and astronomy seem to have absorbed most of his interest. "I visit daily," he writes (April, 1711), "the best mathematicians here in town. I have been with Flamsteed, who is considered the best astronomer in England, and who is constantly taking observations." In a letter written at the end of 1711, or the beginning of 1712, he reports conversations he has had with Flamsteed, and sends a list of the latter's publications, for which Benzelius had asked. He also speaks enthusiastically of his own growing knowledge and hopes of attainment.

"With regard to astronomy," he says, "I have made such progress in it, as to have discovered much which I think will be useful in its study. Although in the beginning it made my brain ache, yet long speculations are now no longer difficult for me. I examined closely all propositions for finding the terrestrial longitude, but could not find a single one; I have therefore originated a method by means of the moon, which is unerring, and I am certain that it is the best which has yet been advanced. In a short time

19

I will inform the Royal Society that I have a proposition to make on this subject, stating my points. If it is favourably received by these gentlemen, I shall publish it here; if not, in France. I have also discovered many new methods for observing the planets, the moon, and the stars; that which concerns the moon and its parallaxes, diameter, and inequality, I will publish whenever an opportunity arises. I am now busy working my way through algebra and the higher geometry, and I intend to make such progress in it, as to be able in time to continue Polhammar's discoveries."

The young student's scientific and literary friends in Sweden often availed themselves of his assistance while he was abroad. At one time it was to procure some out-of-the-way books for the University Library; at another, to purchase scientific instruments, or to ascertain the most approved method of using these. For his brother-in-law he obtained lenses for a 24-ft. telescope, a microscope, and many books, to procure which latter he had to ransack the book-shops and attend auction sales; not, for him, an uncongenial task. The Literary Society of Upsala, also, gave him a number of commissions and instructions, through one of its members, Professor Elfvius, especially enjoining him to watch Flamsteed's method of taking observations, to take note of his instruments, etc. After detailing numerous other requests, the professor concludes one of his letters:

"I recommend the above, and everything else that may be of use in our mathematical studies, to Mr. Swedberg's great desire of acquiring knowledge."

One interesting point upon which Elfvius desired information was as to what Englishmen thought of Newton's *Principia,* which had been before the public something more than twenty years at that time. He himself was not prepared to accept the theory of gravitation, which seemed to him to be "a mere abstraction" and "an absurdity." Swedberg's reply was very guarded. "In this matter," he wrote, "no Englishman ought to be consulted, *quia cæcutit in suis, i.e.,* because he is blind about his own; yet it would be criminal to doubt them."

Mr. Swedberg good-naturedly fulfilled his friends' commissions to the best of his ability, and added to the obligations they thus incurred by volunteering further information and suggestions of his own. He advised the purchase of the *Philosophical Transactions* of the Royal Society, also John Lowth's (? Lowthrop's) *Digest* of the same, Harris' *Lexicon of the Sciences and Arts, The Memoirs of Literature,* several of Sir Isaac Newton's works, and other books. He mentions the publication of Grabe's *Septuagint,* and one or two other theological works; but this is almost the only indication that he took any interest in theology at that time. As a relief from his severer studies, he continued to write poetry, and did not despise the study of English models. He mentions as "eminent English poets, that are well worth reading for the sake of their imagination alone," Dryden, Spenser, Waller, Milton, Cowley, Beaumont and Fletcher, Shakespeare, Ben Johnson, Oldham, Benham, Philip (? Ambrose Philips), Smith, and others; so that for a foreigner he must have gained a considerable acquaintance with English literature.

The young man spent nearly two years in London and Oxford, losing no opportunity of acquiring knowledge. His travels and studies must have involved considerable expense, for which his father does not seem to have been too generous in providing. His father was, in fact, at this time, spending all available money on his own enterprises, and so had little consideration for the lonely and penurious student. As a dutiful son, Emanuel does not chide loudly, but he raises a mild complaint from time to time. "I am on short allowance," he tells Benzelius (April, 1711), "and am not permitted to purchase anything on credit." He writes nine months later: "I have longed very much to see the Bodleian Library, since I saw the little one at Sion

21

College; but I am kept back here on account of *'want of money.'* I wonder my father does not show greater care for me, than to have let me live now for more than sixteen months upon 250 rixdalers (something less than £50) well knowing that I promised in a letter not to incommode him by drawing for money; and yet none has been forthcoming for the last three or fourth months. It is hard to live without food or drink like some poor drudge in Schonen." Again: "Your great kindness, and your favour, of which I have had so many proofs, make me believe that your advice and your letters will induce my father to be so favourable towards me, as to send me the funds which are necessary for a young man, and which will infuse into me new spirit for the prosecution of my studies. Believe me, I desire and strive to be an honour to my father's house and yours, much more strongly than you yourself can wish and endeavour." (Aug., 1712.)

It is to be regretted that these letters are so few and far between; many are evidently missing. Writing from Paris in August, 1713, he refers to a letter he had sent from Holland, whither he went from England, but it has not been found. All that we hear of his stay in that country is from a short reference in this Paris letter.

"During my stay in Holland I was most of the time in Utrecht, where the Diet met, and where I was in great favour with Ambassador Palmqvist, who had me every day at his house; every day, also, I had discussions on algebra with him. He is a good mathematician, and a great algebraist. He wished me not to go away; and, therefore, I intend next year to return to Leyden, where they have a splendid observatory, and the finest brass quadrant I have ever seen; it cost 2,000 new guilders. They are continually making new observations. I will ask permission from the university to take observations there for two or three months, which I shall easily obtain; Palmqvist said the same."

Of his doings in Paris, also, we have but a very meagre record. He met there De La Hire, Varrignon, the Abbé Bignon (a member of the Academy and afterwards Royal Librarian), besides other notables. He observes that:

"Between the mathematicians here and the English there is great emulation and jealousy. Halley, of Oxford, told me that he was the first who examined the variation of the pendulum under the equator; they keep silence about this here; the astronomers here also maintain that Cassini's paper was written before Halley made his expedition to the Island of St. Helena, and so forth."

In Paris and its neighbourhood he spent nearly a year. On leaving, he posted to Hamburg, *via* Lille, and thence into Pomerania, at that time a Swedish province. We hear of him, in his next letter, at Rostock; from which place he sends his brother-in-law a long list of inventions he has either completed or projected. One wonders what some of these were like, and whether the young inventor anticipated the mechanical contrivances of the present age in the same way as, in later years, he anticipated scientific theories that are usually regarded as strictly modern.

The first of these inventions was "the plan of a certain ship, which with its men was to go under the surface of the sea, wherever it chooses, and do great damage to the fleet of the enemy." Another was a device for raising ships with their cargoes by means of sluices, where there is no fall of water. Yet another for setting mill wheels in motion under similar circumstances—*i.e.* when falling water was not available; "the wheel will nevertheless revolve by means of the fire, which will put the water in motion." A magazine air-gun to discharge sixty or seventy shots in succession without reloading, and a flying machine, were further projects of his active brain. The idea of a flying machine he returned to again later; but Polhem seems to have thrown cold water on his schemes, expressing his opinion that "with respect to flying by artificial means,

23

there is perhaps the same difficulty as in making a *perpetuum mobile* or gold by artificial means; although, at first sight, it seems as easy to be done as it is desirable."

His method for finding the terrestrial longitude by means of the moon be regarded as the most important of his early discoveries. Though it was not taken up sympathetically by the learned of his day, he always insisted that it was "the only one that can be given, that it is also the easiest, and in fact the right one." His confidence in it was so great that he republished his pamphlet several times between 1718 and 1766, both in Swedish and in Latin. This little treatise was very favourably reviewed by the *Acta Literaria Sueciæ* for 1720. Its editors declare that it is "superior to all other solutions of this problem which have been hitherto attempted." The *Acta Eruditorum* for 1722, published in Leipzig, also speaks highly of this little work.

In this Rostock letter he expresses a very great desire to return home to Sweden; nevertheless he remained in Pomerania for another nine months, most of the time at the little university town of Greifswalde. What kept him there, unless it was the presence of the king of Stralsund, and a hope that possibly his services might in some way be called upon, it is hard to say; for he had a very poor opinion of the university and its faculty.

At Griefswalde young Swedberg printed a collection of poetical fables in Latin, dealing with the political affairs of his time, under the title of *Camena Borea cum Heroum et Heroidum factis ludens: sive Fabellæ Ovidianis similes sub variis nominibus.* He had been employed upon this for some time as a mental recreation.

The young student's long wanderings were drawing to an end. We can only regret that more of his correspondence at this time, and his own journal especially, have not been preserved. His few letters to Benzelius, from which I have drawn so largely, are full of interest, not only for their record of his studies and achievements, but for the revelation they give of his personal character. Swedenborg has been accused of want of affection and friendliness, but for Benzelius he certainly entertained a very warm regard, and he was deeply attached to his sister Anna; every letter expresses his affection to both, and to "his little brother (nephew) Eric." A very characteristic touch is found in the letter from Rostock (September 6, 1714). He writes: "I have a great longing to see little brother Eric again; perhaps he will be able to make a triangle, or to draw one for me, when I give him a little ruler." "Little brother Eric" was nine years old at this time. His interest in the child continued, for a few years later he wrote: "I hear that his love for mechanics and drawing continues. If he can give the slip to his preceptor, I should like to induce him to follow me; when I would try in every way to promote his welfare, to instruct him in mathematics and other things, should it be desired." It appears that "little brother Eric" did follow his uncle, entering the Board of Mines under his auspices in 1726. On July 13, 1725, his father wrote to Swedenborg: "I acknowledge with all due respect the favour which you have shown towards my Ericus, and which he has received in so many ways from you in Stockholm, both by instruction in physics and mathematics, and more recently by a new present." Eric was then twenty years of age.

Emanuel's stay at Greifswalde was cut short by the arrival of the allied enemies of Sweden before Stralsund, where the king was shut up, which was only fifteen miles distant. "When the siege was about to commence," he says, "I succeeded, under the Divine Providence, in obtaining a passage home in a yacht, in company with Madame Feif [presumably the wife of the Councillor of War], after having been abroad for more than four years" [nearly five, in fact]. Warm work was in prospect around Stralsund, making its neighbourhood unfitted for ladies or students.

CHAPTER II

ANOTHER period of weary waiting and discouragement followed young Swedberg's return to his native country. Full of new ideas and enthusiasm, he thought that some career would surely open to him now. He had many schemes for his country's good, and the enlargement of his own reputation, and was by no means idle; but his efforts to advance the material welfare of Sweden, and to raise her scientific status among the nations, were blocked at all points by conservativeness, vested interests, indifference, and lack of funds, in the same way as his father's attempts at educational and ecclesiastical reforms were frustrated.

His very first undertaking was in connection with his new method of finding the longitude. "The day after to-morrow," he writes to Benzelius, under date, August 9, 1715, "I will travel to the Kinnekulle [mountain], to select a spot for a small observatory, where I intend, toward winter, to make some observations respecting our horizon, and to lay a foundation for those observations, by which my invention on the longitude of places may be confirmed."

He visits the Board of Mines, and observes that the models "are going to ruin as time advances. After six or ten years they will only be good for firewood, unless I choose to prevent that fate by means of a little brass, a little ink, and some paper." Ten years later, when he had a share in the responsibility for the property of the Board, he applied for and obtained an appropriation of fifty silver dalers for the repair of these models, showing that his concern was not simply that of an outside critic.

After his sojourn in more advanced and enlightened countries, he naturally felt the backwardness of his own. He had two great schemes to remedy this. One was the formation of a "Society for Learning and Science," a sort of Swedish Royal Society; the other was the foundation of a Chair of Mechanics at the University of Upsala. He hammered away at this latter idea for years, but without success. His first suggestion was that the existing professors should give up a seventh part of their emoluments, so as to afford an income of 3,000 silver dalers for the support of the new faculty. This proposal naturally met with opposition, and the enthusiastic student afterwards explained that he had meant it more in jest than in earnest; but he had another suggestion ready, which was to reduce the number of professorships in other subjects by not filling up vacancies. "It could be done with the greatest ease," he said, "by dispensing with some of the professorships that are least necessary, *e.g.,* in course of time one professorship might be spared both from theology and medicine, and the professorship of Oriental languages might be transferred either to a professorship of theology, or to the professorship of Greek; so also that of morals might be transferred to the professorship of history; especially as there are few universities where there are so many professorships established."

The bent of Swedenborg's mind was always practical, both as a man of science and as a religious teacher; he could not understand how any one could contentedly rest in mere theory. At the time we are now dealing with, his brother-in-law, Benzelius, was exerting himself to get an astronomical observatory established at Upsala, and received his warm support in the matter. Other people, however, were not so enthusiastic. "I wonder at your friends, the mathematicians," he wrote, "who have lost all energy and desire to follow up so clever a design, as the one you pointed out to them of the building of an astronomical observatory. It is a fatality with mathematicians that they remain mostly in theory. I have thought that it would be a profitable thing if to ten mathematicians there was added one thoroughly practical man, by whom the others could be led to market; in which case this one man would gain more renown and be of more use than all the ten together."

A young man of this disposition could not rest unoccupied. While awaiting the course of events, he started a scientific and technical journal, under the title of "Dædalus Hyperboreus." On the advice of Benzelius, he dedicated it to the King, Charles XII., who professed much interest in the work. First, however, the means of publishing it had to be found, and he appealed to Benzelius to intercede with his father for assistance. He always seemed afraid to approach the latter with demands for money; and, as he was now nearly twenty-eight, the Bishop might well think that it was time he shifted for himself. Thus he wrote to his mediator:

"A single word from you to my father about me, will be worth more than twenty thousand remonstrances from me. You can without any comment inform him of my enterprise, of my zeal in my studies; and that he need not imagine that in future I shall waste my time and, at the same time, his money. One word from another is worth more than a thousand from me. He knows very well that you have the kindness to interest yourself in my behalf; but he knows too, that I am still more interested in my own behalf. For this reason he will distrust me more than you, my dear brother."

All this while the Bishop was using his influence with the King and Court to find his son some employment. But Charles was too busy with other matters, and it was not until the end of the year 1716 that young Swedberg was appointed "Extraordinary Assessor" (that is, an extra assessor, over and above the usual number) at the Board of Mines, the Department of State responsible for the supervision of the great mining industries of Sweden. His fitness for the post was attested by Polhem in a letter to Benzelius dated December 10, 1715. "I find," the great inventor wrote, "that young Swedberg is a ready mathematician, and possesses much aptitude for the mechanical sciences; and if he continues as he has begun, he will, in course of time, be able to be of greater use to the King and to his country in this than in anything else." In another letter, he speaks of "his readiness of resource," and "his other good qualities."

It seems that the King offered the young man three posts to choose from, before he was finally gazetted to the Board of Mines. Though no salary was attached to the office until he attained to full Assessorship, he found the work congenial, and two years later refused the Professorship of Astronomy in the University of Upsala, assigning as his reasons: "(1) I already have an honourable post. (2) In this post I can be of use to my country, and indeed of more practical use than in any other position. (3) I thus decline a faculty which does not agree with my tastes and my turn of mind, by both of which I am led to mechanics, and will be in future to chemistry; and our Board" (he is writing confidentially to his brother-in-law) "is noted for having assessors who know very little on these subjects; for this reason I will endeavour to supply this deficiency, and I hope that my labours in this direction will be as profitable to them as their own may be in another."

There were ulterior reasons, also, for in a later letter, he writes:

"I hope I shall be able to be as useful in the post which has been entrusted to me, and also to secure to myself as many advantages; my present position being only a step to a higher one, while at Upsala I should have noththing more to expect; moreover, I do not believe that the King would like me to give up my present position. With regard to the Board, I will try most diligently to make myself at home in mechanics, physics, and chemistry, and, at all events, to lay a proper foundation for everything, when I hope no one will have any longer a desire to charge me with having entered the Board as one entirely unworthy."

During the early part of his career at the Board of Mines, he was detached at times for special services with his friend and patron Christopher Polhem. The most important of these was connected with the siege of Frederikshald in 1718, when two galleys, five large boats, and one sloop were transported overland from Strömstad to Iddefjord, a distance of fourteen English miles, under Swedberg's direction. Other works were the construction of the great dock at Karlskrona, and the scheme for connecting the North Sea and the Baltic by a canal; which undertaking, however, was never completed, owing to the death of the King, at whose private expense it was to have been executed.

The intercourse of young Swedberg with Polhem was of a very friendly character; so much so that the latter, on the recommendation of the King, promised him his eldest daughter in marriage. From a letter of Swedberg to his brother-in-law, Benzelius, it appears that they were actually engaged; but in the end she was married to another. There was a younger sister, however, to whom the young man became strongly attached, and who in due course was formally betrothed to him. The damsel, it seems, was not consulted, or, at any rate, the match was arranged for her; and it proved that she did not really care for her fiancé. Discovering this, the latter renounced his claim under circumstances that showed high honour and fine feeling on his part. From Robsahm's *Memoirs,* we learn that Emerentia, as she was called, was only thirteen or fourteen years of age when Swedenborg became acquainted with her, and that she could not be persuaded to enter into an engagement; whereupon her father, who loved Swedenborg very much, gave him a written claim upon her in the future, in the hope that when older she would become more yielding, and this contract her father obliged her to sign. She fretted, however, about it so much every day, that her brother, Chamberlain Gabriel Polhem, becoming quite distressed, purloined the contract from Swedenborg, whose only comfort had consisted in daily perusing it, and who therefore quickly missed his treasure. His sorrow at its loss was so evident, that her father insisted on knowing the cause; whereupon he offered to exercise his authority and have the document restored. But when Swedenborg himself saw her grief, he voluntarily relinquished his right; and he left the house with a solemn oath, never again to let his thoughts settle upon any woman, and still less to enter into any other engagement. For some time he ceased to communicate with any of the family.

It was a painful affair to both sides, as appears from a letter of Polhem's to Benzelius, in which he speaks of the interruption of his correspondence with his protégé, and mentions the fact that three of his letters had been returned to him unopened. "I must beg you," he says, "to offer him [Emanuel] my greeting, . . . and also to ask him to favour me with one of his welcome letters, which are the more acceptable in our house, as he has given us sufficient cause to love him as our own son."

The disappointed lover was evidently in a state of great dejection at this time. The light of his life had gone out, and everything looked gloomy in consequence. He writes to Benzelius (October, 1718) ; "Among all my brothers and relatives there is not one who has entertained a kind feeling towards me except yourself; and in this I was confirmed by a letter which my brother wrote to my father about my journey abroad. If I can in any way show a due sense of gratitude, I will always do so. Brother [in-law] Unge does not withhold his hands from any one; at least he has estranged me from my dear father's and my dear mother's affections for the last four years; still this will probably not be to his advantage." Actually, it was his stepmother he was referring to, Swedenborg's father having married again, about one and a half years after the death of his first wife.

Even his scientific pursuits were bringing him no satisfaction. He is discouraged "to find that [his] mathematical discoveries were considered as novelties which the country could not stand." "I wish," he adds (it is a letter to Benzelius that he is writing) "I had some more of these novelties, ay, a novelty in literary matters for every day in the year, so that the world might find pleasure in them. There are enough in one century who plod on in the old beaten track, while there are scarcely six or ten in a whole century, who are able to generate novelties which are based upon argument and reason."

Among the novelties, which his lethargic fellow-countrymen were slow to adopt, were his plans for an astronomical observatory and the foundation of a professorship of mechanics, already mentioned; a scheme for the extensive manufacture of salt in Sweden; a new slow-combustion stove; a new method of discovering mineral veins; a decimal system of coinage, and measures, etc. "Speculations and arts like these," he complains, "are left to starve in Sweden, where they are looked upon by a set of political blockheads as scholastic matters, which must remain in the background, while their own supposed refined ideas and their intrigues occupy the foreground."

In another letter he writes: "It seems to me there is little reward for the trouble of advancing the cause of science; partly on account of the lack of funds, which prevents our going as far into it as we ought, and partly also on account of the jealousy which is excited against those who busy themselves more than other persons with a given subject. Whenever a country leans towards barbarism, it is vain for one or two persons to try to keep it upright."

In sending Benzelius his treatise on the decimal system, in a letter of December 1, 1719, he renews his complaint of neglect and lack of appreciation. "This is the last," he vows, "that I will publish myself, because *quotidiana et domestica vilescunt*, and because I have already worked myself poor by them. I have been singing long enough; let us see whether any one will come forward, and hand me some bread in return." Despairing of recognition at home he proposes to go abroad and seek his fortune as a mining engineer. "For he is nothing short of a fool," he exclaims, "who is independent and at liberty to do as he pleases, and sees an opportunity for himself abroad, and yet remains at home in darkness and cold, where the Furies, Envy, and Pluto have taken up their abode, and assign the rewards, and where labours such as I have performed are rewarded with misery. The only thing I would desire until that time come, is *bene latere* (*i.e.* to find a sequestered place where I can live secluded from the world); I think I may find such a corner in the end, either at Starbo or at Skin[skatte]-berg." At these places he had a partnership in mines and ironworks, inherited from his mother's and stepmother's families.

It was not empty honours that the young man sought; for he and his brothers and sisters had been ennobled by the Queen (Ulrica Eleonora) some six months before this melancholy letter was written. This honour gave him, as the eldest son, a seat in the House of Nobles, one of the four Houses in the Swedish Parliament; and was signalized in the usual way by a change in the family name from Swedberg to Swedenborg, which name we shall hereafter use.

If it was honour he sought, he might have been satisfied with the distinguished favour shown him by Sweden's famous king, Charles XII. He had frequent and intimate

33

intercourse with his Majesty, who condescended to read his *Dœdalus,* to discuss mathematics with him, and to accept his personal assistance in various ways. He writes from Wenersborg, September 14, 1718:

"Every day I had some mathematical matters for His Majesty, who deigned to be pleased with all of them. When the eclipse took place, I took His Majesty out to see it, and talked much to him about it. This, however, is a mere beginning. I hope in time to be able to do something in this quarter for the advancement of science; but I do not wish to bring anything forward now, except what is of immediate use. His Majesty found considerable fault with me for not having continued my *Dœdalus* [which ceased with the sixth number], but I pleaded want of means; of which he does not like to hear. I expect some assistance for it very soon."

These fond hopes were never realized. The King was busy with warlike enterprises, and these, too, were brought to a sudden end by his death at the siege of Frederikshald on the 30th of the following November.

The loss of his royal patron, his unfortunate love affair, his estrangement from his family, and the indifference of nearly every one to his aims and interests, may well have produced a melancholy state of mind. He did not go abroad, however, as he thought he might have to do, but in the summer of 1721 he started upon a lengthy foreign tour, his object being to study the mines and manufactures of other lands that he might render still higher services to his country in his appointed office.

His original plan was to visit Holland, England, France, Italy, Hungary, and Germany; but the tour was chiefly confined to Holland and the German States. He visited all the mines in Saxony and the Hartz mountains, and was entertained in a princely manner by Duke Ludwig Rudolf von Brunswick-Lüneburg, who not only paid all his expenses, but presented him on parting with a gold medal and a large silver coffee-pot, besides bestowing upon him other marks of favour.

While on this tour he published several scientific and speculative works: at Amsterdam *Prodromus Principiorum Rerum Naturalium,* etc., being a treatise on chemistry and physics; *Nova Observata et Inventa circa Ferrum et Ignem,* etc. [New Observations on Iron and Fire]; *Artificia nova mechanica Receptacula Navalia et Aggeres Aquaticas construendi,* etc., a work on the construction of docks and dykes: and a second edition of his "New Method of finding the Longitude"; at Leipzig, *Miscellanea Observata circa Res Naturales,* etc., being "Miscellaneous Observations" on geology, mineralogy, etc. It speaks for the backward condition of things in Sweden, that Swedenborg found it necessary to publish most of his works abroad; partly on account of expense, partly that they might be better printed, and partly to escape the criticism of the Press Censor, whose views were apt to be narrow. When he published his Rules of Algebra (the first in the Swedish language) he questioned his brother-in-law as to whether there was any one in Upsala who knew enough of the subject to read his proofs for him!

In July, 1722, Swedenborg was at home again, full of new projects for enhancing the material prospects of his native land; projects to be met as before with scanty encouragement, and not a little active opposition from interested parties, easy-going conservatives, and jealous officials. Among the latter must be reckoned Urban Hjärne, Vice-President of the Board of Mines, who had an old quarrel with Swedenborg's father, and made the young man uncomfortable at times in consequence.

As the outcome of his studies and observations abroad, Swedenborg laid before the Board, and also before King Frederic direct, proposals for increasing the yield of copper from the ore, for improvements in the manufacture of steel, and for giving encouragement to the manufacture of iron, "the interests of copper being protected at the expense of the iron interest." On these, as on other such matters, he held large and liberal views, as witness his opinion of trade secrets. Referring to the difficulty he sometimes had in gathering information abroad, he wrote: "According to my simple notions, there ought to be no secrets at all in metallurgy; for without such knowledge it is impossible for any one to investigate nature."

On July 15, 1724, Swedenborg, being then thirty-six years of age, was appointed an ordinary assessor of the Board of Mines, with a yearly salary of 800 silver dalers. It was not until 1730 that he received the full salary of 1,200 dalers, so that he was but meanly paid for his great services. From the records of the Board he appears to have been assiduous in his duties, and the value of his labours was recognized on several occasions by his colleagues. But he occupied himself with a great deal more than his official work; he was constantly gathering material for further publications, and by the beginning of 1733 he had the manuscript of several important scientific and philosophical works ready for the press. He petitioned for nine months' leave of absence that he might get them printed at Dresden and Leipzig, which was granted by Royal Decree.

The works in question were his *Opera Philosophica et Mineralia,* three heavy folio volumes with numerous copper-plates, and a *Prodromus Philosophiae ratiocinantis de Infinito,* etc., some account of which will be found in a later chapter. The expense of publishing the former, which must have been very great, was borne by Swedenborg's former patron, the Duke of Brunswick-Lüneburg. The work was very favourably received, and portions of the second part, dealing with the manufacture of iron and steel, were reprinted separately, and even translated into French, during the author's lifetime.

The publication of these works won for Swedenborg a European reputation, and brought him into correspondence with some of the leading scientists and philosophers of the day. The Academy of Sciences of St. Petersburg invited him to become a corresponding member in 1734, and he was one of the first elected members of the Royal Academy of Sciences in his own country.

Swedenborg has left us a somewhat detailed account of his journeyings at this time; a matter-of-fact document, presenting many points of interest. It proves the truth of what Counsellor Sandels said, that "nothing ever escaped him that merited the attention of a traveller."

"It would be too prolix," notes Swedenborg, "to mention all the learned men I visited, and with whom I became acquainted during these journeys, since I never missed an opportunity of doing so, nor of seeing and examining libraries, collections, and other objects of interest."

His observations ranged from such important matters as the fortifications of a town, to the method of constructing fences in Schonen. Wherever he goes, he visits the libraries, museums, picture galleries, churches, monasteries, asylums, theatres, and especially manufactories. He has remarks upon mining; blast furnaces; vitriol, arsenic, and sulphur works; naval architecture; copper and tin manufactures; paper mills; plate glass and mirrors; as well as upon anatomy, astronomy, magnetism, hydrostatics, literature, and the social condition of the people among whom he finds himself.

His experience under Charles XII had taught him how culture and science languish under a military régime. The condition of the Royal Library in Berlin, therefore, could have given him little surprise. The books, he says, were "mostly old; not many are purchased at the present time, no money being obtainable for this purpose." He remarks also that most of the books are old in the Ambrosian Library at Milan, in the Vatican, and in the Library of San Lorenzo, Florence, but without the same explanation. He was essentially a modern man, whose nature was to look forward rather than backward, and so he took little interest in things from an antiquarian point of view. He was inspired by the new-born love of science and progress, and was eager to study all the latest developments. Hence he cared little for missals and breviaries, rare editions and "black letters"; the Ambrosian Library, he said, "is of little value, as it contains only old books." He made one exception, however, in favour of Biblical codices, which he examined with interest.

In matters of religion he was, naturally, observant, visiting churches, both Catholic and Protestant, orthodox and unorthodox; conversing with priests, monks and laymen; and regarding with charitable, though critical eyes, all developments of the religious instinct. He frequently remarks on the impressiveness of the Roman ritual, at the same time noting its sensuous character. Swedenborg's father had been accused of pietism; he himself was fully alive to the evils of forced religious sentiment. "The town" [of Copenhagen], he remarks, "is infected with pietism or quakerism; and they are crazed enough to believe that it is well-pleasing to God to do away with oneself and others; of which many instances are on record."

In many ways Swedenborg showed a broader and more open mind than his father. The latter looked with little favour on the stage, and complained to the King on one occasion that money was being paid to actors and actresses, which might have been devoted to the restoration of his ruined cathedral. Swedenborg, on the other hand, continually visited the theatres and opera-houses, and criticized the performances there. He even descends to such details as to tell us that the best harlequins come from Bergamo. Still he was in no sense a man of pleasure; wherever he went he had humanity in view, and, in a sense, the theatre was as much an object of study to him as the church.

It must be admitted that Swedenborg was not a connoisseur of art. His remarks on painting and sculpture show an astonishing ignorance of the great artists, and a want of appreciation of what is admirable in art. This ignorance he shared with most of his contemporaries; or, indeed, derived from them, for his judgment was chiefly formed by reading, and the taste of the time was false in the extreme.

He was a man of his time, also, in that he showed little appreciation of natural scenery. He tells us of the hidden wealth of the mountains, but not of their outward glory and majesty; he describes his journeys by sea and river, but never a word of the dancing waves and changing light that give endless variety to the one, or the windings that bring ever new beauties to view on the other; he notes the careful construction of the fences, but sees not the flowers of the field that they enclose; he is struck by "an extraordinary fine illumination" at Leghorn, but disregards the rising and setting of the sun. His thoughts were engaged with the nature and origin of things rather than their appearances; he was full of awe and reverence for the wonders of creation, but his æsthetic faculty was dormant or untrained. He was at this period essentially a man of science and practical affairs; though new faculties were rapidly developing within him.

CHAPTER III

SWEDENBORG THE PHILOSOPHER

DURING the middle period of his life, beginning with his return to Sweden in 1734 from the visit mentioned at the end of the last chapter, Swedenborg was chiefly interested in philosophical speculations: these were based upon an extraordinarily wide knowledge of natural science. J. D. Morell, in *The Speculative Philosophy of Europe in the Nineteenth Century,* says of Swedenborg's philosophy, "Few persons who have only listened to vague rumours respecting this philosophy, would imagine that it commenced in a collection of facts, far greater than those of which the father of experimental science himself had any conception." (Vol. i, p. 317.) His investigations ranged from the composition of matter to the seat of the soul in the human body; and his studies embraced mathematics, physics, mechanics, astronomy, metallurgy, chemistry, geology, magnetism, and anatomy. Nor was his knowledge a mere smattering; of several of these subjects he may be said to have acquainted himself with all that was to be known in his time. His speculations were daring and profound. In his *Principia,* the first part of his *Opera Philosophica et Mineralia,* mentioned in the previous chapter, he put forth an elaborate theory of the origin of things, and propounded the nebular hypothesis, many years before Kant, Herschel, and Laplace. In the works which we are now about to consider he rose to higher themes, and strove to fathom the mystery of the human soul, and its relation to its instrument, the body; at the same time touching upon many other profound subjects.

To this middle period belong three works, *Œconomia Regni Animalis (Economy of the Animal Kingdom),*

Regnum Animale (The Animal Kingdom), and *De Cultu et Amore Dei (The Worship and Love of God)*. The term "Animal Kingdom" in the first two titles is somewhat misleading: the Latin means "the Kingdom of the Anima," that is, of the soul. Before considering their contents, we will follow him in the journeys he undertook to gather material and to publish these works, of which journeys we fortunately possess some brief but most interesting records.

On July 10, 1736, he left Stockholm, travelling by way of Norrköping and Helsingborg to Copenhagen, where he spent some time, and met many learned and otherwise noted persons, some of whom were acquainted with his previous works and gratified him by speaking favourably of them. There, and elsewhere, he visited many places of interest, such as the great dry dock then in process of construction at Copenhagen, porcelain works at Hamburg, etc. Although he was preparing for flights into the highest regions of human thought, he maintained his old interest in the practical affairs of life, as he did, indeed, to the very end of his career.

An important note announces that he has commenced the study of Christian von Wolf's philosophical works; and he remarks with evident satisfaction that the author seems to make reference to himself in one of them. He had made the acquaintance of Wolf shortly before this, and the two philosophers corresponded from time to time.

We get a curious bit of information concerning Osnabrück, a town which contained three Roman Catholic and two Evangelical churches, to the effect that "they have alternately a Catholic and Evangelical bishop;" an extraordinary and impossible arrangement, one would have thought.

At Amsterdam he was struck by the avarice of the people —"the whole town breathed of nothing but gain;" and he speculates as to the cause of the wonderful prosperity of the Dutch. When in Rotterdam, a few days later, he recorded his thoughts upon the subject in his diary. "I have considered," he wrote, "why it was that it has pleased our Lord to bless such an uncouth and avaricious people with such a splendid country; why He has preserved them for such a long time from all misfortunes; has caused them to surpass all other nations in commerce and enterprise; and made their country a place whither most of the riches not only of Europe, but also of other places flow. The principal cause seems to me to have been that it is a republic, wherein the Lord delights more than in monarchical countries; as appears also from Rome. The result is that no one deems himself obliged and in duty bound to accord honour and veneration to any human being, but considers the low as well as the high to be of the same worth and consequence as a king or emperor; as is also shown by the native bent and disposition of every one in Holland. The only one for whom they entertain a feeling of veneration is the Lord, putting no trust in flesh; and when the highest is revered most, and no human being is in His place, it is most pleasing to the Lord. Besides each enjoys his own free will, and from this his worship of God grows; for each is, as it were, his own king and ruler under the government of the Highest; and from this it follows again that they do not, out of fear, timidity, and excess of caution, lose their courage and their independent rational thought, but in full freedom and without being borne down, they are able to fix their souls upon, and elevate them to, the honour of the Highest, who is unwilling to share His worship with any other. At all events, those minds that are borne down by a sovereign power are brought up in flattery and falsity; they learn how to speak and act differently from what they think; and when this condition has become inrooted by habit, it engenders a sort of second nature, so that even in the worship of God such persons speak differently from what they think, and extend their flattering ways to the Lord Himself, which must be highly displeasing to Him. This seems to me the reason why they above other nations enjoy a perfect blessing; their worshipping mammon for their God, and striving only after money, does not seem to be consistent with a constant blessing; still there may be ten among a thousand or among ten thousand, who ward off punishment from the others, and cause them to be participants with themselves in temporal blessings."

Remarkable sentiments these for one who had enjoyed the confidence of several monarchs, and to whom "Their Majesties at Carlsberg" had been "very gracious" only a few weeks before, on his taking leave of them to proceed on this same journey; whose father, moreover, had been a staunch upholder of the "divine right"; but Swedenborg always formed his own judgments, and did not fear to express them.

From Rotterdam our traveller went to Dort and Antwerp; thence by "treckschuyt" (canal boat) to Brussels, a portion of the journey which roused him to unwonted enthusiasm. "It was a splendid and most beautiful trip. During the whole journey we had plantations of trees on both sides; people also were more civilized, so that in contrast with their politeness the boorishness and heaviness of the Dutch became very evident." It was doubtless pleasant travelling, the "treckschuyt" being a capacious vessel, "forty ells long, and six ells wide, with five rooms, *i.e.* cabin, kitchen, and other apartments," while "on the forward deck was an awning, under which people could sit."

Among his fellow-passengers were two monks, one of whom "stood on deck for four hours in one position, and during the whole of this time said his prayers devoutly." Swedenborg viewed such, as it would seem to most, excessive piety with his accustomed charity. He presumed that the prayers were for those travelling in the boat, and remarked: "Such prayers must certainly be agreeable to

43

God, so far as they proceed from an honest and pure heart, and are offered with genuine devotion, and not in the spirit of the Pharisees."

While he was prepared to find good in every one and in every church, he did not shut his eyes to ugly facts that came under his notice. He speaks approvingly on several occasions of the spirit of devotion apparent in the Roman Catholic churches; but he cannot help observing the contrast between the wealth of the Church and the wretchedness of the people. "Everywhere," he says (he is in France now), "the convents, churches, and monks are wealthiest and possess most land. The monks are fat, puffed up, and prosperous; a whole proud army might be formed of them without their being missed; most of them lead a lazy life; they try more and more to make all subject to them; they give nothing to the poor except words and blessings, and on the other hand, insist on having everything from the indigent for nothing. Of what use are these Franciscan monks? Others again are slim, lean, supple; they prefer walking to riding on horse-back or in a carriage; they are willing that others should enjoy themselves with them, are witty and quick at repartee, etc." Péronne, he tells us "has many large and handsome churches," but "the houses are miserable; the convents magnificent; the people poor and wretched." Roye, also, "is a miserable town."

Later in his journal he explains the cause of the general poverty, and gives some statistics of the ecclesiastical bodies. "I understand," he says, "that the great revenue of France obtained by the system of taxation called tithing, amounts to 32 millions [livres], or nearly 192 tons of gold, and that Paris on account of its rents contributes nearly two-thirds of that sum. In the country towns this tax, it is said, is not properly collected, as the rents are reported at a lower figure than they amount to in reality, so that scarcely 3 per cent is collected. I am told besides that the ecclesiastical order possesses one-fifth of all the property in the

State, and that the country will be ruined, if this goes on much longer."

"In France there are 14,777 convents and from 300,000 to 400,000 members of religious orders, who possess 9,000 palaces or mansions; 1,356 abbots, 567 abbesses, 13,000 prioresses, 15,000 chaplains, 140,000 pastors and curates, 18 archbishops, and 112 bishops; 776 abbots and 280 abbesses are appointed by the king. There are also 16 heads of Orders."

With all this apparatus, religion does not appear to have had much influence in public or private affairs. In enumerating the various departments of the State, he tells us that "The Comte de Maurepas, Secretary of State, transacts almost everything that concerns the affairs of the interior and the exterior, except what has reference to war; the Comte de Florentin, that which concerns religion, *which is very little*." Of the kind of theology in vogue we get an idea from an entry in his journal dated October 17, 1736. "I was in the Sorbonne, and heard their disputations in theology, which were carried on pretty well . . . ; the whole discussion consisted of syllogisms." He visited many churches and monasteries; heard the king's chaplain preach, who "gesticulated like an actor; yet he preached in a very superior style;" discussed the adoration of saints with an abbé; visited the hospitals; attended the opening of Parliament; and lost no opportunity of studying the life and religion of the people. He was frequently at the opera and theatres, comments upon the pieces, and mentions the distinguished actors and actresses who took part in them.

In the midst of all this his mind was deeply occupied with his new works. Pacing in front of the Hotel de la Duchesse, in Paris, he speculates on the form of the particles of the atmosphere. On September 6th, he writes: "I made the first draft of the introduction to the Transactions, viz., that the soul of wisdom is the knowledge and acknowledgment of the Supreme Being." The next day

"I treated on the subject that 'now is the time to explore nature from its effects.'" He is referring to the passage in his introduction to *The Economy of the Animal Kingdom,* in which, after speaking of the wonderful accumulation of scientific knowledge in modern times that was waiting for some sound theory to unify and interpret it, he exclaims:

> The time is at hand when we may quit the harbour and sail for the open sea. The materials are ready; shall we not build the edifice? The harvest is waiting; shall we not put in the sickle? The produce of the garden is rife and ripe; shall we fail to collect it for use? Let us enjoy the provided banquet; that is to say, from the experience with which we are enriched, let us elicit wisdom. . . . But to launch out into this subject is like embarking on a shoreless ocean that environs the world. It is easy to quit the land, or to loose the horses from the starting-post; but to attain the end or reach the goal is a labour for Hercules. Nevertheless we are bound to attempt the abyss, though as yet we must proceed like young birds that, with the feeble strokes of their new-fledged wings, first essay their strength, and from their nests try the air, the new world into which they are to enter.

The goal towards which our author was thus buoyantly, and somewhat self-confidently, directing his steps, was nothing less than the discovery of the soul, as he explains in the following passage from his introduction to *The Animal Kingdom.*

> I intend to examine, physically and philosophically, the whole anatomy of the body. . . . The end I propose to myself in the work is a knowledge of the soul; since this knowledge will constitute the crown of my studies. . . . In order therefore to follow up the investigation,

and to solve the difficulty, I have chosen to approach by the analytic way; and I think I am the first who has taken this course professedly.

To accomplish this grand end I enter the arena, designing to consider and examine thoroughly the whole world or microcosm which the soul inhabits; for I think it is in vain to seek her anywhere but in her own kingdom. . . .

I am determined to allow myself no respite, until I have run through the whole field to the very goal, until I have traversed the universal animal kingdom to the soul. Thus I hope, that by bending my course inwards continually, I shall open all the doors that lead to her, and at length contemplate the soul herself: by the Divine permission.

To attain the necessary knowledge of human anatomy was the principal object of his long sojourn abroad at this time. In Holland, France, and Italy he pursued his studies, reading up the best authorities in libraries, attending lectures and demonstrations, and using, to some extent, the scalpel himself. He preferred in general, however, to accept the teaching of the great anatomists as to the facts, and to base his theories on their conclusions, for reasons explained in the following extract from his introduction to *Economy of the Animal Kingdom*:

In the experimental knowledge of anatomy our way has been pointed out by men of the greatest and most cultivated talents, such as Eustachius, Malpighi, Ruysch, Leeuwenhoek, Harvey, Morgagni, Vieussens, Lancisi, Winslow, Ridley, Boerhaave, Wepfer, Heister, Steno, Valsalva, Duverney, Nuck, Bartholm, Bidloo, and Verheyen, whose discoveries far from consisting of fallacious, vague, and empty speculations, will for ever continue to be of practical use to posterity.

Assisted by the studies and elaborate writings of these

illustrious men, and fortified by their authority, I have resolved to commence and complete my design; that is to say, to open some part of those things, which it is generally supposed Nature has involved in obscurity. Here and there I have taken the liberty of throwing in the results of my own experience; but this only sparingly, for on deeply considering the matter, I deemed it best to make use of the facts supplied by others. Indeed there are some that seem born for experimental observation, and endowed with a sharper insight than others, as if they possessed naturally a finer acumen; such are Eustachius, Ruysch, Leeuwenhoek, Lancisi, etc. There are others again who enjoy a natural faculty for contemplating facts already discovered, and eliciting their causes. Both are peculiar gifts and are seldom united in the same person. Besides I found when intently occupied in exploring the secrets of the human body, that as soon as I discovered anything that had not been observed before, I began (seduced probably by self-love) to grow blind to the most acute lucubrations and researches of others and to originate the whole series of inductive arguments from my particular discovery alone; and consequently to be incapacitated to view and comprehend, as accurately as the subject required, the idea of universals in individuals, and of individuals under universals. Nay, when I essayed to form principles from these discoveries, I thought I could detect in various other phenomena much to confirm their truth, although in reality they were fairly susceptible of no construction of the kind. I therefore laid aside my instruments and restraining my desire for making observations, determined rather to rely on the researches of others than to trust to my own.

With this digression we turn again to the journal of Swedenborg's travels. He left Paris at three o'clock on a

March morning of 1738, and travelled by diligence and "treckschuyt, which is here called *diligence par eau*," to Lyons, attentively observing everything on the road. Ten days later he started for Turin by way of Mont Cenis, an arduous journey in those days, and at that season of the year. "We had to undergo great fatigue," he writes, "and our lives were endangered by the snow which had fallen the previous night, which was so deep that our mules had fairly to swim in it, and we were obliged to dismount. It was fortunate that our party consisted of twelve persons besides six monks of the Carmelite Order, and that we had an attendance of from fifty to sixty porters who paved a way for us." There was no Mont Cenis tunnel then!

Other dangers were encountered during this Italian tour. On the journey from Turin to Milan he was abandoned by his *vetturino,* and compelled to travel in the sole company of another who was somewhat of a desperado. The fellow flourished a stiletto from time to time in a threatening manner, and would probably have used it had he thought Swedenborg worth robbing. On a sea journey from Leghorn to Genoa, he was again in danger, from Algerian pirates.

He was in Turin at Easter, 1738; and witnessed the Maundy Thursday and Good Friday processions. On the former day, he records: "I saw their magnificent processions, of which I counted nine; altogether there were from twenty to thirty. They had a great number of large wax tapers; six flogged themselves so that the blood streamed from their bodies; others bore a cross of considerable weight; others had their arms stretched out; others, again, bore the insignia of crucifixion; lastly, a machine furnished with a large number of candles was carried, on which Christ was represented together with Mary. . . . On Good Friday evening they have another great procession, with a machine, on which are Christ lying in a shroud, the head of John the Baptist, and Mary with a sword through her heart."

49

Swedenborg met with plenty of such outward signs of the Christian profession, but Christian morality was not so apparent among the people. In Milan he visited the *Ospedale Maggiore,* "one of the finest and largest in existence." "The service in the hospital," he tells us, "is performed entirely by bastards; for foundlings in great numbers are received in a drawer. . . . There are special halls for the wounded, for there is a great number of them, on account of the many [attempted] assassinations." He speaks highly of the general arrangements of the place.

He also visited the principal monasteries. "One which belongs to the order of Ambrosio, is splendidly decorated with paintings; one of these in the hall upstairs may be called a real chef *d'œuvre*; if you are twelve or fifteen steps removed from it, it is impossible to think otherwise than that it stands out from the wall." Swedenborg shared the very common idea that realism is the highest achievement of art. "In the garden a fig-tree was pointed out, where, it is said, Augustine was converted 1400 years ago. Each of the fathers has his domestic and *valet de chambre*; for they all belong to the aristocracy."

At the "large convent for young ladies," which he visited, "I conversed in the parlour with two nuns; I saw their procession and bought their flowers."

On leaving Milan, he joined company with five Carmelite monks who were about to visit Venice on their way to Rome. They can hardly have entered into all his proceedings, for at Verona, as at other places, he visited the opera. He is enthusiastic in his description of what he saw. "A new theatre," he says, "has been built with a hundred and forty boxes. In respect to the shifting of scenes in the theatre, with their decorations, which all represent beautiful palaces and other fine prospects, and also in respect to the singing and dancing, they surpass the French opera to such a degree, that it seems to be mere child's play in comparison with them."

Of the public buildings he seemed to prefer the modern to the ancient, and speaks more of the precious materials of the latter than of the art displayed in their construction. Thus, at Pisa, he tells us: "Much marble is displayed in chapels, churches, and also in some private houses. Their cathedral is entirely of marble on the outside; in the interior are many handsome pictures, sculptures, and ornaments"; the cathedral of Florence he describes as having "a dome which is of marble on the outside and cost eighteen millions [of francs]." "Close by," he says, "is the Church of S. Giovanni Battista, where are sculptures in marble, and statues in bronze." He brought to architecture the eye of the geologist rather than that of the connoisseur. At Padua, he remarks, "the town hall and the other public buildings are old-fashioned"; while of the churches at Vicenza, we learn that the "more recent" churches are especially celebrated for their architecture. His favourite sculptor seems to have been Bernini, and he is apparently oblivious of the very greatest men. He admires the frescoes in the church of Santa Croce in Florence, because they are "so lifelike, that they seem to be in relief."

We note again his apparent insensibility to the grandeur and beauty of natural scenery. On his journey from Florence to Leghorn, he observes that "the road was fine, *but* there were mountains on both sides" (!). And yet Swedenborg was not without imagination, as the works he wrote at this period evince; his imagination, however, was fed by his knowledge of natural science and of classical literature, rather than by outward impressions from the beauties of creation.

If "the proper study of mankind is man," Swedenborg certainly fulfilled his duty in this respect. While he was busy investigating the internal economy of the human frame, he was observing with equal diligence the life of the body politic, and we have many notes on social, political, and religious affairs. At Florence he "witnessed the consecration of seven nuns; they were in white from top to toe. The archbishop performed the ceremony, and changed his head-covering five times; he addressed questions to them, and they answered him in musical cadence; they lay down on the floor under a black cover for a long time; afterwards they received rings, as well as crowns and other things, partook of the sacrament, and then went out in procession with crowns on their heads. Many ladies in bridal array were present, and fine music was played." Two days later (September 9, 1738), he writes: "I witnessed for the third time, in a convent, the consecration of nuns; the ceremonies differed." He tells us of a remarkable monastery in Rome; "its Fathers are called *Hierosolymi;* twelve of them are confined during the whole year; they obtain their food through a trap door; one day in the year they come out: the others meanwhile drive about in carriages."

He describes relics and other treasures in the churches in a matter-of-fact way, without raising any question of their authenticity or value as aids to devotion. Thus, in the church of San Giovanni in Laterano, he tells us: "Many relics are near the altar: the heads of Peter and Paul, under a rich tabernacle or shrine; a famous column of metal filled with stones from the sepulchre of Christ." In Rome, also, he "saw the prison of St. Peter and St. Paul; the door through which the former is said to have been led out by an angel; the stone pillar to which he was bound; the spring which issued close to it; the opening through which he obtained his food, etc." Swedenborg had special opportunities for seeing what was to be seen in Rome, through the influence of his countryman, Count Nils Bjelke, Chamberlain to the Pope, and a senator of Rome. When, in later life, he wrote much about the Roman Catholic Church, he did not depend on mere hearsay.

It was not only ecclesiastical matters that interested him, however. At Leghorn he visited the galleys, and in Venice joined the expedition which accompanied the Doge when he performed the annual ceremony of "wedding the Adriatic."

The diary of this journey ends abruptly on March 17, 1739, but from other sources we learn that Swedenborg returned to Paris about the middle of May. Of his doings from that date until November 3, 1740, when he reported himself again at the Board of Mines, we know very little except that in the interval he published his *Œconomia Regni Animalis* at Amsterdam.

In the early part of 1743, Swedenborg again applied to the King for leave of absence to go abroad to publish a new work. His application was "graciously entertained," but a point of order required that it should first be submitted to the Board of Mines. Accordingly on June 17th he addressed a letter to the governing body, which is specially important to us as evidence that at this period he had no idea of his future mission, no intention of devoting himself to theology, and that the allurements of worldly honour were still before him. "I can assure you," the letter runs, "that I should a thousand times prefer to stay at home in my native country, where it would be a pleasure to me to serve on so illustrious a Board, and to contribute my own small share to the public good; at the same time to watch opportunities for improving my condition, and attend to the little property I have acquired, and thus live at home and have pleasant times, which, as long as my health and means with God's help continue, nothing would disturb—than to travel abroad, exposing myself at my own by no means inconsiderable expense, to danger and vexation, especially in these unquiet times, and undergoing severe brain work and other hard labour with the probability of meeting in the end with more unfavourable than favourable judgments. But notwithstanding all this, I am influenced interiorly by the desire and longing to produce during my life-time something real, which may be of use in the general scientific world and also to posterity, and in this way to be useful to and even to please my native country; and, if my wishes are realized, to obtain honour for it. . . . It is my own chief desire to bring this work to a close, and to return to my country, to my office, and to my property, where I shall in tranquillity and ease, continue my larger work, the *Regnum Minerale,* and thus be of actual use to the public at large in those matters which properly belong to the Royal Board."

Apparently the *Regnum Minerale* was a work which he hoped to undertake after he had completed the publication of the *Regnum Animale* for which he was now again going abroad, but it can only have been an intention, as no MSS. have been found relating to it.

Swedenborg started on his new journey in July, 1743; his journal, however, does not extend beyond August 20th, and contains little of special interest. He met many persons of note, and at Hamburg was presented to Prince Augustus, and Prince Adolphus Frederic, the recently-elected Crown Prince of Sweden. The latter was pleased to look at the manuscript of Swedenborg's new book, and the reviews of his former one. At the various places our author visited, he inspected the churches, fortifications, water works, public buildings, etc., as was his wont. What transpired later in this journey, marking such an unexpected change in his life, will appear in the sequel.

The first two portions of his new work, *Regnum Animale*—it was designed to run some seventeen parts in all—were published at the Hague in 1744. A third part was published in London in 1745; and an immense amount of matter prepared but left unpublished. We must reserve more particular notice of it, and of the other two works mentioned above, for the succeeding chapters.

CHAPTER IV

IN SEARCH OF THE SOUL

SWEDENBORG'S anatomical studies began in early life. In 1719 he submitted to the Royal Medical College a dissertation in Swedish on *"The anatomy of our most subtle nature, showing that our moving and living force consists of tremulations."* In the preparation of this treatise (the manuscript of a portion of which is still preserved in the Diocesan library of Linköping), he says in a letter to Benzelius: "I made myself thoroughly acquainted with the anatomy of the nerves and membranes"; and he claims to have "proved the harmony which exists between it and the interesting geometry of tremulations." He returned to his studies of the structure of the human body again and again, and between the years 1734 and 1743 accumulated a great mass of material for his philosophical treatises.

His object, as I have said, was to discover, if possible, where the living force resides that regulates the economy of the animal kingdom, that is, the kingdom presided over by the *anima,* or soul, to wit, the human body, that wonderful organism which responds to every command and suggestion of the indwelling spirit. Where this living essence resides, and what its nature is, were the objects of his ardent quest.

Swedenborg's quest for the soul was life-long until his intromission into the spiritual world solved for him the mystery that science and philosophy could not fathom. "The subject apparently is the goal of the *Principia,* and still more plainly, of the *Prodromus on the Infinite.* Whether Swedenborg was conscious from an early period of this direction of his labours, is hard to determine;

55

but it is certain that he rose from one study to another, in regular order, without proposing an ultimate end, until he proclaimed his resolution to investigate the soul." (Editor's "Introductory Remarks" to *The Economy of the Animal Kingdom,* pp. xv, xvi.) In the *Principia,* he seemed to recognize that a knowledge of the soul was unattainable by the methods he employed to investigate the hidden forces of nature, for he writes:

> In respect to the soul and its various faculties, I do not conceive it possible that they can be explained or comprehended by any of the known laws of motion; such indeed is our present state of ignorance, that we know not whether the motions by which the soul operates on the organs of the body be such as to be reducible to any rule or law, either similar or dissimilar to those of mechanics. (Part I, Chap. I.)

The laws of physics and chemistry not availing to reveal the mystery of life, he turns to the animal kingdom, and in the organism of its highest subject tries to discover the vital essence, by the study of anatomy and by the aid of certain philosophical doctrines which he has formulated for himself. He writes:

> I am strongly persuaded that the essence and nature of the soul, its influx into the body, and the reciprocal action of the body, can never come to demonstration, without these doctrines [he is referring to his Doctrine of Order, and Science of Universals], combined with a knowledge of anatomy, pathology, and psychology; nay, even of physics, and especially of the auras of the world; and that unless our labours take this direction and mount from phenomena thus, we shall in every new age have to build new systems, which in their turn will tumble to the ground, without the possibility of being rebuilt.

56

This, and no other, is the reason that, with diligent study and intense application, I have investigated the anatomy of the body [in all its parts]. In doing this, I may perhaps have gone beyond the ordinary limits of inquiry, so that but few of my readers may be able distinctly to understand me. But thus far I have felt bound to venture, for I have resolved, cost what it may, to trace out the nature of the human soul. (*Economy of the Animal Kingdom,* Part II, Nos. 213 and 214.)

The outcome of his studies for this purpose was the publication of *The Economy of the Animal Kingdom, considered Anatomically, Physically, and Philosophically;* and the preparation of a great part of the proposed *Animal Kingdom considered Anatomically, Physically, and Philosophically;* the latter being in the nature of a revision and extension of the former. As mentioned, only three parts were published by Swedenborg, though a further part was left in MSS.—whether ready for the printer or still subject to revision cannot be known. Several portions of these MSS. have however been translated and published posthumously, on *Generation,* on *The Brain,* and on *Rational Psychology.*

The *Economy* was translated into English by the Rev. Augustus Clissold, M.A., in collaboration with Dr. James John Garth Wilkinson. The first three parts of *The Animal Kingdom,* all that Swedenborg had actually published, by the latter alone. Each work appeared in two volumes, and they were published successively between the years 1843 and 1846, almost exactly a hundred years after their original issue. To each of them Dr. Wilkinson wrote a lengthy and brilliant introduction which evoked unstinted admiration from Emerson. The latter described Wilkinson as a "philosophical critic, with a co-equal vigour of understanding and imagination comparable only to Lord Bacon's," and declared that these "admirable preliminary discourses . . . threw all the contemporary philosophy of England into the shade." The reader who wishes to know something of Swedenborg's philosophy, and does not want to wade through four large volumes, should at least read Dr. Wilkinson's "Introductory Remarks."

In *The Economy of the Animal Kingdom,* which was the earlier work, Swedenborg deals with the composition of the blood, and its circulation; with the heart, arteries, and veins; with fœtal circulation; and with the brain, especially in regard to its cortical substance and its motion. He also has a chapter on rational psychology, and one on the human soul. The greater part of the work, however, is taken up with the blood and its circulation. "The blood is the life," we are told in the Scriptures; it was because it is "the common fountain and general principle" of the animal kingdom, that Swedenborg regarded it as of primary importance.

> On the nature, constitution, determination, continuity, and quantity of the blood depend the fortunes and condition of the animal life. (Part I, No. 2.)

> The blood is, as it were, the complex of all things that exist in the world, and the storehouse and seminary of all that exist in the body. (*Ibid.,* No. 3.)

> For if all things exist for the sake of man, and with a view to affording him the conditions and means of living, then all things exist for the sake of the blood, which is the parent and nourisher of every part of the body; for nothing exists in the body that has not previously existed in the blood. (*Ibid.,* No. 4.)

It was chiefly, however, because Swedenborg believed that the essential vital principle was contained in the blood that he dwelt at such length upon the nature and offices of the latter. This vital principle he describes as "a most spirituous fluid which is in immediate connection with the soul." The blood is "a concrete of substances of various natures, and more especially of the fluid in which the soul resides, and of which the soul is the life." This spirituous fluid, indeed, he thought must be the soul itself.

If this fluid is regarded as the purest of the organs of the body, and the most exquisitely adapted for the reception of life, then it lives not from itself, but from Him who is self-living, that is from the God of the universe, without whom nothing whatever in nature could live, much less be wise. *This fluid,* in this light, is to be denominated the *spirit* and *soul* of its body. (Part II, No. 245.)

It is the universal force or substance, or the soul of its body, but the red blood is the common substance, or the corporeal soul. (*Ibid.,* No. 205.)

This may seem a materialistic view, and it certainly appears that Swedenborg, at this period, because he saw the necessity of the soul being organic, could not but think that it was a sublimated form of matter. His mind as yet knew nothing about a spiritual substance.

If [he says] we deprive the soul of every predicate that belongs to material things, as of extension, figure, space, magnitude, and motion, we deprive the mind of everything to which, as to an anchor, it can attach its ideas; the consequence is, that everyone is left in doubt whether, after all, the soul be anything distinct from an *ens rationis.* (Part II, No. 216.)

In another place he writes:

It is no matter whether we call the above fluid the spirit or soul, or whether we confine those terms to its faculty of representing the universe to itself, and of having intuition of ends; for the one cannot be conceived, because it is impossible, without the other. (Part II, No. 303.)

The spirituous fluid, or animal spirit, we are told, has

59

its origin in the brain, and is driven to all parts of the body by the pulsations of the latter, for Swedenborg concluded that the brain has a regular motion, as well as the heart.

The motion of the brain is called animation, and the action of the spirituous fluid depends upon it. (Part I, No. 279.)

Every time the brains animate, they drive out their fluid into the fibres and nerves; much as the heart, at every systole and diastole, drives out the blood through its vessels. (*Ibid.,* No. 483.)

To suppose the circulation of this fluid without a motive force, and a real expansion and constriction as a moving cause, would be to imagine the circulation of the red blood through the arteries and veins without the heart. (Part II, No. 169.)

The circulation of this fluid deserves to be called the CIRCLE OF LIFE. (*Ibid.,* No. 168.)

The whole aim of *The Economy of the Animal Kingdom* was to discover the nature of the soul and its operation in the body.

According to our proposition the intercourse between the soul and the body may be ascertained by a diligent and rational anatomical investigation combined with psychological experience. (*Ibid.,* No. 309.)

His conclusions are summed up in a fine passage towards the end of the work. It is too long to quote in its entirety, but the following extracts may suitably close this brief notice.

We have often said above, that in regard to substance the soul is a fluid, nay, a fluid most absolute; produced by the aura of the universe; enclosed in the fibres; the matter by which, from which, and for which, the body exists; the super-eminent organ. . . . Also that its nature, or operations collectively, regard this fluid as their subject; and that these operations, in so far as they are natural, cannot be separated [from the fluid] except in thought; so that nothing here occurs but appears to be fairly comprehended under the term matter.

"But," he asks, "pray, what is matter?" and proceeds to discuss this question with his unfailing care and penetration.

If it [matter] is defined as extension endued with inertia, then the soul is not material; for inertia, the source of gravity, enters the posterior sphere simply by composition, and by the addition of a number of things that through changes in the state of active entities have become inert, and gravitating; for instance, all the mere elements of the earth, as salts, minerals, etc. . . . When, according to the rules of the doctrine of order, I have shown what matter is, what form is, what extension is, and what a fluid is, we shall confess that the controversy is about the signification of terms, or the manner in which something that we are ignorant of, is to be denominated. . . . But tell me whether the ideas of the animus [the lower degree of the mind] are material, or not? Perhaps they are, inasmuch as images, and even, the very eyes, are material. . . . Still material ideas not only agree but communicate with immaterial; are they then any ideas at all before they partake of the life of the soul? Apart from this, are they not modifications? If they are modifications, or analogous to modifications, then I do not understand in what way an immaterial modification is distinguished from a material modification, unless by degrees, in that the immaterial is higher, more universal, more perfect, and more imperceptible. . . . But as for the more noble essence or life of the soul, it is not raised to any that is more perfect, because it is one only essence; but the soul is an organism formed by the spirituous fluid, in which respect greater and lesser exaltation may be predicated of it. This essence and life is not created, and therefore it is not proper to call it material; so for the same reason we cannot call the soul material in respect to its reception of this life; nor therefore the mind, nor therefore the animus, nor the sight, nor the hearing, nor even the body itself so far as it lives. For all these live the life of their soul, and the soul lives the life of the spirit of God, who is not matter, but essence; whose esse is life; whose life is wisdom, and whose wisdom consists in beholding and embracing the ends to be promoted by the determinations of matter and the forms of nature. Thus both materiality and immateriality are predicable of the soul. (Part II, No. 311.)

The section on "The Human Soul," from which these extracts are taken, is a very remarkable study, elevated in tone and profound in its speculations: Dr. Spurgin, a former President of the Royal College of Physicians, declared it to be "a production unparalleled for excellence in the whole compass of human philosophy;" and S. T. Coleridge refers to it in terms of the highest praise. Nevertheless, Swedenborg himself was not satisfied with his conclusions. The more deeply he investigated, the more the soul seemed to evade him; its activities were manifest in every movement of the human body, from the inmost and most subtle, to the visible outward actions; yet still it eluded his grasp.

I could not but think [he writes] with mankind in general, that all our knowledge of it was to be attempted either by a bare reasoning philosophy, or more immediately by the anatomy of the human body. But on making the attempt, I found myself as far from my object as ever; for no sooner did I seem to have mastered the subject, than I found it again eluding my grasp, though it never absolutely disappeared from my view. . . . Thus did I seem to see, and yet not to see, the very object, with the desire of knowing which I was never at rest. But at length I awoke as from a deep sleep, when I discovered, that nothing is further removed from the human understanding than what at the same time is really present to it; and that nothing is more present to it than what is universal, prior, and superior; since this enters into every particular, and into everything posterior and inferior. What is more omnipresent than the Deity, —in Him we live and are, and move,—and yet what is more remote from the sphere of the understanding? (*The Economy of the Animal Kingdom,* Part II, No. 208.)

He was not dismayed, nevertheless. Dissatisfied with his present work, he would search yet more deeply. He continued to study and write in preparation for a still more important work to be entitled *The Animal Kingdom,* the original plan of which embraced seventeen parts, dealing, more or less, with the anatomy of the whole body, and putting forth many philosophical suggestions. He published two parts at the Hague in 1744, as already mentioned, and a third in London the following year. The work was never completed, for reasons that will presently appear.

In the Prologue to this great work he says:

Not very long ago I published *The Economy of the Animal Kingdom.* . . . and before traversing the whole field in detail, I made a rapid passage to the soul and put forth an essay respecting it. But on considering the matter more deeply, I found that I had directed my course thither both too hastily and too fast,—after having explored the blood only, and its peculiar organs. I took the step impelled by an ardent desire for knowledge.

63

The Animal Kingdom, then, was to remedy the defects and supply the deficiencies, of the *Economy.*

What was Swedenborg's object in writing these works? He was anything but a barren speculator, as we have seen, —he aimed at practical ends in all his labours. What, then, did he desire to accomplish by these high philosophical studies? Secure in his own faith in God and spiritual things, he was appalled at the prevalent materialism of his time. There were many then, as now, who tried to persuade themselves that God was an abstraction, and the soul a theological assumption. The existence of a Divine Being, he considered, was "a necessary truth" in all sound philosophy; but in regard to the soul, he hoped to demonstrate its existence and nature by an analytic study of "its kingdom" the body.

To those who deprecated such peering into spiritual mysteries, who held that "all those things which transcend our present state are matters for faith and not for intellect," he replied:

I grant this; nor would I persuade any one who comprehends these high truths by faith to attempt to comprehend them by his intellect: let him abstain from my books. . . . But these pages of mine are written with a view to those only who never believe anything but what they can receive with the intellect; consequently who boldly invalidate, and are fain to deny, the existence of all supereminent things, sublimer than themselves, as the soul itself, and what follows therefrom—its life, immortality, heaven, etc. . . . For these persons only I am anxious; and, as I said before, for them I indite, and to them I dedicate my work. For when I shall have demonstrated truths themselves by the analytic method, I hope that those debasing shadows, or material clouds, which darken the sacred temple of the mind, will be dispersed, and that thus at last, under the favour of God, who is the Sun of Wisdom, an access will be opened, and a way laid down, to faith. (Prologue, No. 22.)

The scheme of *The Animal Kingdom* was to describe in great detail all the organs of the body, dwelling on their uses; and, on the basis of the collected facts, to establish principles which should give the mind access to the secret of life and the conscious soul. For his facts Swedenborg relied on the works of the greatest anatomists of the age, under some of whom he had sat as a pupil. The collection of extracts from their writings to be found in this and the earlier work is in itself of great value, as the publications of the old anatomists are not easily accessible.* He also quotes largely from the *Biblia Naturæ* of John Swammerdam, in regard to the anatomy of insects.

His object was still to locate the soul, and to describe its operations; for "as yet," he says, "her mode of being and her nature are almost absolutely unknown," and proceeds,

I know, it will be whispered in my ear by many of the most accomplished philosophers of the day, that it is vain and useless to enter the recesses and interiors of the human body, with a view to arriving at the soul. . . . But these arguments may be met by a few opposite ones. Inasmuch as the soul is the model, the idea, the first form, the substance, the force, and the principle of her organic body, and of all its forces and powers; or, what amounts to the same thing, as the organic body is the image and type of its soul, formed and principled to the whole nature of the soul's efficiency, it follows, that the one is represented in the other, if not exactly, yet quite sufficiently to the life. . . . Thus, by the body, we are instructed respecting the soul; by the soul respecting the body; and by both respecting the truth of the whole. (Part I, No. 20.)

---

* If any medical reader should wish to consult them, copies of many, or most, of the works from which Swedenborg quotes will be found in the library of the Swedenborg Society, 20 Bloomsbury Way, London, W.C. 1.

Swedenborg's arduous labours enabled him to clear the way, and get a more definite grasp of the problem. He concluded that the centre of the soul's activity is the brain; this receives impressions from outward things, thus originating conceptions, which at length

> put on rational forms, and become intellectual ideas. . . . There is in the cerebrum an eminent sensorium, and intimate recesses therein, whither the sensuous rays of the body ascend, and where they can mount no further; there the soul resides, clad in the noble garment of organization, and sits to meet the ideas emerging thither, and receives them as guests. This high and noble place is the innermost sensorium, and it is the boundary at which the ascent of the life of the body ceases, and the boundary from which that of the soul, considered as a spiritual essence, begins. (Part II, No. 458.)

One evidence of advance we may observe in *The Animal Kingdom*—a clearer recognition of the value of analogy in the pursuit of spiritual truth. Not only does the author perceive that the body is the perfect instrument and analogue of the soul, but he has intimations of the great doctrine of correspondences which plays such an important part in his later works. Thus we read:

> As the blood is continually making its circle of life, that is to say, is in a constant revolution of birth and death; as it dies in its old age, and is regenerated or born anew; and as the veins solicitously gather together the whole of its corporeal part, and the lymphatics, of its spirituous part; and successively bring it back, reflect it with a new chyle, and restore it to pure and youthful blood; and as the kidneys constantly purge it of impurities, and restore its pure parts to the blood; so likewise Man, who lives at once in body and spirit while he lives in the blood, must undergo the same fortunes generally,

and in the progress of his regeneration must daily do the like. Such a perpetual symbolical representation is there of spiritual life in corporeal life; as likewise a perpetual typical representation of the soul in the body. (Part I, No. 293.)

In a note he adds:

In our Doctrine of Representations and Correspondences, we shall treat of both these symbolical and typical representations, and of the astonishing things which occur, I will not say in the living body only, but throughout nature, and which correspond so entirely to supreme and spiritual things, that one would swear that the physical world was purely symbolical of the spiritual world,—insomuch that if we were to choose to express any natural truth in physical and definite vocal terms, and to convert these terms only into the corresponding spiritual terms, we should by this means elicit a spiritual truth . . . in place of the physical truth . . .; although no mortal could have predicted that anything of the kind could possibly arise by bare literal transposition; inasmuch as the one precept, considered separately from the other, appears to have absolutely no relation to it.

Something must be said of Swedenborg's philosophical method, as displayed in these works; a method distinctively his own. Dr. Wilkinson, in his Introduction to the *Economy,* calls Swedenborg the "Synthesis of Aristotle and Bacon." "The ascending method of Bacon, and the descending one of Aristotle," he says, "are, in fact, both realized by Swedenborg, and being connected to each other at either end, they form a legitimate and widening spiral, revolving from the senses to the mind, and from the mind to the senses." (P. xv.) Mr. J. D. Morell remarks in *An Historical and Critical Review of the Speculative Philosophy of Europe in the Nineteenth Century* (Vol. I,

p. 320) that Swedenborg's method "evidently is the inductive and synthetic methods combined. Commencing by observation, his mind seized upon certain high philosophical axioms; and from them reasoned downwards to the nature and uses of particular objects. Perhaps it is the only attempt the world has seen (with the exception of the unsuccessful efforts of Comte) at rising upwards to purely philosophical ideas from positive and concrete facts."

"Swedenborg's mind," it has been truly remarked, "was essentially constructive; whenever it was plunged in a solution of facts, crystallisation at once ensued; by nature he was an architect and no brickmaker. His commentaries on the facts of the anatomists manifested in every way the creative spirit which transforms the inorganic to the organic."

In a paper read before the Royal Swedish Academy of Sciences, on December 14, 1740, Swedenborg explained and defended his philosophic method. He said:

There are two ways by which to trace out those things in nature which lie either open before us, or are hidden from our eyes—viz. the *a priori* which is also called the synthetical method, and the *a posteriori,* or the analytical method. Both are necessary in reflecting upon and tracing out one and the same thing: for in order to do so there is required both light *a priori,* and experience *a posteriori.* Now, while the learned among the ancients followed the former light as remotely and profoundly as they possibly could, those at a later period were induced not to accept anything as witness, unless it was confirmed by experience. Hence also some of the learned at the present day seem to have agreed to let thought rest, and to make experiments which would appeal to the senses; yet they did so with the hope and intent that some day experience would be connected with theory: for experience deprived of an insight into the nature of things is knowledge without learning, and a foundation without a building to rest upon it. The observations of the outward senses merely furnish data and give information about things which the understanding ought to investigate, and concerning which it ought to form its judgments; such also is the distinctive quality of a rational being whose superiority over brute animals consists in being able to exercise his understanding in matters acquired by experience.

Swedenborg was very well versed in both ancient and modern philosophy, and quotes widely from many different authors. He was able to see the value and deficiencies of both systems, and endeavoured by combining their methods to frame one of his own that should lead to sound conclusions. The ancients, he saw, were too much given to hypothesis and conjecture; the moderns were slaves to facts and sensism. The editor of the English translation of *The Economy of the Animal Kingdom* writes in his Introductory Remarks, referring to Bacon and Aristotle, "Swedenborg embraces the merits and avoids the imperfections of these writers, and he alone has propounded a science constituted of principles, which as it were spontaneously, are physical in the physical universe and philosophical in the mind of man, and by which we may pass and repass from the one into the other, so as to contemplate the end of creation in connection with the means, and *vice versa*." (P. xv.)

Swedenborg had understood this long before, for in his *Principia* he had said:

> Knowledge without reason, a heap of many things in the memory without judgment to separate and distinguish them, and without the talent of deducing the unknown object of inquiry from certain known data, by means of a rational or geometrical analysis,—in a word, the possession of the means without the faculty

of arriving at the end, does not make a philosopher.
(Part I, No. 3.)

He who is possessed of scientific knowledge, and is
merely skilled in experiment has taken only the first
step to wisdom; for such a person is only acquainted
with what is posterior, and is ignorant of what is prior;
thus his wisdom does not extend beyond the organs of
the senses, and is unconnected with reason; when nevertheless true wisdom embraces both. (*Ibid.*, No. 1.)

On the other hand,

Synthesis, which begins its thread of reasons from
causes and principles, and evolves and unwinds it until
it reaches the effects of the causes, and the phenomena
resulting from the principles, . . . is nothing but a poor,
precocious, and vague analysis. . . . Those who commence
with this species of scholastic exercitation, that is, who
set out relying on mere reasoning, not fortified by the
sure patronage of experience, will never, as I think, attain the goal. (*The Animal Kingdom,* Part I, Prologue,
Nos. 7, 8.)

Neither science nor reason, alone or together, will enable
us to arrive at true philosophic ideas. There is a higher
faculty still, which has been greatly neglected by philosophers, but which Swedenborg has restored to its proper
place,—the faculty of intuition. The mind can *see* truth,
as well as learn it by observation and reasoning.

The rational mind, that is, the intellect, unhesitatingly
distinguishes the truths of things, and the forms conso-
nant to the order of nature—at once to the nature
of the universe, and to that of the intellect itself; for they
sweetly soothe and please, and call forth deeply-hidden
affections; wherefore whenever a truth shines forth, the
mind exults and rejoices. (*The Animal Kingdom,* Part
I, Prologue No. 2.)

And

one truth is not opened without an infinity of other truths being also opened. (*Ibid.*, No. 4.)

To science and reason

"we must add an innate love of truth, an eager desire of exploring it, a delight in finding it, and a natural gift and faculty of meditating thoughtfully and distinctly, and of connecting reasons together acutely: also of recalling the mind from the senses, from the lusts of the body, the enticements of the world and its cares,— all which things are distracting forces,—and of keeping it in its own higher sphere, until it has summed up its reasons, and carried its thoughts to their conclusion. In proportion as by these means we ascend to truths, in the same proportion truths descend to us. Above all things it behoves the mind to be pure, and to respect universal ends, as the happiness of the human race, and thereby the glory of God: truth is then infused into our minds from its heaven; whence as from its proper fountain it all emanates." (*Ibid.*, No. 12.)

Thus if we wish to invite real truths, whether natural, or moral, or spiritual (for they all make common cause by means of correspondence and representation), into the sphere of our rational minds, it is necessary that we extinguish the impure fires of the body, and thereby our own delusive lights, and submit and allow our minds, unmolested by the influences of the body, to be illumined with the rays of the spiritual power: then for the first time truths flow in; for they all emanate from that power as their peculiar fountain. (*Ibid.*, Part II, Epilogue, No. 463.)

When . . . we have been carried up to the principles of things, we may then properly for the first time commence, or rather, return, from principles, and put them forth, as of sufficient authority, by a clear and intelligible definition: for the mind now looks round the whole world as from a mirror, and contemplates all things in a universal manner. Ladders are constructed, and steps interposed, whereby we may equally descend and ascend. (*Ibid.*, Part I, Prologue, No. 13.)

There is a higher truth that comes to us by perception or intuition, and a lower truth that reaches the mind through the senses.

These . . . are so widely separated, that they cannot possibly come together without some uniting medium. Our rational mind is that uniting medium, where mystic meetings are carried on, and sacred covenants ratified. . . . Now since worldly things flow into it from the lowest sphere, through the gates of the senses, and heavenly things, from the highest, through the portal of the soul, hence it is the true centre of the universe. . . . We are organic subjects, through which the lowest things ascend, and the highest descend; and human minds are the very receiving-rooms of both these guests. (*Ibid.*, Part II, Epilogue, No. 465.)

Here is an organon that makes all other philosophical methods seem imperfect and inefficient; and one that will surely in the end harmonize science and religion. "It is then futile to assert that philosophy is not connected with theology; since the contrary is demonstrated by Swedenborg as fairly as any law of matter is demonstrated by Newton. For Swedenborg took facts representing integral nature, and investigated them, and the order and mechanism of structure, and the pervading use of function, was found to be such as in every case to furnish truths relating to the moral or social existence of man." (*The Economy of the Animal Kingdom*, "Introductory Remarks by the Editor," p. lxxvi.) "He wielded with ease the solid masses of learning, and they obeyed new motions and ran in systematic orbits. The naked rocks of science received a quickening climature, and greenness and life came upon them." (*Ibid.*, p. lxxxix.) Materialists "said that science was passionless and inflexible; that it had nothing to do with philosophy or theology; that it observed sequences, and made answerable formulæ, or had a method but not a soul; that it excluded all but material explanations and ideas. But Swedenborg appealed to the same facts as they did, and with a different result. He found nature warm with the same spirit as humanity, and that her sternest laws are plastic when use requires: that hence illiberal logic is not meant to comprehend her. Also that nature is no other than philosophy and theology embodied in mechanics; or more reverently speaking, she is the mechanism or means of which truth and good are the end." (*Ibid.*, p. lxxvii).

It will thus appear that, while Swedenborg recognized the all-importance of a sound basis of facts to any true system of philosophy, he did not rest in mere science, or allow it to enslave him; but rose above the material plane and took large views that enabled him to grasp the inner meaning, and broad applications of his facts. "The maze of nature is inextricable, and offers no escape, unless we can master its leading intersections. . . . Lord Bacon remarks, that "as no perfect view of a country can be taken upon a flat; so it is impossible to discover the remote and deep parts of any science, by standing upon the level of the same science; or without ascending to a higher." From which it would appear that the evolution of the highest science is requisite *a priori,* to give life and validity to the whole remainder of knowledge." (*Ibid.*, p. xxxvii.) This is what Swedenborg aimed at; how far he succeeded it is for the reader to judge.

Swedenborg's scientific and philosophical works are said to have had a large sale, and he placed them freely at the service of those who "possess understanding, and are interested in such subjects"; but they seem to have met with a cold reception in their author's own day; to all appearance, they were "forgotten as soon as published." There is evidence that some of his contemporaries assimilated and worked upon his ideas, but we meet with no frank acknowledgment of his services to science and philosophy until our own times. He does not appear to have looked for any better reception for his works; and therefore he showed neither bitterness nor disappointment. He was not indifferent to the appreciation of his contemporaries, but few writers have allowed the praise of men to influence them so little.

Of what consequence is it to me, he asks, that I should persuade any one to embrace my opinions? Let his own reason persuade him. I do not undertake this work for the sake of honour or emolument; both of which I shun rather than seek, because they disquiet the mind, and because I am content with my lot; but for the sake of the truth, which alone is immortal. (*The Economy of the Animal Kingdom,* Part II, No. 218.)

If he looked for little recognition from his own generation, he was possessed with the firm consciousness, which is often exhibited by unappreciated genius, that the time would come when he would be better understood. Hence he prefixed the following motto, from Seneca, to his *Economy*: "He is born to serve but few, who thinks only of the people of his own age. Many thousands of years, many generations of men are yet to come: look to these, though from some cause silence has been imposed on all of your own day; then will come those who may judge without offense and without favour."

At the same time as he was engaged upon *The Animal Kingdom* Swedenborg was writing another work of a different and somewhat remarkable character, entitled *De Cultu et Amore Dei* (*The Worship and Love of God*),

74

the first two parts of which, after adding an unusual number of footnotes, he eventually published in 1745. A third part was never published and indeed was not even completed in MS.

It is a little difficult to understand the meaning and intention of this work; but the wisdom and beauty embodied in it are unmistakable. Swedenborg himself said of this work that it was written "under the leadership of the understanding, and according to the thread of reason," and, in reply to a querist who asked him how the book was to be regarded, stated that "it was certainly founded on truth, but somewhat of egotism had introduced itself into it, as he had made a playful use in it of the Latin language, on account of his having been ridiculed for the simplicity of his Latin style in later years. For this reason he did not regard it as *equal* to his other works." It does not properly belong to the category either of his scientific or his theological works, but holds a distinct place of its own.

A summary of its contents gives a poor idea of the book itself, but a few selections will convey something of its literary charm and depth of wisdom. Most readers of the book will be struck by the mixture of poetic fancy and profound penetration which it exhibits.

It essays to give an account of creation, first describing the birth of the planets from the sun. Our own earth, when it had at length broken free from the nebulous ring which surrounded the sun, and from which it had its origin, was gradually prepared for the advent of life, the germs of which existed as

small eggs collected at its surface, or small seeds of its future triple kingdom—viz. the mineral, the vegetable, and the animal. These seeds or beginnings lay as yet unseparated in their rudiments, one folded up in another, namely, the vegetable kingdom in the mineral kingdom, which was to be the matrix; and in the vegetable kingdom, which was to serve as a nurse or nourisher, the animal kingdom; for each afterwards was to come forth distinctly from its coverings. Thus the present contained the past, and what was to come lay concealed in each, for one thing involved another in a continual series; by which means this earth, from its continued auspices, was perpetually in a kind of birth. (Para. No. 15.)

The earth, we are told, gradually receded from the sun, its annual and diurnal rotations occupying an increasing length of time as it removed further and further from the parent orb. At the time when life first appeared, the year was no longer than our present month, and the day not more than two hours in duration. The effect of this rapid rotation was to equalize the climate, the seasons merging into one another so as to from a perpetual spring. These halcyon days are described in a passage which may serve as an example of the poetic style of the book:

The proximate atmosphere itself, or air, breathed the most grateful temperature in consequence of receiving so copious a light and alternate heat, and at the same time, being warmed by fruitful dews exhaled from the bosom of the earth; for as yet there was no furious wind, no Boreas to disturb the air with his stormy whirlwind; nor as yet did the smallest cloud intercept the splendour of the sun and of the stars; but the face of everything was serene, and zephyrs only, with their gentle fannings, appeased the murmurs of the winds. (Para. No. 17.)

The earliest forms of vegetable life were herbs and lowly flowers, which clothed the surface of the earth with beauty; after these, shrubs and plants; and finally, trees. From the vegetable world proceeded the primal forms of animal life, the earliest being insects; from the shrubs were produced eggs which were nourished among their branches, and eventually hatched into birds; while the quadrupeds "were in like manner produced from viviparous forests," the branching horns of many of them indicating their arboreal origin! Lastly came man, the product of the Tree of Life,

> which bore a small egg, the most precious of all, in which, as in a jewel, nature concealed herself with her highest powers and stores, to become the initiaments of the most consummate body. (Para. No. 32.)

Written at the transitional period of Swedenborg's life, *The Worship and Love of God* gathers up many of the ideas found in his earlier works, and reaches forward to the high truths which he was henceforth to expound. Geometry is still to him the most fascinating of sciences, and in a suggestive note he returns to his "doctrine of forms," classifying geometric forms in an ascending series from angular forms, "the form proper to earthly substances," through circular, spherical, spiral, and vortical, to the celestial, the geometry of the heavens. From the doctrine of forms he ascends to that of order and degrees, and to the doctrine of correspondences, foreshadowed in *The Animal Kingdom*. We read:

> Such is the established correspondence, that by natural and moral truths, by means of the transpositions only of the expressions that signify natural things, we are introduced into spiritual truths, and *vice versa,* and thus, as it were, from one Paradise into another. For the sake of illustration, let one or two examples suffice, as first, *Light reveals the quality of its object, but the quality of the object appears according to the state of the light, wherefore the object is not always such as it appears.* . . . Now if instead of light we take intelligence, the quality of the object of which is the truth of a thing; since intelligence is universally allowed to be spiritual

77

light, this conclusion follows: *Intelligence discovers the truth of a thing, but the truth of a thing appears according to the state of the intelligence; wherefore that is not always true which is supposed to be true,* etc. (Footnote to para. No. 55.)

Again:

Nothing in any case exists in nature which does not in a type resemble its origin, or soul; and as this origin is from heaven (for all uses, as was said, are ends designed by heaven), therefore things natural and things celestial must of necessity agree with each other, according to the order first induced, or the most perfect order; and this in such a manner, that it is allowable to take a view of one from the other; for if we unfold natural things, and in their place transcribe celestial or spiritual things, congruous truths result. (Footnote, para. No. 64.)

Those familiar with Swedenborg's remarkable work on *The Divine Love and Wisdom,* published eighteen years later, will recognize the germs of many of the profound ideas it embodies in the work before us. An exhaustive comparison is out of the question, but I may point out some of the more striking of these anticipations.

That all life is spiritual, that spirit is substance, and that, as the origin of all things, God Himself is the only true and real substance, is clearly taught in a note to paragraph No. 47:

The soul is so real a substance, that all the substances of the body, which enjoy active life, are from it, and are called substances, but compounded ones; for every compound is only an aggregate of its simple substances; nor is anything truly a substance but the Supreme, which is therefore called a simple substance.

Another great principle, that no substance is without

form is stated in so many words in a note to para. No. 49. Many of these great philosophical principles have been added in notes, which are quite a valuable part of the book. As it was not Swedenborg's custom to write footnotes, the probability is that the many footnotes in this volume were added at a later date than the first script, possibly after his intromission to be described in the next chapter.

Whether we speak of forms or substances, it amounts to the same thing, since no substance produced from God is given without a form, whence it derives its faculties of acting, and its qualities.

That creation is an emanation from God as the essential substance, and not a making of something out of nothing is strongly insisted upon in both works. In the earlier one we read:

It is impossible for anything to exist from what has no being, and out of nothing, nothing can be made. (Para. No. 61.)

A leading proposition in *The Divine Love and Wisdom* is that "the love or will is the very life of man." In *The Worship and Love of God,* we read:

Without love there is no life, and the life is of such a quality as is the love. (Para. No. 67.)

The essential connection between goodness and truth, and the influence of the will upon perception and belief, are demonstrated in both works. We read in *The Worship and Love of God*:

All truths concentrate in goodness, consequently expand themselves, as it were, into circumferences from goodness, as from a centre. (Note to para. No. 53.)

Again:

Our loves . . . hold the reins, and excite and govern

our minds; by them we are drawn, and then we follow. (Para. No. 59.)

In both books, too, it is taught that all life and wisdom are derived, and that the way to true philosophy is to keep the mind open to influences from within and above.

There are only two ways of access to the mind, namely, from above, and from beneath; the way from above is through the soul and its temple; this way is sacred. . . . This way is open only to the Lord of light, and to His love; but the latter, or inferior way, is the only one through which he [the prince of this world] can creep, and exert his influences. (Para. No. 71.)

Our minds are such as to be capable of turning two ways, as upon hinges, namely, inwards and outwards, or upwards and downwards; for there are, as it were, two ways or places of reception of two guests. (Para. No. 56.)

Those "whose wisdom is grounded only in the delusive *lumen* of nature" cannot see spiritual truth because they persistently look downwards and outwards instead of upwards and inwards.

They suffer themselves to be convinced by nothing, but by the testimony of the external senses; and what is wonderful, they reject from their belief the clearest agencies and effects, unless they see them also in a substance; wherefore when they look into truth from this connection and order, the chain snaps asunder, at its first link, and thus their view remains fixed in mere earthly objects, or in matters which are born from the ultimate form. (Para. No. 95.)

Turning again to the narrative part of this book, Adam is instructed in the nature of true wisdom by heavenly intelligences. The leader of the celestial "wisdoms" teaches him that supreme things, or things superior in order, flow into inferior things, and these into ultimate things, but not *vice versa;* hence inferior things derive their powers and perfections, or thence flow all the qualities and abilities of inferior things. When this order is established, then there is nothing so complicated and abstruse which is not explained and unfolded, for it is the light itself which sees, and the living force itself which acts. . . . But it is altogether otherwise if this order be inverted, that is, if liberty be given to nature to break in, without leave, into the higher and sacred recesses of life. (Para. No. 66.)

The Worship and Love of God is full of profound and brilliant thoughts, but we can only cull one or two more of aphoristic character.

We really here live and walk as little universes, and carry both heaven and the world, consequently the kingdom of God, in ourselves. (Para. No. 70.)

Love, when it is ardent, desires nothing more vehemently, or seeks more intently, than such a connection of its nature—viz. that it may be another's not its own, and conceiving that only to be its own, which is reflected from another into itself. (Para. No. 80.)

What is life? Is it not to understand what is true, and to relish what is good? (Para. No. 74.)

Life has ordained nature to be a consort with itself, and to exercise power accordingly. (Para. No. 66.)

Let us not, then, I pray, immerse our rational views in empty sophisms, or rather in mere shades, . . . by asking, whether our minds and souls are material, or whether they are extended, so as to fill spaces, and whether their activities are to be measured by times or the velocities of times, and the like; for matter is only an expression, the attributes and predicates of which ought to be defined absolutely to all sense and apprehension, before it can be demonstrated according to what understanding those forms and their activities are to be perceived. (Note to para. No. 53.)

The reader will be able to form some opinion from these extracts of the high philosophy of this little book. In point of theology it is more or less orthodox—the doctrine of a personal Trinity seems to be acepted, and even that of substitution, which afterwards its author so strongly repudiated. Swedenborg had as yet no idea that he was to be given a mission as a religious revelator; his aim in this and his other philosophical works seems to have been to establish the Divine origin of creation and the reality of spiritual things. That he was alive to the necessity of reform in the Church, however, appears from the allegorical description of her condition at the conclusion of Part I.

The Worship and Love of God marks the transition from philosophical reasoning to spiritual perception in the mind and work of Swedenborg. As the editor of the English translation of *The Economy of the Animal Kingdom* wrote in his introduction, "Here his mingled physiological and psychological endeavours terminate. Henceforth, he discerned the soul, neither through the dark glass of science, nor through the mists of philosophy, nor through the curtains of nature, but in a manner more rare and homely, viz. by spiritual sight and experience, rightly apprehended by a prepared or spiritual mind." (Pp. xvi, xvii.)

CHAPTER V

THE *Regnum Animale,* Part III, and *De Cultu et Amore Dei,* Parts I and II, were published in 1745; in 1749 appeared the first volume of *Arcana Cælestia.* A more complete contrast than this latter work and his previous publications afford could scarcely be imagined. His literary style has been discarded for a level unrhetorical prose; philosophical speculation has given place to confident statement in regard to spiritual matters, though without a trace of egotism; while theological orthodoxy is superseded by the widely different system of doctrine usually associated with the author's name. The same subject—the creation, and the early history of the human race—is dealt with in the *Arcana Cælestia* as in *The Worship and Love of God,* but the treatment is totally different. In the earlier work, the story of the creation is accepted as literal history, though interpreted somewhat freely in accordance with the speculative ideas of the author; in the new book, it is regarded as a Divine allegory, the only consistent interpretation of which is shown to be spiritual. Whence has come this remarkable change? The explanation is given by Swedenborg in the concluding paragraph of the Introduction to the *Arcana Cælestia.* After asserting that the Sacred Scripture contains a spiritual sense, he proceeds:

> That this is really the case, in respect to the Word, it is impossible for any mortal to know, however, except from the Lord. Wherefore it is expedient here to premise, that, of the Lord's Divine mercy, it has been granted me, now for several years, to be constantly

and uninterruptedly in company with spirits and angels, hearing them converse with each other, and conversing with them. Hence it has been permitted me to hear and see things in another life which are astonishing, and which have never before come to the knowledge of any man, nor entered into his imagination. I have there been instructed concerning different kinds of spirits, and the state of souls after death,—concerning hell, or the lamentable state of the unfaithful,—concerning heaven, or the most happy state of the faithful,—and particularly concerning the doctrine of faith which is acknowledged throughout all heaven: on which subjects, by the Divine mercy of the Lord, more will be said in the following pages.

By many persons this extraordinary claim is regarded as an indication of mental aberration; but of those who have given serious study to the author's subsequent writings, most have not hesitated to accept it fully. In no other way can they account for the wonderful spiritual insight which these works display. The validity of this claim will not be discussed here, but the reader's attention is invited to the most remarkable psychological revelation ever given to men—the record, in Swedenborg's own words, of the gradual opening of his spiritual sight.

Granting the possibility of such an intromission into the world of spirit, we should scarcely expect it to occur suddenly, without preparation, and without premonitory signs. If we accept Swedenborg's own statements, such preparation and such signs were not wanting. Indeed, at the close of his life, he was able to declare, in the *True Christian Religion,* his last published work, written 1770-71, that he had been prepared from his earliest youth for the holy office to which God had called him; but it was not until 1743 that he began to have direct intimations of the great change that was about to come over him.

When in the early part of that year he made application to the Board of Mines for leave of absence to go abroad and publish his *Regnum Animale,* it is evident that he had no thought of such a revolutionary change in the order of his life.

In conversation with Carl Robsahm many years later, he remarked: "I, for my own part, had never expected to come into that spiritual state, in which I am now; but the Lord selected me for this work, and for revealing the spiritual meaning of the Sacred Scriptures, which He had promised in the Prophets and in the book of Revelation. My purpose previously had been to explore nature, chemistry, and the sciences of mining and anatomy."

In a letter to the Rev. Thomas Hartley, written towards the close of his life, Swedenborg assigns the year 1743 as the date when his spiritual sight first began to be opened. But it was only in April, 1745, as he tells us in several places, that he was finally able to have full intercourse with angels and spirits, speaking with them as man with man. There is no doubt that the process of intromission was a gradual one; in the *Adversaria,* No. 183, he says that "at first I had dreams during a number of years, when I learned something of their real signification"; and in the *Spiritual Diary,* No. 2951, we are told of remarkable dreams, visions, and extraordinary lights seen and voices heard, and, finally, direct speech with "a certain spirit"; while in *Heaven and Hell,* No. 130, we read, in reference to the spiritual light in the Heavens:

> I was elevated into that light interiorly by degrees, and in proportion as I was elevated, my understanding was enlightened, till I was at length enabled to perceive things which I did not perceive before, and, finally, such things as I could not even comprehend by thought from natural light.

Swedenborg kept a private diary of his experiences during a part of this time, the very existence of which was unknown until 1858, when the manuscript was acquired by the Royal Library, Stockholm. It had been in the possession of Professor Scheringson, of Våsterås, who died in 1849 in his ninetieth year, and it had lain for nearly ten years longer unnoticed among his papers. The Royal Librarian, Mr. G. E. Klemming, published the diary in 1859, under the title of *Swedenborg's Drömmar (Swedenborg's Dreams)*, 1774; and caused much excitement thereby among the disciples of the seer. By some its authenticity was questioned, others doubted the wisdom and justice of publishing so private a record; but the genuineness of the document is now fully established, and its value as a unique psychological study is held to justify the revelation of such intimate self-confidences, notwithstanding the opportunity some of the entries have given for unfriendly criticism.

Let us reverently examine this solemn record, recognizing the fact that "we are penetrating the inner secrets of a man's life deeper and more completely, perhaps, than has been done in the case of any other man that ever lived." Though the diary only covers the short period from March 24, 1744, to October 27 of the same year, embracing however a brief record of some earlier dreams, we have a most complete picture of a soul laid bare. No priest ever heard a more sincere confession, or pronounced pardon to a more humble penitent. We have seen how upright and blameless before the world this man's life had been; yet he cast himself before his Lord as the vilest and most unworthy of mortals. Though he had not been guilty of flagrant sin, he knew that the love of evil still lurked within him, as within us all, ready to be stirred into act by temptation; and that wayward thoughts prompted to lust, to pride, to self-confidence. The deepest evils are not those that appear outwardly, as insidious and fatal diseases often lurk in an apparently healthy body. Only by severe temptations can interior evils be extirpated, and such temptations Swedenborg underwent.

Apparently, most of the experiences noted down in this diary came to him during the night-time, hence his method of dating them. In the day-time he was as other men. "All the while," he says, "I was in society constantly as before, and no one could observe the least change in me."

> I found [he writes, April 7 x 8] that I was more unworthy than others and the greatest sinner, for this reason, that our Lord has granted me to penetrate by thought into certain things more deeply than many others; and the very source of sin lies in the thoughts I am carrying out; so that my sins have on that account a deeper foundation than those of many others; and in this I found my unworthiness and my sins greater than those of other men.

Intellectual pride seems to have been one of his besetting faults, for under the same date he writes:

> I saw a book-shop, and immediately the thought struck me that my work would have more effect than that of others; yet I checked myself at once; for one serves another, and our Lord has more than a thousand ways by which to prepare a man, so that each and every book must be left to its own merits, as a means near or remote, according to the rational condition of every man. Still arrogance at once crops up: may God control it, for the power is in His hands!

On another occasion he had been attending a lecture at the Royal College of Surgeons, London, "when I was rash enough," he says, "to think that I should be mentioned as one of those who understood anatomy best; I was glad, however, that this was not done."

On April 8 x 9 we read:

I entreated Christ's mercy for cherishing so much pride and arrogance, by which I flatter myself.

He confesses (April 13 x 14) that "I am inclined to boast of my work." Some months later (October 6 x 7) he writes:

Afterwards I lighted upon these thoughts, and received this instruction, namely, that all love for whatever object, as, for instance, for the work upon which I am now engaged—whenever such an object is loved [for its own sake], and not as a medium for the only love, which is to God and Jesus Christ, is a meretricious love. He acknowledges on several ocasions that he is inclined to resist God's will and choose his own course.

There was something in me that prevented my submitting myself to God's grace as I ought to have done, thus suffering Him to do with me according to His good pleasure. (April 10 x 11.)

He felt that a change was coming over his life, and that a new and higher work lay before him. He was reluctant, however, to give up his philosophical studies, in which he took such delight, and on which he was inclined to rest his fame: and yet he saw that such a sacrifice would have to be made, if he accepted the mission offered to him.

Intellectual pride was not the only form of temptation that assailed him. The inmost depths of his soul were disturbed with such thoughts, that he came to feel he was "only evil and that continually." In the *Diary* for April 11 x 12, he writes:

I perceived in myself . . . that in every particular thought, and even in that which we consider pure, an infinite quantity of sin and impurity is contained, and likewise in every desire which enters from the body into the thoughts; these spring from deep roots. Although therefore, a thought may appear pure, it, nevertheless, is a fact that a person may think in a certain way from timidity, hypocrisy, and many other causes, as may also be traced out by an exploration of the thoughts; so that on this account man is so much the more unable to free himself from sin, and there is not a single thought which is not very much alloyed with uncleanness and impurity. . . . I have, indeed, observed that our whole will into which we are born, and which is ruled by the body and introduces thoughts, is opposed to the Spirit . . . and hence it is that we are dead to everything good, but to everything evil we are inclined from ourselves. Even his very virtues were a source of temptation.

While I was thinking, as is often the case, suppose some one should consider me a saint, and on that account think highly of me; nay, suppose, as is done by some simple-minded people, he should not only revere but also adore me as one whom he considers a holy man or a saint; in this case I found that in the zeal in which I was, I was willing to inflict upon him the greatest possible pain, rather than that sin should be laid upon him. I saw also that I must entreat the Lord with the most earnest prayers, not to have any share in so damnable a sin, which would then be laid to my charge. (April 7 x 8.)

He experienced the conflict which arises between the flesh and the spirit under stress of severe temptation; and he believed that his temptations came from an outside source. He even felt at times that malign spirits had taken possession of him, and were endeavouring to force him to the commission of evil "which he would not"; but he never lost faith or courage, and prayed vehemently for deliverance from his tormentors. He realized, also, that his prayers were answered, and often rose from the depths of despondency to heights of conscious victory. After a period of "most severe temptation," so that he could

89

scarcely control the ungodly thoughts that arose in his mind, he wrote:

> Yet I can affirm that I never was of better courage than to-day, and that I was not in the least faint-hearted and pained as on previous days, although the temptation was most severe. The reason is, that our Lord has given me this strong faith and confidence, that He helps me for the sake of Jesus Christ and according to His own promise; so that I then experienced what effect such faith has. (April 19 x 20.)

Feeling himself to be under the hand of God, he submitted patiently to his trials, and disciplined himself with the severity of a mediæval saint.

> The whole day of the 9th [April] I spent in prayer, in songs of praise, in reading God's Word, and fasting; except in the morning when I was otherwise occupied.

If he was often in a state of gloom and depression, he had his times of exaltation also.

> I experienced so much of the Lord's grace when I resolved to keep my thoughts in a state of purity, as to feel an inmost joy. . . . I was not allowed to mention the large measure of grace which had fallen to my lot; for I perceived that on the one hand it could serve no other purpose than to set people thinking about me either favourably or unfavourably, according to their disposition towards me; and on the other hand, it would not be productive of any use, if the glorification of God's grace served to encourage my own self-love.
>
> The best comparison I could make of myself was with a peasant elevated to power as a prince or king, so that he could have whatever his heart desired; and yet there was something in him which desired to teach him that he himself knew nothing. By this comparison,

however, it is seen that it is Thy hand [O God] which causes this great joy. (April 7 x 8.)

Again and again he prays for the grace of humility or gives thanks for having attained something of it. Describing one of his temptations, he says:

This have I learned, that the only thing in this state— and I do not know any other—is, in all humility to thank God for His grace, and to pray for it, and to recognize our own unworthiness, and God's infinite grace.

He says again:

Very often I burst into tears, not of sorrow, but of inmost joy at our Lord's deigning to be so gracious to so unworthy a sinner; for the sum of all I found to be this, that the only thing needful is to cast oneself in all humility on our Lord's grace, to recognize one's own unworthiness, and to thank God in humility for His grace. (April 7 x 8.)

To do God's will became the desire of his heart. He writes:

I have for my motto God's will be done; I am Thine not mine; as therefore I have given myself from myself to the Lord, He may dispose of me after His own pleasure.

Again:

I pray to God that I might not be my own, but that God might please to let me be His.

Describing a vision, in which he saw a profusion of gold, he says:

It denotes that the Lord, who disposes all things, gives me in spiritual and worldly matters all that I need, whenever like a child I cast my care upon Him.

In all his work, he recognizes himself "simply as an instrument."

His consciousness of the Divine leading became stronger as time advanced. He says (October 12 x 13):

I discovered I am in such a state that I know nothing on this subject (*i.e.* on religion)

and, on the previous day, he tells us:

I have no knowledge about religion, but have lost all.

It was necessary that he should be emptied of all self-will and preconceived ideas, before he could become a fitting instrument for the work before him.

These dreams and visions were often accompanied by violent tremors, prostration, trances, sweatings, and on one occasion, at least, by swooning. During their continuance he enjoyed preternatural sleep, often lasting from ten to thirteen hours. Doubtless the system was exhausted by the strain put upon it—for all this time he was doing hard literary work during the day—and Nature asserted her demands. We cannot wonder, either, that he became so absorbed as sometimes to pass his friends in the street, and not return their salutations.

These things, the reader will be inclined to think, are common experiences with all enthusiasts. Granted; but then Swedenborg was never anything but the very reverse of an enthusiast, and there were aspects of his case that differed radically from these common experiences. Far from being a victim of religious excitement, we find him watching and studying his own case with the eye of a scientific observer. He was well aware that people are sometimes led away by emotion to imagine all kinds of things, and was careful to guard himself against such extravagances. He observed (October 6 x 7):

How easily human beings may be led astray by other kinds of spirits [*i.e.* evil spirits], who represent themselves to men according to the quality of the love of each.

Of one of his visions, he remarks:

Our Lord knows best what all this means;

and, again:

God grant that I do not mistake in this; I believe I do not.

After a night of horrid dreams and bodily tremors, he says:

I begin thinking whether all this was not mere phantasy;

so it is evident that he was not a prey to his own imaginations.

Swedenborg's case is indeed unique. We can understand the ignorant, or the fanatic, or the unstable mistaking hallucinations for realities; but not a man living an active life in the world, a mathematician and logician, and a devotee of natural science. Nor was there any sudden "conversion" to account for the change that came over him. Nor was there any evidence of a weakening of his mental faculties or any mental disorder, for at the time these strange events were happening he was engaged in writing and publishing philosophical works which have been acknowledged by some of the most brilliant intellects of our time as revealing astounding mental powers; and he continued to write and publish, for nearly thirty years, other works, which are thoroughly sane and consistent, and, to those who have most carefully examined them, bear evidence of more than mortal wisdom. The explanation most easy to credit was Swedenborg's own.

There is something touching and beautiful in the thought of this middle-aged philosopher thus renouncing his life's ambitions, and in childlike obedience to what he saw to be a call from God, turning his back upon the wisdom of the world which had been as meat and drink to him. A friend of kings and princes, and an intellectual prince himself, we see him now, a stranger in a strange land, all alone in the darkness of the night, pouring out his soul in prayer to God, and singing simple hymns, such as he had probably learnt at his mother's knee. A favourite one was " Jesus is my best of friends." It is, indeed, a remarkable picture.

A word as to his theology at the time of these self-revelations. Swedenborg was educated in the evangelical doctrines of the Lutheran Church, and does not seem to have questioned their adequacy until middle life, excepting on the subject of faith alone, on which his father also held broader views than most of his clerical brethren. This diary shows that the son still held by his early teaching. The doctrine of a personal Trinity appears again and again; the distinctive offices of the Father, the Son, and the Holy Ghost, being accepted in a strictly orthodox manner. He prays to God for Christ's sake, and pleads the blood and merits of the Saviour. He deprecates allowing the understanding to be mixed up with matters of faith, averring that "faith is separated from our understanding and resides above it." After his full enlightenment, he had a vision of a magnificent temple in heaven, over the portal of which was written: "Now it is allowable to enter intellectually into the mysteries of faith," and he constantly insisted thereafter that faith is impossible where reason is ignored.

Signs of coming change appear already, particularly in his views of the nature and unity of God, and the supreme Divinity of Jesus Christ. In an early entry, we read: "Christ, in whom dwells the fulness of the Godhead, must alone be addressed in prayer. . . . He is omnipotent, and the only Mediator." And, again, a prayer quoted above, was put into his mouth, beginning: "O thou Almighty Jesus Christ."

At this time he had no clear idea of the mission to which he was to be called, but several passages show that he had some foreshadowing of it. On April 21 x 22 he writes:

> Because it seemed to me that I was so far separated from God that I could not yet think of Him in a sufficiently vivid manner, I came into a state of doubt whether I should not direct my journey homewards. Yet I gathered courage and perceived that I had come [to Holland] to do that which was best of all, and that I had received a talent for the promotion of God's glory; I saw that all had helped together to this end; that the Spirit had been with me from my youth for this very purpose; wherefore I considered myself unworthy of life, unless I followed the straight direction. I then smiled at the other seducing thoughts; and thus at luxury, riches, and distinction, which I had pursued.

This remarkable diary ends with the entry of October 26 x 27; but we have later experiences related in other places. The most important of these is the account given by Carl Robsahm, from Swedenborg's own description, of how the Lord appeared to him, some time in April, 1745. There is no need to quote the particulars, which have already appeared in several former biographies; but the concluding part of the account is important as it marks the turning point in our author's life. The experience definitely determined the character of his succeeding years.

A man appeared to him in a vision while he was at the inn after dinner, and somewhat alarmed him. According to Robsahm, Swedenborg's statement continued as follows:

> I went home, and during the night the same man

revealed Himself to me again, but I was not frightened now. He then said that He was the Lord God, the Creator of the world, and the Redeemer, and that He had chosen me to explain to men the spiritual sense of the Scripture, and that He Himself would explain to me what I should write on this subject; that same night also were opened to me, so that I became thoroughly convinced of their reality, the world of spirits, heaven, and hell, and I recognized there many acquaintances of every condition of life. From that day I gave up the study of all worldly science, and laboured in spiritual things, according as the Lord had commanded me to write. Afterwards the Lord opened, daily very often, the eyes of my spirit, so that, in the middle of the day, I could see into the other world, and in a state of perfect wakefulness converse with angels and spirits.

A stupendous claim, stated simply and clearly, without a trace of any such feelings or language as can be considered mystical or enthusiastic. *If* Swedenborg was thus favoured, we ought certainly to find evidence of it in his works, and to these we must turn for the only satisfactory answer to the question.

CHAPTER VI

SEER AND THEOLOGIAN

WE have further insight into the development of Swedenborg's mind and life at the transition period in his *Adversaria,* a note-book of his Biblical studies written between 1745 and 1747, and in his *Spiritual Diary* which records his experiences from day to day among the inhabitants of the spiritual world. Neither work was published by himself, so we cannot regard them in the same way as those he actually published. They were intended for his own private use; but, read with proper discretion, and in the light of his published teachings, they are full of interest, and help us to understand his published works. Some uncertainty is still apparent in the theological views embodied in these records, but there is evidence of growing knowledge and of full confidence in his Divine mission.

The *Adversaria,* says Dr. R. L. Tafel, "marks the second step which Swedenborg took in the investigation of the Divine Word. The exploration of the merely literal sense he did not carry further than the third chapter of Genesis. . . . He returned to the first chapter of Genesis with a view of discovering there, not the creation of the natural world, but the creation and establishment of the Kingdom of God.

"He now recognized the existence of an interior sense in the Word of God, in the following words, in the *Adversaria* (i., No. 23) :

> That in the Mosaic account of creation there is everywhere a double meaning of the words, viz. a spiritual as well as a natural, appears clearly to the apprehension of every man from the tree of life and the tree of knowl-

97

edge in the midst of the garden; for life and knowledge are spiritual, and yet are attributed to a tree, for this reason, that whatsoever originates in the ultimate parts of nature, on account of deriving its origin from heaven, involves something celestial in what is terrestrial, or something spiritual in what is natural; and it does so on this ground, that everything that is represented in the Divine mind, cannot but be carried out in reality in the ultimate parts of nature, and be formed there according to the idea of heaven. There results hence a correspondence of all things, which, with the Divine permission, we shall follow out in its proper series."

The *Adversaria* furnishes an example of Swedenborg's amazing industry. Written within two years, it filled nine considerable volumes when published at Tübingen, by Dr. Immanuel Tafel, Professor of Philosophy, and Librarian to the University, between 1842 and 1854. Such a literary *tour de force* is almost without a parallel.

About this time also our author was engaged upon his copious Biblical indexes, which occupy some two thousand pages of MS., and contain besides a concordance of passages for ready reference, a dictionary of correspondences and other notes. All this was preparatory to future works.

The *Spiritual Diary* contains notes of a large number of things heard and seen by Swedenborg in the spiritual world, together with many doctrinal explanations of them, or suggested by them. The record extends from February, 1747, to April 29, 1765; but the entries are not regular, and many are without date. The early portion, moreover (up to October 9, 1747), is missing, and the nature of its contents is only known to us from the author's index.

The character of the *Spiritual Diary* is very different from the *Dream Book* already referred to. Instead of strange dreams and incomprehensible, or dimly comprehended, visions we have a sober account of things seen and heard, extraordinary enough in some cases, but no longer so perplexing to the beholder and auditor. It is a traveller's descriptive notes of an unknown country.

To most uninitiated readers the *Spiritual Diary* will seem strange and unconvincing. But it goes without saying that any account of such experiences must seem incredible to most persons, and more or less strange to all. To understand them, we need some acquaintance with the author's spiritual philosophy. It is unfortunate that many persons have drawn their limited knowledge of Swedenborg from his private diaries, which they had not the capacity to understand, through ignorance of his systematic teachings. So they have concluded that he is erratic and visionary, and that there is little to be learnt from him. Studied with proper doctrinal aids, these remarkable records are full of interest, and worthy of attentive consideration. The reader who is willing to accept such aid, and to set aside his prejudices, will have the realities of the spirit life presented to him forcibly and reasonably, very different from the imaginations of Dante or Milton. Let him remember, however, that what he reads are private memoranda of extraordinary experiences, and he will be in a position to form a reasonable opinion on the matter. But a just judgment of the man and his teachings must be based on his known life and published works, to the further consideration of which we now proceed.

Swedenborg retained his position as Assessor of the Royal Board of Mines until the middle of 1747, when he retired on a pension of half of his salary. The documents relating to his retirement, which have been preserved to us, are of great importance as evidence of his undoubted sanity and mental capability at the time he was undergoing the remarkable experiences we have just been considering.

The Board of Mines in Swedenborg's time consisted of a president, who always belonged to the highest order of nobility, two councillors of mines, and about six assessors, of whom Swedenborg was one. In the spring of 1747, that is, more than two years after his full intromission into the next world, one of the councillors retired, and Swedenborg was unanimously recommended as his successor by his colleagues. Instead of accepting the position, he addressed a memorial to the King in the following terms. The memorial is dated June 2, 1747:

"Most mighty and most gracious King,—Your Royal Majesty's Board of Mines, at your behest, have sent in their humble proposition with regard to the vacant place of Councillor of Mines on their Board and they have most humbly proposed me for this office *in primo loco*; but as I feel it incumbent on me to finish the work on which I am now engaged, I would most humbly ask Your Royal Majesty to select another in my place for this position, and most graciously release me from office. . . .

"It is my humble wish, that you graciously release me from office, but without bestowing upon me any higher rank; which I most earnestly beseech you not to do. I further pray that I may receive half of my salary, and that you will graciously grant me leave to go abroad, to some place where I may finish the important work on which I am now engaged.

"I remain with deep respect, my most gracious Sovereign, Your Royal Majesty's most humble and dutiful subject.

EMAN. SWEDENBORG."

A Royal Decree releasing Swedenborg from his office, "which he has hitherto filled with renown," and agreeing to continue to pay him half his salary, was issued on June 12th, and on the 15th was handed in to the Board.

"All the members of the Royal Board regretted losing so worthy a colleague, and they asked the Assessor kindly to continue attending the sessions of the Board until all those cases should be adjudicated that had been commenced during his attendance at the Board, to which the Assessor kindly assented." (Minutes of Board, June 15, 1747.)

The final leave-taking was on July 17th. In the minutes for that day the following entry appears:

"Assessor Swedenborg, who intends as soon as possible to commence his new journeys abroad, came up for the purpose of taking leave of the Royal Board. He thanked all those at the Royal Board for the favour and kindness he had received from them during his connection with the Board, and commended himself to their further friendly remembrances.

"The Royal Board thanked the Assessor for the minute care and fidelity with which he had attended to the duties of his office as an Assessor up to the present time; they wished him a prosperous journey and a happy return; after which he left."

Thus ended Swedenborg's long connection with the Board of Mines. His reason for retiring while still in the full vigour of life was not only that he might have more time to devote to his new work, but that his mind might not be distracted unnecessarily by worldly concerns; for the spiritual influences by which he was now guided were withdrawn in the degree in which he allowed himself to be immersed in worldly concerns. He writes in his *Spiritual Diary* (March 4, 1748):

Whereas now I have been almost three years, or thirty-three months, in that state in which, my mind being withdrawn from corporeal things, I could be in the societies of spiritual and celestial [spirits], and yet be like another man in the society of men, without any difference, which spirits also wondered at;—when, however, I intensely adhered to worldly things in thought, as when I had care concerning necessary expenses, about which I this day wrote a letter, so that my mind was for some time detained therewith, I fell, as it were, into a corporeal state, so that the spirits could not converse with me as they also said, because they were as though absent [from me]. A case rather similar occurred before; whence I am enabled to know that spirits cannot speak with a man who is much devoted to worldly and corporeal cares;— for bodily concerns draw down, as it were, the ideas of the mind and immerse them in corporeal things.

No one has insisted more strongly than Swedenborg on the necessity of an active life in the world to a healthy religious condition, and as a preventive of the delusions sometimes induced by evil spirits; but his own case was abnormal, as he always maintained. He did not retire from the world that he might give himself up to lonely contemplation, or to secure his own salvation; but because he felt himself called to a great mission, which required his whole time and energies.

Swedenborg did not remain long in his own country after his retirement, though there is no record of the date when he commenced his new journey. He was in Holland, as a memorandum of accounts in his commonplace-book shows, in November, 1747, and remained there until October, 1748. A further memorandum records that he "took lodgings [in London] on November 23, 1748, for six shillings per week for half a year; if the rooms are taken for a whole year there is a deduction of thirty-two shillings, so that the whole rent amounts to fourteen pounds;" a modest sum for a noble philosopher and friend of kings to pay.

The object of Swedenborg's coming to London was to arrange for the publication of the first volume of *Arcana Cœlestia,* an exposition of the spiritual sense of Genesis and Exodus. The work was issued anonymously, by John Lewis of Paternoster Row, and, it is to be feared, fell very flat on the market. From an undated entry in the *Spiritual Diary* (No. 4422, in all probability September or October, 1749), we learn that only four copies were sold in two months; but this was only to be expected in such a careless and sceptical age. The book also being published in Latin, only appealed to the learned, who would not be likely to lend a ready ear to the lucubration of an anonymous foreigner. The few who did read, however, must have been astonished at what met their eyes. They had surely never seen the like before!

A brief preface maintained the spiritual content of the Holy Scriptures, and showed that without a knowledge of their internal meaning, they were like "a body without a soul."

It is impossible, the author continued, whilst the mind abides in the literal sense only, to see that it is full of such spiritual contents. Thus, in these first chapters of Genesis, nothing is discoverable from the literal sense, but that they treat of the creation of the world, and of the garden of Eden which is called Paradise, and also of Adam as the first-created man; and scarcely a single person supposes them to relate to anything besides. But that they contain *arcana* which were never heretofore revealed, will sufficiently appear from the following pages; where it will be seen that the first chapter of Genesis, in its internal sense, treats of the NEW CREATION of man, or of his REGENERATION, in general, and specifically of the most ancient church; and this in such a manner, that there is not a single syllable which does not represent, signify, and involve something spiritual.

As we shall discuss the contents of *Arcana Cœlestia* in another place, there is no need to say more here, than to point out the striking difference between the character of its statements, and those contained in the *Diaries, Adversaria,* etc. Here there is no uncertainty, hesitancy, or doubt; but a calm unfolding of positive truth. We notice a change in some of the terms employed, which are now crystallized into the forms they will hold throughout the long series of subsequent works. Thus, the appellation of the Divine

Saviour in *The Worship and Love of God* was the "Only Begotten" or "Son of God"; in the early part of the *Spiritual Diary*, as in the greater part of the *Adversaria*, it is "God-Messiah," whereas in *Arcana Cœlestia* and all later works the term "Lord" is used. In commencing the exposition of the internal sense of Genesis, he writes:

In the following work, by the LORD is solely meant Jesus Christ, the Saviour of the world, who is called the Lord; without other names. He is acknowledged and adored as the Lord throughout all heaven, because He has all power in heaven and earth. (No. 14.)

This doctrine of the exclusive Divinity of Jesus Christ is the key-note of all Swedenborg's theology.

Mr. Benjamin Worcester, in his *The Life and Mission of Emanuel Swedenborg,* p. 272, remarks that "the style of the *Arcana* differs materially from that of the earlier *Adversaria*. It is no longer that of an explorer, just discovering, or about to discover, or just hearing things entirely new to him. It is now that of a master, full to overflowing with knowledge that had become familiar to him, and that lay broadly and clearly under his view, from which he had only to choose what would be most intelligible and most useful to his readers. He no longer doubts whether what he writes is quite correct and to be printed. It is apparent that he is writing and printing under clearly recognized authority. Yet the careful student finds some minor points, though marvellously few, in which the author's later experience of twenty years developed additional clearness and slight modifications."

A second volume of *Arcana Cœlestia* was issued in 1750, in parts, both in Latin and English, and was announced in a lengthy advertisement by the publisher. "This work," he said, "is intended to be such an exposition of the whole Bible as was never attempted in any language before. The author is a learned foreigner, who wrote and printed the first volume of the same work but last year, all in Latin, which may be seen at my shop in Paternoster Row, as above mentioned. . . . This, then, may be said of our author. He has struck out a new path through this deep abyss, which no man ever trod before; he has left all the commentators and expositors to stand on their own footing; he neither meddles nor interferes with any of them; his thoughts are all his own; and the ingenious and sublime turn he has given to everything in the Scriptures, he has copied from no man; and therefore, even in this respect, he has some title to the regard of the ingenious and learned world."

The work, we are told, was printed in "a grand and pompous manner" and sold at an extremely low price. "It is the generous author's absolute command that it should be so, who, it is plain, wants neither purse nor spirit to carry on his laudable undertaking."

Notwithstanding small encouragement in the way of sales, the publication went on year by year until the work was completed in the year 1756, eight quarto volumes, all in Latin, except, as stated, that the second volume was issued with an accompanying English translation.

Meanwhile Swedenborg was gaining new experience, and planning further works. He resided for the most part in Stockholm, sending his manuscript from time to time to Mr. Lewis in London. He took an active part in the parliament of his native country, and went about as usual among his friends, few, if any, knowing of his extraordinary experiences, or guessing that he was the author of these strange Latin tomes.

In 1758 he again journeyed to London, where he published four small works, *De Telluribus, etc.* (*The Earths in the Universe*), *De Ultimo Judicio* (*The Last Judgment*), *De Nova Hierosolyma et ejus Doctrina Cœlestis* (*The New Jerusalem and its Heavenly Doctrine*), a treatise, *De Equo Albo* (*On the White Horse of the Apocalypse*), and a larger one, perhaps the best known of all his writings, *De*

105

Coelo et ejus Mirabilibus et de Inferno (Heaven and Hell).
All these were remarkable works, and excited considerable
interest and curiosity. Between 1757 and 1759 he also began
writing a voluminous exposition of the best part of the Book
of Revelation, on similar lines to the *Arcana Cœlestia,* but
carried it no further than the beginning of chapter XIX.
The work was never completed, and was replaced later (in
1766) by a smaller one entitled *Apocalypsis Revelata (The
Apocalypse Revealed.)* The MS. of the earlier work was
published posthumously, and in its English form, under the
title *Apocalypse Explained,* fills six large octavo volumes,
and is treasured by students of Swedenborg for its abundant
exegetic material.

In the spring of 1762, this wonderful old man, now
seventy-four years of age, set out on another expedition,
this time to Amsterdam, to which city he was about to
transfer his publishing; probably, suggests Dr. Tafel, because of the rejection of his teachings by the clergy and the
leading men of England. At any rate, he published nothing
further in England except a pamphlet on *De Commercio
Animæ et Corporis (The Intercourse of the Soul and the
Body)*, which appeared in 1769.

At Amsterdam were published the following works: In
1763, *Doctrina Novæ Hierosolymæ de Domino (Doctrine of
the Lord)*, *Doctrina Novæ Hierosolymæ de Scriptura Sacra
(Doctrine of the Sacred Scripture)*, *Doctrina Vitæ pro
Nova Hierosolyma (Doctrine of Life)*, *Doctrina Novæ
Hierosolymæ de Fide (Doctrine of Faith)*, *Continuatio de
Ultimo Judicio (Continuation Concerning the Last Judg-
ment)*, *Sapientia Angelica de Divino Amore et de Divina
Sapientia (Divine Love and Wisdom)*. In 1764 appeared
*Sapientia Angelica de Divina Providentia (Divine Provi-
dence*; in 1766, *Apocalypsis Revelata (Apocalypse Re-
vealed)*; in 1768, *Deliciæ Sapientiæ de Amore Conjugiali
(Conjugial Love)*, the first of his revelatory works to which
Swedenborg attached his name; in 1769, *Summaria Ex-*

positio Doctrinæ Novæ Hierosolymæ (*A Brief Exposition of the Doctrine of the New Church*; and, last, though not least, in 1771, *Vera Christiana Religio* (*The True Christian Religion*). All these treatises, like his other theological works, were written in Latin.

Two other publications of a different character may be mentioned as belonging to this period, which show that, with his transcendental studies, he had not ceased to take an interest in mundane affairs. The transactions of the Royal Academy of Sciences of Stockholm, for April, May and June, 1763, contain a paper by Swedenborg, in Swedish, on the inlaying of marble; and in 1776, our author republished, in Amsterdam, his *New Method of finding the Longitude of Places on Land and Sea.*

All these publications necessitated many journeys between Sweden and Holland, or England, which were undertaken quite alone and without mishap, from his seventy-fourth to his eighty-fourth years. Nothing but a strong conviction of his Divine mission could have induced him, at such a time of life, to risk the perils and discomforts inseparable in those days from travel by sea and land, and to endure the loneliness of a life of protracted exile. When he started on his last expedition he was in his eighty-third year, yet he fearlessly undertook the journey, confident that God would protect him and preserve his life until his work was finished. He lived to see his *Vera Christiana Religio* (*True Christian Religion*) delivered from the press, and to write an appendix to it, as well as one or two other brief papers. For some reason, possibly at the invitation of English receivers of his teachings, of whom there was now a small but growing number scattered up and down the country, he crossed over to London in July, 1771, and remained there to the close of his life.

When once it became known that Swedenborg was the author of these remarkable books, and that he professed to have open intercourse with spirits and angels, he became

107

the object of much interest and curiosity. "Unexpectedly to everybody," wrote Jung-Stilling, "this intelligent, learned, and pious man began to have intercourse with spirits. He made no secret of this, but frequently at table, even in large companies, and in the midst of the most rational and scientific conversations, would say, 'On this point I conversed not long ago with apostle Paul, with Luther, or some other deceased person.' It can easily be imagined that the persons present opened their mouths and eyes, and wondered whether he was in his sound senses. Still occasionally he has furnished proofs, against which no objection can be raised. The veracity of these relations has been impugned, and the good gentleman has even been charged with imposture; but this charge I deny emphatically. Swedenborg was no impostor, but a pious Christian man. These proofs that he had actually intercourse with spirits are generally known concerning him." When questioned, he spoke freely of his experiences, but never obtruded them on others. The Rev. Nicholas Collin, Rector of the Swedish Church in Philadelphia, stated that, in Stockholm, "no one presumed to doubt that he held some kind of supernatural intercourse with the spiritual world," and, indeed, many had had striking evidence of the fact. He constantly asserted his Divine commission, fearless of the ridicule that his claim sometimes brought upon him. Count Höpken once asked Swedenborg why he had published the memorable Relations which seemed to throw so much ridicule on his doctrine, otherwise so rational, and whether it would not be best for him to keep them to himself, and not to publish them to the world. Swedenborg replied that he had orders from the Lord to publish them, and that those who might ridicule him on that account would do him injustice, "for," said he, "why should I, who am a man in years, render myself ridiculous for fantasies and falsehoods"? Even to the King he insisted upon the truth of his asseverations. In a memorial dated May 10, 1770, protesting against the ban that had been placed upon his books by the Consistory of Gothenburg, he wrote:

That our Saviour visibly revealed Himself before me, and commanded me to do what I have done, and what I have still to do; and that thereupon He permitted me to have intercourse with angels and spirits, I have declared before the whole of Christendom, as well in England, Holland, Germany, and Denmark, as in France and Spain, and also on various occasions in this country before their Royal Majesties, and especially when I enjoyed the grace to eat at their table in the presence of the whole royal family, and also of five senators and others; at which time my mission constituted the sole topic of conversation.

To Count Tessin he said that

God had granted him revelations of this kind, that he might lead the world away from darkness and error, which of late had increased to such a degree, that the very existence of God was in effect denied.

But Swedenborg did not trust to mere asseveration to convince the world of the truth of his doctrines and visions. In the same memorial to the Swedish King to which we have referred above, he appeals to his critics' reason, and truthfully says that in his writings

much may be found which has never before been discovered except by real vision, and intercourse with those who are in the spiritual world. . . . That our Saviour permits me to experience this, is not on my own account but for the sake of a sublime interest which concerns the eternal welfare of all Christians.

There can be no question of the seriousness of Swedenborg's claim. Count Höpken wrote: "He answered me that he was too old to sport with spiritual things, and too much concerned for his eternal happiness to yield to such foolish notions, assuring me, on his hopes of salvation, that imagination produced in him none of his revelations, which were true, and from what he had heard and seen."

CHAPTER VII

THEOLOGICAL TEACHINGS

To APPRECIATE the theological reformation that Swedenborg instituted, we must consider the state of the current theology of his day. "Towards the middle of the [eighteenth] century," says Leslie Stephen, "the decay of the old schools of theology was becoming complete"; the creed of orthodoxy was practically dead, having proved itself "incapable of satisfying the instincts of various classes of the population, and the perception of its logical defects was the consequence, not the cause of the gradual break-up." Swedenborg was as fully alive to the moral insufficiency of the theology of his time as to its logical defects: and set himself (acting, as he states, under a Divine injunction) to rehabilitate it in both respects. Two oft-quoted aphorisms of his will suffice to convey an idea of the position he takes: "All religion has relation to life and the life of religion is to do good;" (*Doctrine of Life*, No. 1). "Now it is allowable to enter intellectually into the mysteries of faith." (*True Christian Religion*, No. 508.) He propounded a rational theology as the groundwork and motive power of a good and useful life.

Swedenborg explains:

> The reason why but few at the present day have religion is: First, because it is not known that the Lord [*i.e.* Jesus Christ] is the Only God in person and in essence, in whom is a Trinity: when yet the whole of religion is based on the knowledge of God, and on His adoration and worship. Second, because it is not known that faith is nothing else but truth; and because it is not known whether that which is called faith is truth, or not.

111

Third, because it is not known what charity is, nor consequently what good and evil are. Fourth, because it is not known what eternal life is. (Preface to *Canons of the New Church.*)

Swedenborg believed that he was Divinely commissioned to supply the true knowledge that was so conspicuously lacking; and his works contain a new theology, which even those who do not accept his views cannot deny to be both rational and practical. If regarded as his own achievement, one can only wonder at the profound insight he displays, and his immense daring in attempting such a task; but we prefer to look upon it otherwise, and to accept his statement that he was only an instrument in the great work he undertook.

Swedenborg's theological teachings are to be found scattered throughout his Writings, but the following are especially devoted to systematic statement of them: *The True Christian Religion, The New Jerusalem and its Heavenly Doctrine, The Four Leading Doctrines, namely, of the Lord, of the Sacred Scripture, of Life* and *of Faith, The Divine Providence,* and *A Brief Exposition of the Doctrine of the New Church.* It will be impossible to examine all of these in detail; the better plan will be to give a general summary, with particular references when necessary.

The foundation stone of the whole system is the doctrine of the supreme Divinity of Jesus Christ. Although St. Paul asserted that "in Him dwelleth all the fulness of the Godhead bodily," and the early Christians accepted that view implicitly, the doctrine was not clearly understood and consequently had been lost sight of for fifteen hundred years. The stumbling-block of a Trinity of persons had blinded the eyes to the absolute truth. Swedenborg teaches that, instead of Jesus Christ being only the second member of a Divine Trinity of Persons, the whole Trinity is centred in one Divine Person—Himself. The Father is the inmost principle of the Divine, which no man hath seen or can know,—the exhaustless, ineffable Love of God; the Son is the manifestation of the Divine, the Divine Wisdom revealed to us in "the Word," as it has come to men in different forms, especially as "the Word made Flesh"; the Holy Spirit is the effluent energy of Divinity, proceeding from the Father through the Son, that is, from Divine Love through Divine Wisdom, and operating in man to inspire, to console, and to sanctify. All these constituents were embodied in the person of the Divine Saviour, as He Himself taught when He declared that the Father dwelling in Him was the doer of His beneficent works; and when He breathed on His disciples and said, "Receive ye the Holy Ghost." (John xx. 22.) Again, speaking of the promised Comforter, He said, "I will not leave you comfortless: I will come to you." (John xiv. 18.)

The teaching of any church as to the nature and character of God forms necessarily the central principle of its theological system. Upon the ideas that we entertain of God will depend our conception of His relation to His creatures, and their duty to Him.

In consequence of separating the Divine Trinity into three persons, each of which is declared to be God and Lord [says Swedenborg] . . . a sort of frenzy has infected the whole system of theology, as well as the Christian church, so called from its Divine founder. . . . Men's minds are reduced by it into such a state of delirium that they do not know whether there is one God, or whether there are three. They confess but one God with their lips, while they entertain the idea of three in their thoughts; so that their lips and their minds, or their words and their ideas, are at variance with each other: the consequence whereof is that they deny the existence of any God. This is the true source of the naturalism which is now so prevalent in the world. For I appeal to experience, while the lips confess but one God, and the mind entertains the idea of three, whether such confession of the lips, and such an idea in the mind, do not mutually tend to destroy each other? Hence if there be any conception of God left in the understanding, it is that of a mere word or name, destitute of any true perception which implies a knowledge of Him. (*True Christian Religion,* No. 4.)

The restitution of the true doctrine of Trinity in Unity necessitated a restatement of the doctrine of the Atonement; since, if there are not three persons in the Trinity, it is impossible for one of these to offer Himself as a sacrifice to the clamant justice of another. The doctrine of the Atonement as taught by Swedenborg is that set forth by St. Paul, when he wrote to the Corinthians: "God was in Christ, reconciling the world unto Himself." God is ever waiting to be gracious and can need no reconciliation to His creatures; they, however, need to be reconciled to Him, before they can be fitted to dwell in His presence, and it was to effect this reconciliation,—to bring back the wandering sheep to the fold,—that God came into the world as Christ. He took upon Himself human nature, that therein He might be "tempted in all points like as we are," and so might conquer and subdue the spiritual enemies that kept man in bondage. He became the champion of lost humanity, and made recovery possible when evil seemed to have become paramount. In this view of the Atonement, there is no substitution of the innocent for the guilty; yet all the merit belongs to the Saviour.

Swedenborg rejects all schemes of salvation that do not involve reformation of character; yet he is emphatic in his teaching that man has no power to procure his own salvation, though gifted with absolute freedom to choose the good and reject the evil. Good actions should be done by man "as of himself; nevertheless under the belief that they

114

are from the Lord operating with him and by him." (*True Christian Religion*, No. 3.)

The necessity of perfect freedom in spiritual matters is strongly insisted upon. Man is subject, he tells us, to influx from both good and evil spirits, but the Lord preserves a perfect equilibrium between these influences, which only the man himself can disturb.

> In this equilibrium every man is kept as long as he lives in the world; and by means of it he is kept in that liberty of thinking, of willing, of speaking, and of doing, in which he can be reformed. (*Divine Providence.* No. 23.)

No spiritual acquisition can be permanent that is not appropriated in freedom; hence salvation is impossible without man's voluntary co-operation, for otherwise "a man would have nothing whereby he could reciprocally conjoin himself with the Lord." (*True Christian Religion*, No. 485.)

The acceptance of the doctrine of man's absolute spiritual freedom dispels many common misconceptions in regard to the work of salvation. Hope of reward or fear of punishment, though they may set the thoughts towards higher things, can produce no real spiritual change; no more can miracles, visions, or intercourse with the dead, because they may force belief against the will and the reason. We often hear of persons being brought to a knowledge of sin and of their need of salvation, on a bed of sickness; it will be surprising, therefore, to many to learn that no one can be "reformed in states of bodily disease" (*Divine Providence*, No. 138) for then the mind is abstracted from the world, and is not in the same rationality as during active life.

The whole question is summed up in the statement that, "No one is reformed in states that are not of rationality and liberty" (*Divine Providence*, No. 138), a dictum which has a very wide bearing. If this be true, those who submit their reason to priests and dogmas for the sake of peace, and, as they think, their soul's salvation, are woefully misled. The peace they attain is a spurious peace and their hope of salvation by these means is illusory. Equally deluded are those who seek the seclusion of the cloister or the hermit's cell, or in any way withdraw themselves from active life in the world, for their soul's benefit. They are simply paralysing spiritual growth, and endangering their hoped-for happiness.

The life which leads to heaven is not a life withdrawn from the world, but one lived in the world; a life of piety without a life of charity [*i.e.* good-will to others]— which is only possible in the world—does not lead to heaven; but a life of charity, which consists in acting sincerely and justly in every duty, engagement, and work, from an interior, that is, from a heavenly origin; and such an origin is in that life when man acts sincerely and justly because it is agreeable to the Divine Laws. Such a life is not difficult, but a life of piety alone without charity is difficult, and yet it leads *away* from heaven as much as it is commonly believed to lead *to* heaven. (*Heaven and Hell,* No. 535.)

This passage sums up Swedenborg's doctrine of life and salvation.

Since salvation is the attainment of spiritual health, it is evident that eternal rewards and punishments cannot be arbitrarily bestowed. Before we can go to heaven, heaven must have come to us; and no one will go to hell, who has not first received hell into his soul.

The states of the interiors make heaven, and that heaven is within every one, and not out of him. (*Ibid.,* No. 33.)

It can in no case be said that heaven is out of any one,

but that it is within him. . . . This plainly shows how much he is deceived who believes that to come into heaven is only to be elevated amongst angels, without any regard to the quality of the interior life, and thus that heaven may be conferred on any one by an act of unconditional mercy; when the truth is, that if heaven is not within us, nothing of the heaven which is around can flow in and be received. (*Ibid.*, No. 54.)

Swedenborg's descriptions of the other life are so important and enlightening that they demand more extended notice in a special chapter. We shall refer here to only one other point, namely, his statement that the future life is continuous with this; that there is but a short semi-conscious interval between the death of the body and the commencement of the spiritual existence. This disposes of the idea that the dead of past generations are reserved for future judgment at the "great assize" to be held at the end of the world.

What then is the Last Judgment, of which we read in the New Testament? It was commonly taught that, in fulfilment of His promise, Christ would come again in the clouds of the material firmament, and summon all mankind, "both the quick and the dead," before Him for judgment. After the judgment had taken place, the saints would be caught up into the clouds with their Lord, and the world would be destroyed by fire. A new heaven and a new earth would then be established, in which Christ should reign for ever and ever. Swedenborg shows that this is a misconception of the teaching of the Gospels, due to a literal interpretation of figurative language; and he makes the astounding statement that the Last Judgment has already taken place, having come "without observation," as foretold. This stupendous event took place, he tells us, in the year 1757, and was a spiritual occurrence. In the world of spirits, or intermediate state, there were at that time collected myriads of spirits who had not yet passed to their eternal homes. The majority of these were diabolical or hypocritical, and their influence on the inhabitants of this "lower earth" was such, that if they had not been brought into order, they would have quickly destroyed all spiritual life among men. To avert such a catastrophe, a general judgment was executed upon them, and a reign of order established in the intermediate world. Swedenborg affirms that he was permitted to witness this judgment, and that the prophecies of the Gospels and the Revelation were fulfilled before his eyes. The powers of evil were placed under restraint; and the influx of new spiritual forces among men was made possible. The remarkable progress of the world since that time is a direct outcome of this judgment. Those who would deny this to be the cause, must be prepared to suggest some better reason for the unprecedented changes that have marked the history of the past hundred and seventy-five years.

In his work entitled *The Last Judgment,* Swedenborg shows, by logical argument and Scriptural proofs, that the Last Judgment and the End of the World could not take place as anticipated. It would be physically impossible for all mankind who have lived from the beginning of time to be assembled on this earth at Christ's appearance, so that "every eye should see Him"; the only place, therefore, where a general judgment could take place is the "World of Spirits," in which those who have passed from this world are assembled together, awaiting removal to their final places. The "End of the World" so often spoken of in the authorized version of the New Testament is a mistranslation of the Greek term, and should be rendered "The Consummation of the Age," which rendering at once puts a new construction upon the passages in question. The consummation of an age, Swedenborg tells us, is the end of a Church or Dispensation, which takes place when it has become corrupted to such an extent that "there is no faith because there is no charity." That was the condition of the Christian Church in the middle of the eighteenth century, and therefore its consummation was then effected.

What evidence have we that this Last Judgment has really taken place? Swedenborg declares himself to have been an eye-witness.

It is impossible, he says, for any man to know when the Last Judgment is accomplished, for every one expects it on the earth, accompanied by a change of all things in the visible heaven and on the earth and with the human race therein. Lest therefore the man of the Church from ignorance should live in such a belief, and lest they who think of a last judgment should expect it for ever, whence at length the belief in those things which are said of it in the sense of the letter of the Word must perish, and lest haply, therefore, many should recede from a faith in the Word, it has been granted me to see with my own eyes that the Last Judgment is now accomplished; that the evil are cast into the hells, and the good elevated into heaven, and thus that all things are reduced into order, and consequently the spiritual equilibrium, which is between good and evil, or between heaven and hell, is restored. (*The Last Judgment*, No. 45.)

If the Last Judgment was a spiritual event, it is needless to say that the Second Coming of Christ is to be interpreted spiritually also. The Church has been looking for a physical reappearance of its Divine Founder for nearly two thousand years, until faith and hope are almost exhausted; but it has looked in vain, because it has misunderstood the prophecies. As the Jews looked for a conquering Messiah, and did not recognize the promised deliverer in the meek and gentle Jesus; so Christians have rested their faith on the appearance of a visible Judge, and have been disappointed in their expectations. Both erred in reading the prophecies too literally. Christ, indeed, has come, but not as men have expected Him. His First Advent was the revelation of the Divine in human nature,—"the Word was made flesh": the Second Coming is in the spirit, a revelation to men of the inner glory of the Divine Word. The "clouds of heaven," from which the manifestation comes forth, are appearances of truth, which obscure the clear shining of the Wisdom of God. The literal sense of Scripture is full of such appearances, arising from the limitations of the mental and moral condition of those through whom the Scriptures were given. Thus, to the evil, God appears angry and vengeful; simple minds think of God and Christ as separate Persons, and so on. There are other appearances, also, which arise from the metaphorical style in which the Scriptures are written, spiritual things being embodied in natural images.

The Second Coming of Christ is thus something inward and spiritual,—a coming "not with observation," as He Himself foretold. It is an unfolding of the inner meaning of the First Advent, and of all Divine revelations. Of this Second Coming Swedenborg declared that he was the instrument. Through him was revealed the spiritual sense of the Divine Word, shining through and illuminating the letter, and dissipating its mysteries and obscurities. Of this doctrine of the spiritual sense of Scripture we shall speak more fully in a later chapter.

It will be seen that Swedenborg was no mere critic of the current theology. While he attacked the corruptions that had marred and mutilated the pure gospel of Christ, he was enabled to reveal its spiritual truth as it is known in heaven, a system that is at once consistent, rational, practical, and in many ways new. Theology with him is truly a science, based upon revealed knowledge and the facts of human experience, confirmed by reason, and ministering to the practical needs of life.

The religion that Swedenborg teaches is eminently wholesome and manly. It does not require that men shall withdraw themselves from the world, and deny themselves the pleasures it offers; such pleasures, however, must not be pursued from selfish motives, but as aids and stimulants to useful labour. True religion affects the whole man, soul and body, heart and intellect, thoughts, motives, words, and deeds. In most religious systems the intellect is subordinated to a faith in mysterious dogmas; but Swedenborg announced the emancipation of the intellect in spiritual matters, and taught that reason is the inseparable handmaid of faith; thus he elevated our ideas of faith; at the same time he enlarged our conceptions of charity and good works. Charity, he tells us, is not a mere sentiment; nor are its offices limited to the service of the poor and needy, but consist in "doing good to our neighbour daily and continually, not only to our neighbour individually, but to our neighbour collectively; and this cannot be effected but by a man's doing what is good and just, in whatever office, business, and employment he is engaged, and with whomsoever he has any connection." (*True Christian Religion,* No. 423.)

Such good works, however, are not to be done with the idea of merit, or hope of reward; the truly charitable "place no merit in their works, for they never think of merit, but only of their duty, which as good citizens they are bound to perform." (*Ibid.*)

In the true Christian religion, as taught by Swedenborg, rewards and punishments have no place as incentives to virtue. All goodness vanishes from men's deeds, however beneficent they may appear, when the thought of merit or reward enters; the good man only desires to be a channel of the Divine beneficence, and humbly acknowledges that all the impulse, all the power, and all the will to do good come from the Lord, to whom therefore all merit belongs. He does not even expect to be rewarded in heaven for his good deeds, but only looks forward to the higher life as affording wider scope for the fulfilment of the Divine Will, and greater opportunities for usefulness. Such is the practical teaching of the doctrines revealed by Swedenborg. They present us with a worthy idea of true religion.

CHAPTER VIII

SPIRITUAL PHILOSOPHY

IN CONSIDERING Swedenborg's system of spiritual philosophy, we are again placed in the dilemma of having either to accept his claim to special enlightenment, or to believe that his ideas were all evolved from his inner consciousness. To many, the latter presents the greater difficulty; but let each one judge for himself. Of the profundity and originality of Swedenborg's teachings on such subjects as the nature and character of God, the origin of evil, the creation and preservation of the universe, the relation of spirit to matter, the constitution of the human mind, and on life and death, there can be no question. His philosophical doctrines pervade the whole of his theological works, but they are set forth especially in *The Divine Love and Wisdom, The Divine Providence, The Arcana Cœlestia, The True Christian Religion,* and *The Intercourse of the Soul and the Body.* The MS. he left uncompleted of *Apocalypse Explained* also contains a great deal of philosophical matter.

The fundamental principle of Swedenborg's philosophy is the substantial reality of spiritual things. Judging by appearances, we speak of the material world as real and substantial, but this is a fallacy of the senses.

A fallacy is an inversion of order, it is the judgment of the eye, not of the mind, it is a conclusion drawn from the appearance of a thing, not from its essence. (*Apocalypse Explained,* No. 1215.)

Thought from the eye closes up the understanding, but thought from the understanding opens the eye. (*Divine Love and Wisdom,* No. 46.)

123

Living in this phenomenal world we cannot help being misled by outward appearances; it is difficult to believe that the things that we see and handle are less real than those which are unseen, yet we can be brought to a rational conviction of this truth.

Appearances are the first things out of which the human mind forms its understanding, and these appearances the mind cannot shake off except by the investigation of cause; and if the cause lies deep, the mind cannot trace it unless it keep the understanding for a long time in spiritual light; but it cannot keep it long in that light on account of the natural light which continually drags it down. (*Divine Love and Wisdom,* No. 40.)

The great spiritual realities are Love and Wisdom.

The idea of men in general about Love and about Wisdom is as of something flying and floating in subtile air or ether; or as an exhalation from something of the kind; and scarcely any one thinks that they are really and actually Substance and Form. . . . Nevertheless the truth is that Love and Wisdom are the real and actual substance and form which constitute the subject itself. (*Divine Love and Wisdom,* No. 40.)

But love and wisdom in man are not self-derived; they are a reflection of the essential attributes of Deity itself.

The Divine Love and the Divine Wisdom are Substance and Form in itself, thus Very Reality and the One Only Reality. . . . He who by some stretch of thought can keep in his mind, and comprehend Esse and Existere in itself, will certainly also follow and comprehend that it is the Very Reality, and the One Only Reality. Very Reality is predicated of that which alone *is*; the One

Only Reality of that from which every other thing is. Now because this Very and this One Only is Substance and Form, it follows that it is the very and the one only Substance and Form. Because this very Substance and Form is Divine Love and Divine Wisdom, it follows that it is the very and one only Love, and the very and one only Wisdom; consequently, that it is the very and one only Essence, as well as the very and one only Life; for Love and Wisdom is Life. (*Divine Love and Wisdom,* Nos. 44 and 45.)

In explanation of the apparently ungrammatical character of the last sentence, it should be stated that, according to our author, "the Divine Love and Wisdom proceed from the Lord as one" (*Divine Providence,* No. 4) just as the heat and light of the sun are inseparably united.

God being thus the One Only Substance, created things derive their being and nature from Him. The idea that the Almighty in the beginning created all things out of nothing is unphilosophical and childish.

Every one who thinks from clear reason sees that the universe was not created out of nothing, because he sees that it is impossible for anything to be made out of nothing; for nothing is nothing, and to make anything out of nothing is contradictory, and what is contradictory is against the light of truth, which is from the Divine Wisdom. . . . Every one who thinks from clear reason sees also that all things have been created out of substance which is substance in itself, for this is very Esse out of which all things that are, can exist; and because God alone is Substance in itself, and thence very Esse, it is evident that the existence of things has no other source." (*Divine Love and Wisdom,* No. 283.)

Swedenborg is careful to point out that nothing of Pantheism is involved in this teaching, though the charge of Pantheism has, nevertheless, been brought against him. In the same paragraph, he continues:

Many have seen this, because reason causes it to be seen; but they have not dared to confirm it, fearing lest they might perhaps be led to think that the created universe is God because from God, or that nature is from itself, and thus that the inmost of nature is what is called God. . . . In what follows it will be seen that, although God has created the universe and all things of it from Himself, yet there is nothing at all in the created universe which is God.

In another place, he says:

That which is created in God by God is not continuous from Him; for God is Esse in Itself, and in created things there is not any Esse in itself. If in created things there were any Esse in itself, this would be continuous from God, and that which is continuous from God is God. . . . Every created thing by virtue of this its origin is such in its nature that it is a recipient of God, not by continuity but by contiguity. Its conjunctivity comes by contiguity, and not by continuity. It is conformable because it has been created in God by God; and because it has been thus created, it is an analogue, and by this conjunction it is as an image of God in a mirror. (*Divine Love and Wisdom,* Nos. 55 and 56.)

God, in His inmost essence, is incomprehensible and unapproachable by either angels or men. To the former He manifests Himself as a spiritual sun, and this spiritual sun is the origin and centre of life in the spiritual world, in the same way as the sun of the solar system is the origin and centre of life on the physical plane. This might be taken to imply that God is impersonal; but, although He is thus objectively manifested to the angels, they are conscious also of intimate personal communion. The appearance of the heavenly sun is in accordance with the law that all the interior states and ideas of spiritual beings are reproduced in corresponding external objects. Thus, since the Lord is the source and centre of their spiritual life, the Divine Love and Wisdom appears externally embodied in a magnificent heavenly luminary. From this spiritual sun, "the first proceeding of the Divine Love and Divine Wisdom," emanate atmospheres which are the media of life to spiritual beings, and by influx and correspondence to the lower world also. These atmospheres are of diminishing intensity the farther they are removed from their origin, and give rise to several degrees of life, essentially distinguished from one another. There are three discrete degrees of spiritual life, to which the three kingdoms of nature correspond.

Creation proceeds from the spiritual sun, operating on the physical plane through the natural sun; that is, from spiritual forces acting through natural forces. We might say that the spiritual sun is the soul of the natural sun, which in itself has nothing of life; like all matter it is dead and inert. Life and force are spiritual; matter is but a medium which enables them to exhibit themselves on the physical plane.

Creation itself can in no wise be ascribed to the sun of the natural world, but all to the sun of the spiritual world; because the sun of the natural world is wholly dead, but the sun of the spiritual world is alive; for it is the first proceeding of the Divine Love and the Divine Wisdom; and what is dead does nothing whatever of itself, but is acted upon. Wherefore to ascribe to it anything of creation would be like ascribing the work of the artificer to the instrument with which the hands of the artificer operate. (*Divine Love and Wisdom,* No. 157.)

The actuality of the natural sun is not from itself, but

from the living force proceeding from the sun of the spiritual world. (*Divine Love and Wisdom,* No. 157.)

Nothing in nature exists except from a spiritual origin. . . . For that which has not in itself an essence does not exist, for it is a nonentity, because there is no esse or being as the ground of its existence. Thus it is with nature; its essence from which it exists is the spiritual, because this has in itself the Divine Esse, and also the Divine power of acting, creating, and forming. (*Apocalypse Explained,* No. 1206.)

Nature and life are two distinct things; nature takes its beginning from the sun of this world, and life from the sun of heaven. (*Ibid.,* No. 1207.)

There is not a hair or thread of wool on any beast, nor a filament of a quill or feather upon any bird, nor a point of a fin or scale on any fish, which is not derived from the life of their soul, thus which is not from a spiritual origin clothed by the natural. (*Ibid.,* No. 1199.)

The living thing disposes the dead thing to compliance with itself, and forms it for uses which are its ends. (*Divine Love and Wisdom,* No. 166.)

Creation, according to Swedenborg, was not simply an initiatory act, but is in continual operation. The reproductive powers of animals and plants are not from any life that is in nature itself, but are simply the means of successive new creations.

It matters not that the continuations are effected by seeds, it is still the same creative force which produces. (*Apocalypse Explained,* No. 1209.)

Seeds are impregnated by the most subtile substances, which cannot be from any but a spiritual origin. (*Divine Love and Wisdom,* No. 310.)

All life being thus derived from the spiritual world, and every material object having behind it a spiritual force, or soul, which produces and sustains it, it follows that spiritual and natural stand to each other as cause and effect, and that there is a constant and intimate relation between the two. This is the basis of the doctrine of "correspondences," as Swedenborg named it. The natural world is an image or mirror of the spiritual world, every object, fact, and phenomenon, representing, or "corresponding" to, some immaterial idea which is its spiritual counterpart. We shall deal with this doctrine in a special chapter, as it is very important, forming as it does the groundwork of all Biblical exegesis contained in Swedenborg's works.

Spiritual life is not monotonous and uniform in character, but presents as great variety as life on the physical plane. If the latter is derived from the former, it follows that there must be a corresponding order and arrangement in the manifestations on both planes. The Divine life, as it descends through the spiritual world, is received according to the state and capacity of the subject, and thus presents infinite variety. Broadly, there are three great classes of minds that embrace and manifest the Divine influences according to their kind; these three classes correspond to the three kingdoms of nature, and in the other life form three distinct heavens, termed by Swedenborg, celestial, spiritual, and natural, with three corresponding hells. Within these degrees there are as many varied types as there are of animals, plants, and minerals in the three kingdoms of nature.

The doctrine of degrees is one of a far-reaching character, and is peculiar to Swedenborg among modern philosophers and thinkers. Degrees, he tells us, are of two kinds, discrete and continuous. Discrete degrees are distinct orders of life or capacity, like the three kingdoms of nature; and are related to each other by correspondence. Continuous degrees are varieties of the same order of life, natural or spiritual; and may be illustrated by the classification of animals, plants, and minerals into genera and species. In each kingdom of nature the various forms are connected in a continuous series; but, broadly speaking, the three kingdoms are only related to each other by analogy. The correspondence which we have seen to exist between natural and spiritual things will enable us to understand the degrees that mark the development of man's mental and moral nature. The human mind is not the simple instrument that it is sometimes thought to be, but exhibits a marked trinal division both in its moral and intellectual aspects. Truths may be apprehended in three different ways: by the learning of facts or doctrines; by the process of reasoning; or by perception; and these three different modes of apprehension are characteristic of the three degrees of the mind, which are the scientific, or the faculty of memory; the rational, or cogitative; and the intellectual, or perceptive faculty. To these three mental degrees belong three corresponding classes of moral qualities. There are good deeds which are done from a sense of duty, in a spirit of simple obedience; others which the doer performs from principle or a conviction of what is right; and others, again, which are prompted by feelings of love, kindness, or generosity.

Such is a simple outline of this doctrine. When a clear conception of it has been formed, it is seen to be full of philosophic suggestion.

To return to the subject of Creation, Swedenborg does not favour the idea that new forms of life are developed merely by accidental variation, change of environment, or natural selection, or by all of these together. New forms indicate new characteristics, and hence new spiritual causes. Development is spiritual in the first instance; external influences are, at best, but secondary causes.

For the dead thing to act upon the living thing, or for the dead force to act upon the living force, or, what is the same, for the natural to act upon the spiritual, is entirely contrary to order, and therefore to think that it does so is contrary to the light of sound reason. The dead thing, the natural thing, may indeed in many ways be perverted or changed by external accidents, but still it cannot act upon life; but life acts into it, according to the change of form which has been induced. (*Divine Love and Wisdom,* No. 166)

The spiritual principle acts into the natural and thereby produces its effects, as the principal cause does by its instrumental cause. (*Apocalypse Explained,* No. 1197.)

The gradual evolution of the higher from the lower, therefore, apart from spiritual influx, is impossible.

Swedenborg has important observations on instinct and reason, and the difference between animals and men. Instinct is not simply habit hereditarily transmitted as materialists maintain, but is spiritual in origin.

There is some spiritual principle which leads in all such cases. (*Ibid.,* No. 1198.)

The life of animals, as of man, is from the spiritual world, and thence, also, their instincts are derived.

The distinction between men and the lower animals is stated concisely in *The Intercourse between the Soul and the Body,* where we read:

A man is a man, because his understanding can be raised above the desires of his will, and thus, from above, can know and see them, and also govern them; but a beast is a beast, because its desires impel it to do whatever it does. (No. 15.)

At greater length the difference between men and animals, and the reason why only the former are immortal, is explained in the following passage, which for clearness

131

and cogency could not be paralleled from the observations of any other writer on the subject:

Man is spiritual and at the same time natural, whereas a beast is not spiritual but natural. Man is endowed with will and understanding, and his will is the receptacle of the heat of heaven, which is love, and his understanding is the receptacle of the light of heaven, which is wisdom; but a beast is not endowed with will and understanding, but instead of will has affection, and instead of understanding, knowledge (*i.e.* knowledge appertaining to its life). The will and understanding with man can act as one, and they can act not as one, for man from his understanding can think what is not of his will, being able to think what he does not will, and *vice versa;* but with a beast affection and knowledge make one, and cannot be separated; for a beast knows what appertains to its affection, and is affected by what appertains to its knowledge; and inasmuch as the two faculties, which are called knowledge and affection, with a beast, cannot be separated, therefore a beast cannot destroy the order of its life, and hence it is that it is born into all the science of its affection. But the case is otherwise with man; his two faculties of life, which are called understanding and will, can be separated, as was said above, therefore he can destroy the order of his life, by thinking contrary to his will, and willing contrary to his understanding, and hereby he also has destroyed it; hence it is that he is born into mere ignorance, that from it he may be introduced into order through knowledges by way of the understanding. The order into which man was created, is to love God above all things and his neighbour as himself, and the state into which man has come since he destroyed that order, is to love himself above all things, and the world as himself. Because man has a spiritual mind, and this is above his natural mind, and his spiritual mind is capable of intuition into such things as appertain to heaven and the church and also such as appertain to the State in respect of moral and civil laws, and these things have reference to truths and goods, which are called spiritual, moral, and civil, besides the natural things of knowledge, and to their opposites, which are falses and evils, therefore man can not only think analytically, and thence draw conclusions, but also receive influx through heaven from the Lord, and become intelligent and wise: this no beast is capable of —what it knows not being from any understanding, but from the knowledge belonging to its affection, which is its soul.

Inasmuch as man has a spiritual mind, and at the same time a natural mind, and his spiritual mind is above his natural mind, and the spiritual mind is such that it is capable of the intuition and love of truths and goods in every degree, both conjointly with the natural mind and abstractedly from it, it follows that the interiors of man which are of either mind, can be elevated to the Lord by the Lord, and be conjoined to Him; hence it is that every man lives eternally. This is not the case with a beast, which does not enjoy any spiritual mind; but only a natural, hence its interiors, which contain only knowledge and affection, cannot be elevated by the Lord, and conjoined to Him: wherefore a beast does not live after death. A beast is indeed led by a certain spiritual influx falling into its soul, but inasmuch as its spiritual cannot be elevated, it cannot be otherwise than that this is determined downwards, and regards such things as appertain to its affection, which have reference only to the things of nourishment, habitation, and propagation, and that from the knowledge of its affection it knows them by means of sight, odour, and taste.

Inasmuch as man, by virtue of his spiritual mind, has the capacity to think rationally, therefore he also has the faculty of speech, for to speak appertains to thought from the understanding, which can see truths in spiritual light; but a beast, which has not any thought from understanding, but only knowledge from affection, is only able to utter sounds, and to vary the sound of its affection according to its appetites. (*Apocalypse Explained,* No. 1202.)

Of the Divine Omnipotence and man's free will, of the origin of evil, and other subjects which have distracted the spiritual philosopher in every age, Swedenborg presents rational and adequate explanations. He shows that there is no real conflict between Omnipotence and free-will. Although God is all-powerful, He does not operate arbitrarily, but by law; and it is part of the Divine law that man shall be free in spiritual matters. He is held in equilibrium between forces of good and of evil, and must make his choice between them. At the same time the ability and will to do good are from the Lord alone, though it is given to man to feel that they are from himself. All he can do, however, is to dispose his mind and heart to receive the Divine influences. The origin of evil is in man's free-will, which enables him to pervert the Divine blessings; all evil is the perversion of what was once "very good." These subjects have been alluded to in our last chapter, and are discussed at length in *The True Christian Religion.* It is impossible here to do more than refer to them, or to touch upon other interesting points.

Swedenborg's spiritual philosophy is so totally different from anything else of the kind, that the unaccustomed reader finds himself at first in a strange land, and may depart again without having obtained so much as a glimpse of its beauties, sceptical even of their existence. Let him sojourn long enough to acquire the language and accustom his eyes to the new scenery, and he will surely be repaid. Dropping metaphor, we may express our conviction that the clear logical statement, and luminous exposition of deep matters, which he will find as he pursues his studies, can scarcely fail to win his assent to the author's assertion, that "now it is allowable to enter intellectually into the mysteries of faith." (*True Christian Religion,* No. 508.)

The principles that Swedenborg has elucidated have a very wide bearing; they are applicable, indeed, to all the great subjects that have exercised the human mind from time immemorial. A new light is thrown upon all of these problems, and a new order is brought into the region of philosophic inquiry.

CHAPTER IX

EXPOSITORY WORKS

SWEDENBORG'S principal expository works are *The Arcana Cœlestia,* the first theological work that he published; and *The Apocalypse Revealed.* The ground covered by these only includes the Books of Genesis and Exodus, and the Book of Revelation; but incidentally they touch upon almost every part of Scripture. They are bulky treatises, the *Arcana* in the latest English translation filling twelve large octavo volumes, and *The Apocalypse Revealed,* two. Besides these two works and the small expository treatise *The White Horse,* he left unpublished in MS., some fragmentary notes, a *Summary Exposition of the Prophets and Psalms* and *The Apocalypse Explained.* The last two were published as posthumous works many years after his death. *The Apocalypse Explained* was nearly lost to the world altogether, a portion of the manuscript having narrowly escaped destruction by fire. This manuscript had, indeed, an adventurous history from the time it left the custody of the Swedish Royal Academy of Sciences in 1783, until its return to its proper home there in 1842.

It is stated that Mr. C. F. Nordensköld obtained the loan of this and other manuscripts of Swedenborg's from the secretary of the Academy, and brought them to England with a view to publishing what he thought desirable. The papers came into the hands of Mr. Henry Peckitt, a retired physician and apothecary, who, in his enthusiasm for the new doctrines, undertook the whole cost of publishing *The Apocalypse Explained.* While the first volume was in the printer's hands, and the manuscript of the second was being prepared for the press by Mr. Peckitt, a disastrous fire destroyed his house, with the contents of his valuable library; and the precious manuscript was given up for lost. A fireman, however, had hastily thrown it into the street, where it was picked up by a neighbour. On regaining possession of it, Mr. Peckitt carried it to the meeting-room of the Theosophical Society (as the few disciples of Swedenborg then called themselves), and, throwing it on the table, burst into a flood of tears. When he had recovered his self-possession, he explained: "There! the greatest treasure which I had in my house is preserved in safety; and for the sake of that, I willingly submit to my great loss."

On the death of Mr. Peckitt, the custody of the manuscript passed to two of his friends, by whom the nature of the original trust does not appear to have been understood; for they subsequently sold it to Mrs. Peckitt, and it remained in the Peckitt family until 1828, when it was handed over to the Swedenborg Society by Mr. Henry Peckitt, Junior. When it was discovered that it really belonged to the Swedish Academy of Sciences, it, with other manuscripts that had been missing for many years, was returned to the Librarian. This action led to a very pleasing exchange of courtesies between the two bodies.

With this digression we may proceed to consider the contents of this and the other works mentioned above.

First, it may be well to say something about Swedenborg's general teachings respecting the Bible. He regards it in the strictest sense as a Divine revelation, but he tells us that the early chapters of Genesis are purely allegorical in character and do not describe the creation of the universe and the history of the first human pair, as commonly supposed. The Bible is truly the "Word of God," though in its outward form it appears like a human book. Within the historical narratives of individuals and nations, however, and in the gospels, prophecies, and poetical books, is enshrined an interior spiritual sense; or, rather, a series of spiritual meanings, one within the other, like the various enfoldings of a flower.

> In its ultimate sense, the Word is natural; in its interior sense, spiritual; and in its inmost, celestial; and it is Divine in every sense. (*Doctrine of the Sacred Scripture,* No. 6.)

It is indeed, the Divine Truth taking form as it descended from God through the heavens to the earth.

> In its first origin the Word is purely Divine; when this passed through the Heavens of the Lord's Celestial Kingdom it was Divine Celestial, and when it passed through the Heavens of the Lord's Spiritual Kingdom it was Divine Spiritual, and when it came to man it became Divine Natural; hence it is that the natural sense of the Word contains within it the spiritual sense, and this the celestial sense, and both a sense purely Divine, which is not open to any man, nor even to any angel. (*Apocalypse Revealed,* No. 959.)

The spiritual sense can be comprehended by men in some degree, but the celestial sense

> can scarcely be unfolded, for it does not fall so much into the thought of the understanding, as into the affection of the will. (*Doctrine of Sacred Scripture,* No. 19.)

It is adapted to the perception of the celestial angels, with whom the Divine law is received "in their inward parts," and written "in their hearts."

In thus attributing a heavenly meaning to the Scriptures, Swedenborg does not detract from the value of the literal sense: indeed, he raises it to a much higher degree of esteem than is bestowed upon it even by fundamentalists; for he teaches that the books of the Bible are not mere human compositions but a veritable embodiment of the wisdom of God, inexhaustible by the highest angels, but adapted, also, to the comprehension of the simplest minds. Everything needful for salvation, he tells us, is contained in the literal sense, and from the literal sense the doctrine of the Church should be derived and confirmed. In the literal sense, indeed, "the Word is in its fulness, its holiness, and its power." What need, then, to supplement this with a spiritual sense? Because the natural sense is written according to appearances, and is often obscure and misleading; and because the spiritual meaning amplifies and emphasizes the truth of the letter, while it explains the mysteries and apparent contradictions of the same.

In no part of the Bible is a knowledge of the spiritual sense more helpful than in dealing with the early chapters of Genesis. It is objected by sceptics that these contain false science and imaginary history, while they present an unworthy idea of God as an unjust, resentful, and arbitrary Being. In the spiritual sense, however, all these difficulties disappear, and criticism is disarmed. As Bishop Colenso remarked: "Let it be once freely admitted that these stories of the first chapters of Genesis, whatever they may teach of Divine, Eternal Truth, and whatever lessons may be drawn from them by a devout mind, are in their present form and structure mythical descriptions, where their narrative is an imaginative clothing for ideas, and so are not to be regarded as teaching unquestionable matters of historical fact which occurred in primitive times; and then such a comparison, as we must now make, between the statements of the Bible and well-known facts of science, would be superfluous and uncalled for." (*The Pentateuch*, etc., Part IV, p. 85.)

No better example of Swedenborg's exegetical method could be afforded than his explanation of these early chapters of Genesis. Truly he brings light into dark places. Instead of treating the opening chapter as an account of the beginning of created things, he takes us at once into spiritual regions, and interprets the record as descriptive of the new creation or regeneration of man. The unregenerate condition, when man is immersed in the things of sense and self, and oblivious of his better nature, is typified by the dark and formless void, over which the Spirit of God brooded, to bring into it order and life. The end and purpose of the spiritual creation, as of the physical, is the formation of man in the image and likeness of God. The spiritual man is the human soul when all its faculties are fully developed and duly subordinated, and it lives according to the Divine laws. To attain to this state, the soul requires to pass through various stages of development, which process is represented by the six days of creation.

> The times and states of man's regeneration, in general and in particular, are divided into six, and are called the days of his creation: for by degrees he is elevated from a state in which he possesses none of the qualities which properly constitute a man, until little by little he attains to the sixth day, in which he becomes an image of God. (*Arcana Cœlestia,* No. 62.)

Briefly, the six states of man's regeneration are these. The first is a condition of darkness and vacuity; for man is born in total ignorance of all that belongs to his spiritual life. The creation of light, and the division of light from darkness, represent the first dawn of spiritual knowledge, and the recognition of the difference between the worldly and the heavenly life; such a state as Bunyan describes in Christian, when he was first aroused to a sense of sin and the necessity for a change of life.

> The second state is when a division takes places between those things which are of the Lord, and such as are proper to man. . . . Thus the things which belong to the external man are separated from those belonging to the internal. (*Arcana Cœlestia,* No. 8.)

The term earth, throughout the Bible, has reference to the external man or natural degree of life, and heaven to the internal man or the spiritual degree of life.

> The third state is that of repentance, in which the man, who is being regenerated begins to discourse piously and devoutly, and to do good actions, like works of charity, but which nevertheless are inanimate, because they are supposed to originate in himself. These good actions are called tender grass, and also the herb yielding seed, and afterwards the tree bearing fruit. (*Ibid,* No. 9.)

The gathering together of the waters represents the storing up of spiritual knowledge. Water in its various forms is an apt emblem of truth. The sea, or ocean, the great reservoir of the waters of the earth, stands for the memory, which is the omnivorous receptacle of knowledge of all kinds: a storehouse from which the intellectual faculties constantly draw to stimulate the growth of ideas, which, with the practical uses that result from them, are the spiritual counterparts of the various forms of vegetable life.

In the fourth state the life is ruled by the great principles of love and faith, represented by the sun and the moon. The stars are particular knowledges of spiritual truth which serve to guide the life when the greater lights are obscured. In this stage of regeneration, the indefinite ideas of the earlier states have given place to clear and distinct conceptions of truth and duty.

The correspondence of the heavenly bodies to the guiding principles of the higher life is almost self-evident. The sun is constantly used in the Bible as a type of the Lord, especially as to His Divine love, and, by the poets, of any powerful controlling influence. The moon, receiving her light from the sun, and shining upon the world when the rays of the latter are withdrawn, is a fitting representative of faith, which cheers and illumines the night-time of the soul. The stars, although they give little light, by their apparent fixity of position relative to each other, serve to guide the mariner or wayfarer. We have guiding stars to direct us on our heavenward road also.

The fifth day of creation was marked by the production of fishes and birds; while the creation of the higher mammals is assigned to the sixth.

> After the great luminaries are kindled and placed in the internal man, and the external thence receives light, then he who is being regenerated begins first to live. Heretofore he can scarcely be said to have lived, inasmuch as the good which he did was supposed by him to have been done of himself, and the truth which he spake to have been spoken of himself; and since man of himself is dead, and there is in him nothing but what is evil and false, therefore whatsoever he produces from himself is not alive, in consequence of his inability to do good which is good in itself. . . . Now that he is vivified by love and faith, and believes that the Lord operates all the good which he does and all the truth which he speaks, he is compared to the *creeping things of the water,* and to the *fowls which fly above the earth,* and also to *beasts,* which are all animate things, and are called *living souls. (Arcana Cœlestia,* No. 39.)

Fishes and birds represent a comparatively low grade of spiritual life, in which faith is the predominating element; the higher animals typify the life in which love is more active. Man, the crown and epitome of the whole creation, stands for the regenerated soul, perfect in its degree, as reflecting the image and likeness of the Creator, and exercising dominion over his own powers and capacities (the lower animals) by God-given strength and authority.

This is a very brief statement of the spiritual meaning

of the first chapter of Genesis, as explained by Swedenborg. We may take a broader view of the subject, also. All that is here applied to the individual man, applies equally to man in a corporate sense. The days of creation not only speak of the regeneration of the individual soul; they have an interior historical meaning also, which describes the formation of the human principle in the race. Swedenborg states, and science confirms his assertion, that mankind in primitive times was little distinguished from the lower animals; the spiritual principle which now differentiates men from brutes was implanted gradually, during successive generations; and this development of the higher consciousness in the race is also shadowed forth in the account of the creation of the world given in the first two chapters of Genesis.

The work of creation finished, we are told that God rested from His labour on the seventh day. God is said to rest when man's life has been brought into harmony with the Divine life, and there is no longer opposition or conflict. Although it is for each individual to work out his own salvation, the truth is that every effort towards righteousness is the Lord's work. When this work is over, and the man no longer resists the Divine Will, the Sabbath state has been reached, in which both God and man enter into their rest.

The Sabbath state of the race is represented by the Garden of Eden. Creation being finished, and everything having been declared to be "very good," we are told that "the Lord God planted a garden eastward in Eden; and there He put the man whom He had formed." There has been much speculation as to the probable site of this garden, but all such speculation is futile. It is a "garden of the soul" and not any material paradise that is described. Under a variety of beautiful symbols the happy condition of mankind is depicted when they followed the appointed order of their lives, and delighted to do the Divine will.

It was a childlike condition of absolute dependence on God, but one not destined to last, as the sequel of the story shows.

We are given to understand that everything in Eden was good: the trees were "pleasant to the sight and good for food," and the animals were gentle and harmless. Yet one tree and one animal appear to have been evil; the tree of knowledge of good and evil was forbidden to be even touched, and the wily serpent was the cause of the transgression of this commandment. What do these things mean?

The temptation of Eve, and through her of Adam, was not the work of a crafty reptile temporarily endowed with speech, but was of the nature of all human temptations. "Let no man say when he is tempted, I am tempted of God: for God cannot be tempted with evil, neither tempteth He any man; but every man is tempted, when he is drawn away of his own lust, and enticed." (James i. 13, 14.) The serpent is a type of this lust,—of the lower, sensual nature that delights to grovel on the earth, and which, if listened to (this serpent can talk very seductively), inevitably leads to a fall from virtue.

The tree of knowledge of good and evil, again, was no earthly tree, but represents mere worldly knowledge and the impressions of the senses. This kind of food is dangerous to the higher life of man, when it comes to be regarded as in the "*midst* of the garden."

It is allowable to obtain a knowledge of what is true and good by means of every perception derived from the Lord [the trees of the Garden], but not from self and the world, or to inquire into the mysteries of faith by the senses or from science, for in this case the celestial principle is destroyed." (*Arcana Cœlestia,* No. 126.)

Everything in this story being symbolical, it follows that Adam and Eve are not to be regarded as two individuals:

they are representatives of the race, or of human nature
in the abstract, Adam standing for its intellectual, and
Eve for its emotional, side. We can see now why the woman
was first tempted, and through her the man: it is desire
that leads a man astray and warps the judgment to its
wishes. Man's desire for independence led him to trust
in his own self-derived intelligence, rather than in the
Divine guidance represented by the tree of life. After
the fall access to the tree of life was denied to him: not
that the highest blessings were arbitrarily withheld but
man's own actions rendered him incapable of receiving
them.

Among other misconceptions that have arisen from putting a literal interpretation on these parabolic stories, is
the idea that the need to labour for one's daily bread was
laid upon man as a curse, on account of Adam's dis-
obedience. Work, the source of the truest satisfaction, the
greatest blessing in life next to love, a curse sent by God!
None but an idler by nature could really entertain such
a thought. The Eden condition was not one of ease
and idleness; the man was placed in the garden "to
dress it and to keep it." What, then, is the meaning of
the curse? First, let us premise that God never curses;
the solemn malediction pronounced is but a truthful statement of the condition to which man had reduced himself
by his rebellious action. The blasted ground is the human
heart, which was no longer "an honest and good heart"
that brought forth abundantly, but one filled with thorns
and thistles that choked the Word and rendered it un-
fruitful. So, from that time any progress in the spiritual
life has only been through much toil and struggling.

The history of Cain and Abel, again, presents many
difficulties, if we regard it as describing actual occurrences. We cannot help feeling that the treatment of Cain,
prior to his fratricidal act, was not altogether just: he
offered what he had to the Lord, yet he was rejected and

145

his brother preferred. In the spiritual sense this inequality does not appear; we see Cain as the representative of merely intellectual faith, apart from charity, for the fruits of the earth, as we have seen, stand for things of the intellect; while Abel typifies love or charity, and his offering, the worship that springs from the good affections of the heart, the "firstlings of his flock." Where mere faith and formalism prevail, love is slain.

The story of the Flood has given occasion to the rationalist for much animadversion; but when it is interpreted, spiritually, all his objections are groundless. It is not a physical deluge that we have to consider, but a flood of monstrous evils and falsities that overwhelmed the Church in ancient times. Noah and his family represent those who had not succumbed to the prevailing heresies and immoralities; a "little remnant," in fact, such as is found in all times of spiritual decadence, among whom a revival of religion takes place. These were supported, in the midst of the general demoralization, by adherence to true doctrine and godly life. Noah, we are told, was "a preacher of righteousness." Right principles or doctrines form the spiritual ark, which bears us up when the floods of iniquity threaten to overwhelm us.

Literalism sees in the account of the tower of Babel another instance of Divine judgment, and the origin of the diversity of language. We know now that the many tongues by which men convey their thoughts to one another did not originate in this way, but by gradual evolution from the earliest forms of speech. Therefore, if the story of Babel has any ground of truth, it must be read in some other than the verbal sense. It is really a Divine parable, telling us of the efforts of evil and misguided men to circumvent the Divine order of life and climb up to heaven some other way. The tower of Babel is a citadel of false doctrine, having the brick of man-made schemes of salvation, and the fiery bitumen of unholy passions, instead of the solid stone of Divine truth, and the firm-set mortar of uniting love.

Up to the time of Abraham, the Biblical account consists of myths, or allegorical story; afterwards there is an evident basis of historical truth; but the events are so selected and recorded as to convey a continuous spiritual meaning. The history of the patriarchs, of the sojourning of the Israelites in Egypt, their miraculous deliverance, their wanderings in the wilderness, and their final settlement in the promised land, convey deep, spiritual lessons for all times and peoples. Not only this, but in their inmost sense they have reference to the great work which the Saviour accomplished in redeeming mankind and in glorifying His human nature during His life upon earth. We cannot here give more than a hint of these things.

Swedenborg's explanation of the *Book of Revelation* is consistent with his explanation of *Genesis* and *Exodus* in his *Arcana Cœlestia*, inasmuch as it is based upon the same "science of correspondences." The same types occur, both in the Book of Genesis and in the Apocalypse, and indeed throughout the Sacred Scriptures, and have the same meanings assigned to them. In the light of the spiritual sense, the apparently heterogeneous mass of symbols becomes a connected account of spiritual events.

Many have expounded this prophetical book which is called the Apocalypse; but none of them have understood the internal or spiritual sense of the Word, and therefore, they have applied the various particulars in it to the successive states of the church, with which they have become acquainted from history; besides which, they have applied many of them to civil conditions. Hence it is that those expositions are for the most part conjectures, which never can appear in such a light as would admit of their being established as truths; wherefore, as soon as they are read, they are laid aside as mere opinions. . . . All things which are written in the Apocalypse are expressed in a style similar to that in which the prophetical parts of the Old Testament are written, and, in general, in which the whole Word is written, and the Word in the letter is natural, but in its inward contents it is spiritual, and being such, it contains a sense within it which does not at all appear in the letter. (*Apocalypse Explained,* No. 1.)

What, then, does the spiritual sense in the Apocalypse discover to us?

The book opens with the description of a wonderful vision of the glorified Saviour, as seen by the aged apostle. We cannot accept this as a picture of the actual person of Deity, but rather as a comprehensive representation, seen in the spiritual world, of the Divine perfections. The head of dazzling whiteness, the feet like glowing brass, the covering garment, the golden girdle, the sword proceeding from His mouth, and the seven stars in His right hand, all have a definite signification and shadow forth some quality of Divinity, or some form of Divine activity.

The seven Churches are not seven particular Christian organizations, though the apostle's message may have been addressed to such at first, but stand for all classes of those who receive the Gospel. Their various defections describe the different forms of heresy and evil that have wrought corruption in the Church; for the Apocalypse is the book of judgment of the first Christian dispensation. A great part of it is taken up with a prophetic forecast of this judgment.

Protestant theologians have been agreed in regarding Babylon as a type of the perverted Romish Church; Swedenborg gives it a spiritual meaning: the judgment pronounced upon Babylon is not alone upon a particular section of the corrupted Church, but upon all who pervert the truths of religion for the sake of gaining dominion over others. There are many such outside the Roman communion, but the subjection of the laity to the priesthood, and the assumption of almost Divine powers by the latter, are such striking characteristics of the Romish system, that they cannot be overlooked.

Protestant heresies are equally condemned in the Book of the Revelation. The great red dragon stands for the immoral doctrine of salvation by faith alone, which, as destructive of all spiritual enlightenment, is represented by the monster drawing down the stars with his tail. This dragon stood before the woman who was about to give birth to a child, that he might devour it as soon as born. Women in general correspond to affection, and the woman here represents those in the decadent church who still retain a love of what is good and true, among whom a new church will arise. The spiritual dragon vehemently opposes the pure doctrine of this new church, symbolized by the man-child.

The triumph of the good and true, and the inauguration of a new dispensation, are set forth in the marvellous vision of the holy city, New Jerusalem, descending from God out of heaven. Cities in the Bible always represent systems of doctrine, true or false. As a great city, Babylon typifies the corrupt system of the Romish Church, so, the New Jerusalem describes in vivid symbols the beauty and consistency of the doctrines of a True Christian Religion. The foundations of precious stones are the great fundamental principles of religion, full of light and beauty; the wall great and high, truths that protect from the assaults of evil; the gates of pearl, introductory truths, like the two great commandments, that lead the soul to the heavenly state represented by the golden streets of the holy city; the river of the water of life flowing from the throne through the street of the city, the continual influx of living truth from the Lord: and so with all the other objects described; each has its inherent signification.

Stated in this brief and bare manner, it may seem to the reader that the interpretation of these Divine symbols is arbitrary and inconclusive; but further study will satisfy him that it is based, as Swedenborg taught that it was based, upon a principle that is universal and, by creation, resident in the nature of things. It would be easy to show, for instance, that stone throughout the Scriptures stands for truth, especially the hard facts of knowledge. Recognizing this correspondence, we can see why the Israelites were commanded to build altars of unhewn stones; that is, to offer worship from unsophisticated truth; why the tower of Babel was built of brick instead of stone; how David vanquished the Philistine giant by means of a smooth stone from the brook; we can understand the meaning of the stone that destroyed the composite image which Nebuchadnezzar saw in his dream; of the "head stone of the corner"; of the rock upon which the wise man built his house; and of the other rock, the declaration by Peter of Christ's Divinity, upon which the true Church is founded.

Space will not permit of further elaboration of the subject, but what has been written will serve to give a general idea of Swedenborg's exegesis. The reader will probably admit that his method is ingenious and the result interesting; but if he once grasps the great principle of correspondence, upon which the spiritual interpretation of Scripture is based, he will come to see that the method is also true and the result inevitable: that, in fact, Swedenborg has not given us an ingenious system, but revealed to us the facts of an unalterable law, under which "the invisible things of Him from the creation of the world are clearly seen, being understood by the things that are made." (Rom. i. 20.)

CHAPTER X

THE SCIENCE OF CORRESPONDENCES

THE doctrine of Correspondences, to which reference has been made in the preceding chapter, is based upon the fact that everything outward and visible has an inward and spiritual cause. Speech, or written language, for example, is the outward embodiment of thought. Without thought, it is needless to say, speech and writing would never have come into existence. That is why the lower animals have no language, beyond an absolutely limited range of expressive sounds. There is an exact correspondence between thought and expression, whether the latter take the form of articulate speech, writing, art, or music. Where a knowledge of this correspondence is wanting, the outward form loses its meaning, as, for example, a foreign language, to one unacquainted with its symbols and accidence, is meaningless because the vivifying thought is separated from its corresponding outward expressions. For many years the Egyptian hieroglyphics, and the cuneiform inscriptions, were meaningless signs, until the discovery of the key to them restored the lost correspondence between inward idea and outward expression, and now the ancients, though dead, still speak to us through their peculiar forms of writing.

Written signs, and even verbal speech, are in some degree arbitrary; it would, indeed, be possible to invent a language, in which symbols that were absolutely arbitrary were alone employed, though no historical language has arisen in this way. In this artificial language there would still be a correspondence, but a purely conventional one; whereas in natural languages the forms employed have originally been derived from the ideas it has been desired to convey, and thus they are truly symbolical. There is a form of language, however, in which correspondence is perfect, and which is understood by all; to wit, the language of emotion. We need not be familiar with the French tongue to know when a Frenchman is angry, or pleased, or in distress: though we may not understand a word he is saying, we can read the expression of his face, and can gather from his gestures and tone of voice, the state of his mind. In a sincere person, the face is a perfect expression of the mind, and even a hypocrite cannot prevent his character from appearing to some extent in his features. And, not only the features, but the whole body, with its movements and gestures, expresses the nature of the man, for the spirit forms the body into its own likeness; not completely, it is true, in this state of existence, but perfectly in the spiritual world, where the correspondence between the internal and the external is complete.

As the bodily form expresses the character of man's spirit, so also the works of his hands declare his inward nature. No history is so true as that which is written in the art of a people. Architecture is an embodiment of national life, and even the fashioning of everyday objects of utility reveals something of the character and ideals of a community. In fact, every act of man is the outcome and expression of his soul, and corresponds to the latter in a manner more or less perfect.

If the deeds and works of man thus reveal his inward character, so also are the wisdom and goodness of God set forth in His works: not in a general sense merely, as ministering to the needs and pleasures of His creatures, but in a most particular manner, every object being an embodiment and mirror of some quality of Divinity. That the objects of nature are in some way symbolical of spiritual things is generally recognized. In notes to Chapter iv. of his *Science of Correspondences Elucidated,* the Rev. Edward Madeley gives a striking series of quotations from ancient and modern authors in support of this view. The whole Universe is, indeed, "the Time-vesture of the Eternal," and symbolical in every detail. "All visible things are emblems," because they are created in correspondence with Divine ideas. The "Science of Correspondences" is the science that enables us to understand their inner reality.

Not only is there a correspondence between the outward creation and the spiritual world, there is also an intimate relation between nature and the spirit of man. The ancients described man as a microcosm, or a universe in little. The full significance of this comparison has only been made known to us by Swedenborg. As outward nature is the embodiment of Divine ideas, and man was created "in the image and likeness of God," there is a correspondence of all things in man with all things of the physical universe. There is a mental and spiritual heaven and earth; there are spiritual sun, moon, and stars; there are mountains, hills, valleys, and plains of the soul; there are spiritual trees, flowers, and tender herbs, also thorns, thistles, and poisonous plants; there are spiritual beasts, birds, reptiles, and insects; in fact, everything which we see around us has its counterpart in our spiritual natures.

Without entering into great detail, let us see how this doctrine of correspondences works out. The heavens and the earth—what is above us, and what is beneath our feet,—clearly exhibit the dual nature of man, his spiritual part and his earthly part. In his spiritual heaven are the lights that illumine his soul, and enable him to walk without stumbling,—the greater lights of love and faith, and the lesser lights of knowledge and precept. Light and darkness themselves are correspondents of truth and error, as every one plainly perceives. The earth is man's lower nature, the natural man; barren and unproductive apart from the higher influences which are continually operating upon it, but fruitful and beautiful when these are allowed free scope. The sunshine of love and the light of truth bring forth beautiful thoughts, ideas, and perceptions, which, with their practical realization in good works, are the analogues of vegetable life with its trees, plants, blossoms, and fruits. The animals which inhabit this mental earth, are the various affections and desires of human nature, whether good or bad. We have within us, *in posse,* if not in active life, all the good and evil animals that range the world, innocent lambs, mild and harmless sheep and cattle, swift and strong horses, gentle doves and sweet singing birds; also fierce and destructive creatures, rapacious birds, and slimy and venomous reptiles.

The three degrees of the human mind are strikingly presented to us in the three kingdoms of nature. The mineral kingdom, with its rocks, earths, minerals, fluids, and gases, stands for all that is inert and lifeless in human nature— mere knowledge, on the intellectual side, and animal instincts and propensities on the moral side. The vegetable kingdom, as we have seen, aptly typifies intellectual processes, a truth which is recognized in our everyday language. We talk about sowing the seeds of truth; of the germination of ideas, which take root in the mind and grow into orderly systems of truth, like mental plants and trees, bearing fruit ultimately in practical purposes. The animal kingdom presents a series of expressive symbols, relating more especially to moral qualities.

The things in the animal kingdom are correspondences in the first degree, because they *live;* those in the vegetable kingdom are correspondences in the second degree, because they only *grow;* and those in the mineral kingdom are correspondences in the third degree, because they neither *live* nor *grow.* . . . Besides these, whatever the industry of man prepares from them for use, are correspondences; such as food of all kinds, garments, houses, public edifices, and so forth. (*Heaven and Hell,* No. 104.)

All things in general and particular which exist in the created universe have such a correspondence with all things of man in general and in particular, that it may be said that man also is a kind of universe. There is a correspondence of his affections, and thence of his thoughts, with all things of the animal kingdom; of his will, and thence of his understanding, with all things of the vegetable kingdom; and of his ultimate life, with all things of the mineral kingdom. (*The Divine Love and Wisdom,* No. 52.)

The correspondence of outward nature with the human mind and life, is only a limited example of this great law, which extends throughout the universe, both spiritual and physical; for the Divine life descends by various degrees to the material plane in every world, and every plane of life is related to all others by correspondence. Creation, indeed, takes place by a successive unfolding of the Divine, first in the spiritual world, and by influx from that, into the world of nature. A knowledge of correspondences, we are told, is one of the "universal knowledges" essential to a true understanding of creation.

Correspondence [thus] extends itself more widely than man, for the heavens correspond one with another. The second or middle heaven corresponds to the third or inmost; and the first or lowest heaven to the second or middle; the first or lowest heaven corresponds also to the corporeal forms in man, which are called his members, organs, and viscera; and thus the corporeal part of man is that in which heaven ultimately closes, and on which it rests as on its base. (*Heaven and Hell,* No. 100.)

The universal heaven is so formed as to correspond to the Lord, to His Divine Human; and man is so formed that all things in him, in general and in particular, correspond to heaven, and through heaven, to the Lord. (*Arcana Cœlestia,* No. 3624.)

There is a correspondence of sensuous things with natural ones; there is a correspondence of natural things with spiritual ones; and there is a correspondence of spiritual things with celestial ones; and, finally, there is a correspondence of celestial things with the Lord's Divine; thus there is a succession of correspondences from the Divine down to the ultimate Natural. (*Ibid.,* No. 5131.)

It may be useful to explain that the term "natural" in this passage has reference to the natural degree of man's life; but the Divine descends also into material nature, for everything is created and constantly sustained by an inflowing of the Divine life.

The natural world, and all that it contains, exists and subsists from the spiritual world, and both from the Divine. (*Heaven and Hell,* No. 106.)

Since the Divine life descends to man through the celestial, spiritual, and natural heavens, the revelation of God's will and wisdom comes to him in the same way. The Word of the Lord that came to "holy men of old" was the ultimate expression of the Divine Wisdom, accommodated to the low estate of humanity. Hence its form is imperfect and apparently full of blemishes; but it has within it a deeper meaning, or rather, series of meanings comprehended by the several orders of angels. The celestial angels perceive the truth more interiorly than the spiritual angels; the spiritual angels have a clearer comprehension of it than those of the lowest heaven; while these latter are in spiritual light far exceeding that enjoyed by mortals. These several degrees of intelligence are distinct from one another, but are united by correspondence. Divine revelation comes to them all and is ultimated in the written Word of God. The key to the interpretation of the latter is therefore the science of correspondences, for the histories, biographies, prophecies, etc., of the Bible are couched in language that is intimately related to spiritual ideas.

The Word is so written, that every single thing therein, even to the most minute, corresponds to the things in heaven; hence the Word has Divine force; and conjoins heaven with the earth. (*Arcana Cœlestia,* No. 8615.)

One of the most self-evident of correspondences is that of light to truth. We speak familiarly of the light of truth and the light of reason; of throwing light upon a subject; and of the mind being illumined by ideas. The first created thing was light, and the first manifestation of the Divine power in the new creation, or regeneration of man, is the letting in of light in the chaos and darkness of the natural mind. Light is the constant symbol of truth throughout the Bible; the lamp that burnt continually in the sanctuary was a beautiful symbol of true worship, the light which Jesus enjoined His disciples to let shine before men: He declared Himself to be "the light of the world" that shone in uncomprehending darkness; He restored sight to the blind both physically and spiritually: He is, indeed, "our light and our salvation," and is constantly endeavouring to lead us from darkness into light. His Word is a lamp unto our feet, and a light unto our path, and will lead us, if we follow Its guidance, in "the way everlasting." As the Bible opens with the declaration, "Let there be light," so it closes with the promise of light for the righteous in the Holy City.

Accepting, as we cannot help doing, this spiritual meaning of light, many dark places in the Divine Word become clear. When we read, for instance, as we do in numerous passages, that the sun shall be darkened, the moon shall withdraw her shining, or be turned to blood, and the stars shall fall from heaven, we must not think of physical catastrophes, but of love waxing cold, faith forsaking men's minds, and knowledge ceasing, in the dark times of the Church.

The correspondence of light, as I have said, is self-evident: let us take another example that seems, at first sight, arbitrary and unconvincing. Swedenborg tells us that the horse represents the human understanding or intellect. Before attempting to show the correctness of this interpretation, I may remark that we recognize it more or less when we speak of a man riding a hobby, or possessing "horse-sense." The intellect, in fact, adds to our spiritual powers, in much the same way as a horse enlarges our physical ability. It gives us a more commanding view of the world and enables us to progress more swiftly in our undertakings; and in spiritual warfare—the war-horse is a frequent symbol in Scripture—does not the intellect enable us to run down our enemies as a warrior tramples his foes. Our power is increased with our insight.

There are in the Bible many remarkable passages relating to the horse. What is the meaning of the adder biting the heels of the horse, so that his rider shall fall backwards? The serpent tribe, as we have seen, represents the lowest sensual nature of man, while the horse is high intelligence. Man falls from his high estate, when he allows sensuality to mar his intellectual capacities. How often do we see a bright intellect overthrown by the indulgence of sensual appetites! The heel here is the vulnerable part, as in the myth of Achilles, and in the prophecy relating to the serpent and the seed of the woman. (Genesis iii. 15.) What is the spiritual heel but that part of the man which is especially open to temptation, the animal nature or carnal mind? It is to this that the allurements of the senses appeal.

The most remarkable reference to horses and riders in the Bible is the record of the vision seen by St. John of the four riders who appeared at the opening of the first seal. Swedenborg tells us that this represents the gradual decline in the understanding of the Word of God during successive ages of the Church's history. The white horse, with its rider crowned and armed, going forth, conquering and to conquer, typifies the irresistible power of unadulterated truth. The red horse, whose rider, wielding a great sword, had power to take peace from the earth, represents the true understanding of truth destroyed by passion and hatred. The black horse is evidently the antithesis of the white horse, and stands for truth falsified and perverted; while the pale horse, which was ridden by Death, and had Hell in its train, pictures to us a total lack of spirituality, and the consequent extinction of all true knowledge and perception of higher things.

The reader will recall Zechariah's vision of four horses which evidently is similar in meaning to that of St. John; and the description by the latter of another rider upon a white horse, who was called, "Faithful and True," "the Word of God," "King of kings and Lord of lords" and who was followed by the armies of heaven also mounted on white horses. This latter vision strikingly confirms Swedenborg's interpretation, for is it not clear that this is a demonstration of the power and purity of essential truth?

There is another aspect of the doctrine of correspondences that has an important practical bearing. Not only is there a correspondence between the natural and spiritual worlds, and between the several degrees or planes of each, and also between outward nature and the mind of man; there is, or should be, likewise, a correspondence between the internal and external of the man himself, and between the inflowing life of God and the human soul which receives it.

The universal heaven is so formed as to correspond to the Lord, to His Divine Human; and man is so formed that all things in him, in general, and in particular, correspond to heaven, and through heaven to the Lord. (*Arcana Cœlestia,* No. 3624.)

The process of regeneration is, indeed, the bringing about of a correspondence between what is internal and spiritual and what is outward and natural.

159

The work of regeneration is chiefly occupied in making the natural man correspond to the [spiritual] rational. . . . When it obeys, it corresponds; and in proportion as it corresponds, man is regenerated. (*Ibid.*, No. 3286.)

The natural is subjugated when it is reduced to correspondence; and when the natural is reduced to correspondence, it reacts no more. (*Ibid.*, No. 5651.)

But men, spirits, and angels, are so full of iniquity that [absolute] correspondence can never take place to eternity, yet the Lord is always making it more perfect. (*Spiritual Diary*, No. 2158.)

"Without correspondence," we read just before, "there can be no holiness," and elsewhere,

Blessed, after death, is he who is in correspondence, that is, whose external man corresponds to his internal. (*Arcana Cœlestia*, No. 2994.)

Since there is only One who is perfectly holy, we are told that,

In Him alone was there a correspondence of all things which belong to the body with the Divinity, and such a correspondence as was most perfect, or infinitely perfect. . . . Thus He is the Perfect Man, and the Only Man. (*Ibid.*, No. 1414.)

As Divinity and Humanity are united in the person of Jesus Christ our Lord, so must our humanity be brought into harmony with the Divine Spirit operating within us, that the prayer of Jesus may be fulfilled: "Holy Father, keep through Thine own name those whom Thou hast given Me, that they may be one, as We are." "I in them, and Thou in Me, that they may be made perfect in one." (John xvii. 11, 23.)

CHAPTER XI

"THINGS HEARD AND SEEN"

IF SWEDENBORG really enjoyed the privilege of constant association with angels and spirits, as he asserts, we should expect to find evidence of the fact in his works. These should give us new light on spiritual subjects, and positive information in regard to the life to come. As to the new light which Swedenborg has thrown upon theological and philosophical problems, the reader may form some opinion from a perusal of the foregoing chapters: in this chapter we propose to deal chiefly with his revelations of "other-world order."

When we compare the generous and enlightened views in relation to the other life, which are largely held by intelligent people at the present day, with the grossly material and morally revolting ideas of the popular theology of the eighteenth century, we cannot but feel that a distinct advance in spiritual knowledge has been made. To the influence of Swedenborg this change must be largely, if not entirely, attributed. At a time when men—if they believed at all in a future life—believed in the resurrection of the material body; in the arbitrary character of Divine rewards and punishments, and the vindictiveness of the latter; in heavenly joys consisting of perpetual adoration and psalm-singing; in the lost being tortured for ever in material fire and brimstone; and that among the lost were all the heathen who had never heard of Christ, and millions of unbaptized or non-elect infants,—at such a time Swedenborg revealed the spiritual nature of the resurrection, the continuity of the life beyond the grave with the present state of existence; the universality of the Divine benignity, reaching even to the lowest hell; the automatic character

161

of future rewards and punishments; that the spiritual life is a life of activity and usefulness; that the fire of hell is nothing but the burning of evil lusts; that the heathen are as certain to secure salvation as professing Christians, if they live up to the light they possess; and that all children who die, whether baptized or unbaptized, whether Christian or Gentile, are given immediately into the care of the wisest angels and are trained and educated to become angels likewise.

Men in all ages have desired to know the fate of their departed friends,—what their state and condition is; how they are occupied; if they still enjoy any kind of intercourse with the friends from whom they have been sundered by death; and if the latter may look forward to a renewal of the old intimacies, when they themselves are translated to the upper world; but the veil has hitherto been closely drawn. Are we to assume that it must ever remain so? Are there not circumstances in our own times that seem to point to the necessity of some further revelation to prevent the extinction of faith? On the one hand we have a growing agnosticism, and on the other an eager craving on the part of those who still cling to the old beliefs, for more light on the future life. Swedenborg states that he was admitted, by Divine Providence, beyond the veil, and instructed by actual experience in the order of the spiritual world, with the object that men's faith might be sustained, and might rest upon a sure foundation. Let us hear what he says, then, without prejudice. We have the fullest information in his work entitled *Heaven and its Wonders, and Hell: from Things Heard and Seen,* but additional particulars will be found in the chapters interspersed between the expository portions of the *Arcana Cœlestia,* in *Conjugial Love,* and incidentally in other works. In the introduction to *Heaven and Hell,* he writes:

The arcana which are revealed in the following pages,

are concerning heaven and hell, and also concerning man's life after death. The man of the church at this day knows scarcely anything concerning heaven and hell, or concerning his life after death, although they all stand plainly described in the Word; indeed, many who are born within the church deny these things, saying in their hearts, "Who has come thence and told us?" Lest, therefore such a negative principle, which prevails especially amongst those who have acquired much worldly wisdom, should also infect and corrupt the simple in heart, and the simple in faith, it has been granted me to associate with angels, and to converse with them as one man with another; and also to see things which are in the heavens, as well as those which are in the hells, and this for thirteen years; and now to describe them from experience, in the hope that ignorance may be enlightened, and unbelief dispelled. (No. 1.)

The first great principle, of the continuity of existence, is stated in the very earliest words that Swedenborg published on the nature of the other life. In *Arcana Cœlestia* (No. 70) we read:

That I might know that man lives after death, it has been granted me to speak and converse with several persons with whom I had been acquainted during their life in the body, and this not merely for a day or a week, but for months, and in some instances for nearly a year, as I had been used to do here on earth. They were greatly surprised that they themselves, during their life in the body, had lived, and that many others still live, in such a state of unbelief concerning a future life, when nevertheless there intervenes but the space of a few days between the decease of the body and their entrance into another world,—for death is a continuation of life.

Then follows a description of what happens during those few days, based not only upon the information of others but upon his own experience; for, he asserts that he was brought into a condition of bodily insensibility that he might undergo precisely similar states to those of dying persons. The dying, he tells us, are attended during the passage from one world to another by heavenly as well as earthly watchers. Angels from the celestial, or highest, heaven first minister to the passing soul, and keep the mind as far as possible in the pious and holy thoughts which are usually associated with the death-bed. The subject is at this time semi-conscious, and scarcely notices the presence of his angelic ministrants; who themselves are silent, and communicate their thoughts by a subtle influence.

It is a law of spiritual life that persons of diverse nature cannot remain associated together for long; it follows that for such as have not reached the celestial degree of development, the presence of the holy ones who first approach them is found unendurable after a time; so these retire and give place to spiritual angels.

The spiritual angels remain with the man so long as their presence is congenial to him, instructing him in Divine knowledge, and introducing him to the wonderful scenes of his new stage of existence. They, in turn, withdraw if their presence is shown to be distasteful.

When the soul thus separates himself, he is received by good spirits, who likewise do him all kind offices whilst he is in consort with them. If, however, his life in the world was such that he cannot remain associated with the good, he seeks to be disunited from them also, and this separation is repeated again and again, until he associates himself with those whose state entirely agrees with that of his former life in the world, among whom he finds, as it were, his own life. They then, wonderful to relate, live together a life of similar quality to that which had constituted their ruling delight when in the body. On returning into this life, which appears to them as a new commencement of existence, some after a longer and others after a shorter space of time are carried thence towards hell; whilst such as have been principled in faith towards the Lord, are led by degrees from this new beginning of life to heaven. (*Arcana Cœlestia,* No. 316.)

Thus, at the very threshold of his new state of existence the man becomes his own judge, and chooses his own associates. It is an inspiring thought, and one that gives us an overwhelming idea of the Divine benignity, that every one high or humble, saint or sinner, is offered an opportunity of entering the very loftiest sphere of heavenly society, and, when this offer is rejected, is shown one by one all the glories of the kingdom, and invited to choose his own place and share in the same.

When the novitiate has fully entered into spiritual consciousness and returned into his own proper mode of life, he is surprised to find that the new world is little different from the one he has just left; so little indeed, that many refuse to believe that they have died at all. They find themselves possessed of bodies quite as real as those which they had in the world, they meet congenial companions, and see around them objects not unlike those to which they had been accustomed in their earthly life. They enjoy, in fact, a real, substantial existence, instead of living in a disembodied condition, as, before they entered their new stage of life, they probably anticipated they would.

Swedenborg was the first to teach that spirits have substantial, organized forms and perfect sensation. He says:

Care should be taken not to give credence to the erroneous opinion that spirits do not possess far more exquisite sensations than during the life of the body, for I have been convinced to the contrary by experience repeated thousands of times. . . . Spirits not only possess the faculty of sight, they live in such great light that the mid-day light of this world can scarcely be compared

to it. . . . They enjoy the power of hearing also, and
that in so exquisite a degree as vastly to exceed what
they possessed in the body; of which, in my almost constant conversations with them, now for some years, I
have had repeated opportunity of being convinced. The
nature of their speech, and the sense of smell they also
possess, will, by the Divine mercy of the Lord, be considered hereafter. They have, besides, a most exquisite
sense of touch, whence come the pains and torments
endured in hell; for all sensations have relation to the
touch, of which they are merely diversities and varieties.
Their desires and affections, moreover, are incomparably
stronger than those possessed during the life of the body.
. . . Men think, also, after death, far more perspicuously
and distinctly than during their previous life; for in a
spiritual state of being, more is involved in one idea than
in a thousand whilst in the natural life. . . . In a word,
man loses nothing by death, but is still a man in all respects, although more perfect than when in the body.
(*Arcana Cœlestia,* No. 322.)

Not only does man take with him all his powers and
capacities, but also his acquired modes of thought, his beliefs, and his prejudices. Hence many arrive in the new
life with gross misconceptions as to the nature of the happiness of heaven, which they desire to enjoy; and these
erroneous ideas have to be corrected. This is done in the
most effective and thorough way, by allowing them to test
experimentally their own ideals of bliss. In the introduction
to *Conjugial Love,* we have a most interesting description
of such experiences, which is repeated in the *True Christian
Religion* (Nos. 731–752). We are told of spirits who had
looked forward to constant social intercourse with the
wisest and best as their ideal of happiness, and who were
therefore placed in a mansion where they might meet with
such; but in a few days they grew weary of talk and begged

to be let out, which was permitted after they had become thoroughly convinced of the error of their preconceptions, and had been instructed as to the true nature of heavenly joy. Others sought satisfaction in feasting with the patriarchs and apostles, and were granted the semblance of such delight, but were quickly sated. Others again, and these were doubtless a large class, had learnt to regard heaven as a place of perpetual worship, "where congregations ne'er break up, and Sabbaths have no end." Such were permitted to enter a temple and join in the worship there proceeding. At first they were in ecstasies; but after a long period of devotion, their fervour began to wane,—some nodded and slept, others yawned, or cried out to be released, and all were wearied with excess of pious effort. Those who had looked forward to the enjoyment of heavenly dignities, were permitted to assume such, but found no lasting satisfaction in them. All were instructed that heavenly joy

> is the delight of doing something that is of use to oneself and others; and the delight of use derives its essence from love and its existence from wisdom. The delight of use, originating in love through wisdom, is the soul and life of all heavenly joys. (*Conjugial Love,* No. 5.)
>
> To those who do uses faithfully, He gives the love of use, and its reward, which is internal blessedness; and this is eternal happiness. (*Ibid.,* No. 7.)

But is not the "chief end of man" to "glorify God and enjoy Him for ever"? Truly! The glorification of God, however, is something more than psalm-singing.

> It means bringing forth the fruits of love, that is, doing the work of one's function faithfully, sincerely, and diligently, for this is of the love of God, and of the love of the neighbour; and this is the bond of society, and its good. Thereby God is glorified. (*Ibid.,* No. 9.)

167

It need scarcely be said that such experiences do not take place either in heaven or in hell, but in an intermediate state where souls are prepared for their final abodes. At the time when Swedenborg wrote, the doctrine of an intermediate condition had been utterly eliminated from Protestant theology: it was a bold thing, therefore, for him to describe it, especially as he thereby laid himself open to the charge of restoring the false notion of purgatory. With Swedenborg, however, the intermediate state is not a place where those who have neglected the means of salvation on earth may have a second chance; but the theatre of judgment, where the true character of the man is brought to light. The method of this judgment is not that of a criminal court, in which the accused is arraigned before judge or magistrate, and witnesses are called on either side. Here the man is his own judge and his own witness; his scroll of life is unrolled before him, and all his states and experiences recalled; the good that he has done for the love of goodness is confirmed as his own, while works done from the desire for merit or applause are cast aside as dross; evil that has been done and repented of is again brought to mind, to be spurned and blotted out, if repentance has been genuine; while misdeeds that have been done from the love of evil are recalled with a sense of delight, and become confirmed as part of his nature. The truth that men have learned is also confirmed to them if they have made it their own by obedience; while those whose knowledge and profession of truth have only been a cloak to an evil life, are deprived of that wisdom which was theirs only in seeming. Such as have never been instructed in true doctrine, or who have imbibed error unconsciously, have opportunities afforded them of acquiring the truth in which they are deficient. The heathen, and other ignorant persons of good disposition, are carefully instructed in such degree of truth as they are able to receive, and are thus prepared to enter the abodes of angels.

From the above statement, Swedenborg's remark will be understood, that "the Lord casts no one into hell" (*Heaven and Hell,* No. 545); the wicked, however, naturally gravitate thither, as there alone do they find congenial associations. Not only are none sent to hell, but none need remain there who wish to leave. We are told that evil spirits are sometimes granted their desire to enter heaven, but they immediately cast themselves down headlong, unable to endure its atmosphere of purity. Another striking statement of Swedenborg's is that men are not punished for their misdeeds done in the body, but only for continuance in ill-doing. Nor are they punished for evil actions done with good, though mistaken, intention; still less for hereditary evil, except in so far as they have made it their own.

There is nothing vindictive in Divine punishment; indeed, as we have said, there is no such thing, really, as *Divine* punishment; it only appears to be Divine, and the appearance is due to the evil setting themselves against the true order of their life.

> Such is the equilibrium of all and everything in the other life that evil punishes itself, so that there is in evil the punishment of evil. It is similar in respect to falsity, which returns upon him who is principled in it, hence every one brings punishment and torment on himself. . . . The Lord never sends any one into hell, but is desirous to bring all out of hell; still less does he induce torment; but since the evil spirit rushes into it himself, the Lord turns all punishment and torment to some good and use. (*Arcana Cœlestia,* No. 696.)

Thus there is mercy even in punishment.

> The mercy of the Lord involves all and everything done by the Lord towards mankind, who are in such a state that the Lord pities them, each one according to his state; thus He pities him whom He permits to be pun-

ished, and him also to whom He grants the enjoyment of good. It is of mercy that He permits man to be punished, because mercy turns all the evil of punishment into good; and it is of mercy to grant the enjoyment of good, because no one merits anything that is good. (*Ibid.,* No. 587.)

The Lord also provides for the mitigation of the sufferings of those who by their own acts have brought punishment upon themselves.

When the wicked are punished, there are always angels present to regulate its degree, and alleviate the pains of the sufferers. (*Ibid.,* No. 967.)

The common idea that punishment in hell is continuous and incessant is a mistaken one; the evil are only punished when they transgress the bounds within which they are restrained for the sake of outward order, and seek to do injury to others.

The wicked run into the punishment of their evil; but only when their evil has reached its height. Every evil has its limit, though it is different in each individual; this limit it is not allowed them to pass; and when a wicked person does pass it, he brings himself into punishment. (*Arcana Cœlestia,* No. 1857.)

By this means the devils in hell are prevented from rushing into greater depths of wickedness;

for the law in the other life is that no one ought to become worse than he had been in the world. (*Ibid.,* No. 6559.)

Both heaven and hell are ruled by the strictest principles of Divine order. The government of heaven is the natural outcome of the spirit of order that reigns within all: in hell there is necessary coercion and restraint, though liberty is granted so far as it is not abused.

Heaven is divided broadly into three divisions, corresponding to the three degrees of the human mind, the celestial, the spiritual, and the natural; and in each of these heavens there is a further classification into societies, according to the specific characteristics of the inhabitants. There is a triple division also in the hells, and a similar subdivision into infernal associations. In the heavenly societies there is subordination of one to another; there are rulers and leaders and teachers: but there is nothing of the love of place and power that marks earthly governments. Greatness in heaven consists in being pre-eminent in use.

So strictly are individuals and societies subordinated to the general welfare, and so harmoniously related, that the whole of heaven, we are told, appears before the Lord as one man. Every angel, and every society, has a function in this body politic corresponding to some particular organ or constituent of the human body. Those in especial intelligence belong to the head, those in whom love is the ruling principle form the heart, the active spirits are the hands, the critical represent the kidneys, and so on with every detail. Even the skin, hair, and nails have their correlatives.

This doctrine of the *Maximus Homo,* or "Grand Man," as Swedenborg terms it, has been ridiculed by some, because it has not been understood. In order that we may comprehend any spiritual truth, we must, says our author, remove from our minds all ideas of space and time. We are not to regard the Grand Man, therefore, as an immense shape, into whose bodily form are packed away myriads of other human beings; but as representing in its totality the perfection of human qualities. As, in this world, no one man can embody all the possibilities of the race, and each has his own place in the general economy; so in the higher stage of existence every individual is complementary to all the rest, and the full MAN is only seen in the great whole. Hell, it may be added, is, in its totality, a hideous and inhuman monster.

Since time and place cannot be predicated of spiritual things, there is no regular procession of hours, days, and years, or bodily progression from place to place, as in this world. There are times and seasons, but they are spiritual, and mark the changes of state with the individual. There is a spiritual sun, as we have said, but this is stationary, appearing always before the faces of the angels at a middle elevation.

Though there is not bodily progression as in this world, angels and spirits are not bound to one locality. Desire brings presence, and when the desire is strong the passage to another's presence is instantaneous. There is no need for laborious trudging through miles of intervening country, nor for vehicular journeys by sea or land.

Life in heaven, as we have seen, is not a monotonous round of religious exercises, but a scene of busy activity. Since useful service is the ground of heavenly happiness, it follows that there must be occupations in heaven. Every faculty of the mind will find employment, and idleness is not permitted even in hell. There those who are unwilling are compelled to labour, and only receive food as they perform some service.

The occupations of the angels differ from earthly employments, inasmuch as spiritual beings have not to labour for "the meat which perisheth," nor for necessary shelter and clothing, these things being provided for them freely, nevertheless, they find abundant means of employment.

> In heaven there are governments, offices, higher and lower courts of justice arts, and handicrafts. (*Conjugial Love,* No. 207.)

Many of the angels are engaged in uses connected with the administration of government, and with worship; for there is the strictest order in heavenly societies. Art, music, and literature, again, afford congenial occupation to many, though their pursuit does not involve the intense labour, and resulting weariness, that often accompany mental efforts on earth.

> Writings in the heavens [we are told] flow naturally from the very thoughts of the angels, and are executed so easily, that it is as if thought put itself forth; nor does the hand pause for the choice of a word, because the words, whether written or spoken, correspond to the ideas of their thought; and all correspondence is natural and spontaneous. (*Heaven and Hell,* No. 262.)

Heavenly architecture surpasses in beauty and dignity the finest efforts of human builders.

> Such is the architecture of heaven that one might say it is very art itself there; nor is this to be wondered at, because that art itself is from heaven. (*Heaven and Hell,* No. 185.)

Heavenly architecture, however, is not the work of the angels themselves, but takes form, like their other surroundings, from their mental states. That there are constructive arts of various kinds, demanding conscious effort, we gather from several statements. In one place we read of a beautiful vase, which some spirits had made in honour of the Lord; in another, of "pieces of embroidery and knitting, the work of their own hands," which some heavenly maidens presented to three novitiate spirits; and of "scribes, who were writing out copies of the writings of the wise ones of the city," which the same spirits inspected, and "wondered to see them so neat and elegant." These spirits also "were taken to see the wonderful works that are done in a spiritual manner by the artificers." (*Conjugial Love,* No. 207.) Science, too, has its place in heaven, and the study of his surroundings affords delight and satisfaction to the angelic mind. Trees, plants, and flowers exist there in abundance and with a variety unknown upon earth. Swedenborg tells of one who had been a botanist who found

173

himself among most beautiful plantations and most delightful flower beds of immense extent.

He strolled through the plain, and not only looked at them [the flowers] one by one, but also gathered them and held them close to his eye. . . . He declared that flowers of plants are to be seen there in vast abundance, such as are never seen in the world, and are scarcely comprehensible here by any effort of imagination; and that each one sparkles with an incomprehensible splendour because they are from the light of heaven. (*Arcana Cœlestia,* No. 4529.)

Education, as will readily be understood, forms an important part of the angels' activities, since all novitiate spirits have to be instructed, and initiated into their new life, especially those who, like the heathen, have lacked the means of true knowledge in this world, as well as all infants and young children.

There are societies whose duties consist in taking care of children; other societies whose duties are to instruct and educate them as they grow up; others which in like manner instruct and educate the young, who are of a good disposition from education in the world, and who thence come into heaven; others which teach the simple good from the Christian world, and lead them in the way to heaven; others which perform the same office for the various Gentile nations; others which defend novitiate spirits, or those who are newly arrived from the world, from the infestations of evil spirits; some, also, are attendant on those who are in the lower earth [the inferior region of the world of spirits]; and some are present with those who are in hell, to restrain them from tormenting each other beyond the prescribed limits: there are also others who attend upon those who are being raised from the dead. (*Heaven and Hell,* No. 391.)

Angels, again, perform important offices as "ministering spirits, sent forth to minister for them who shall be heirs of salvation." (Hebrews i. 14.)

> Angels of every society are sent to men, that they may guard them, and withdraw them from evil affections and consequent evil thoughts, and inspire them with good affections, so far as they are willing to receive them from freedom. (*Heaven and Hell,* No. 391.)

We have many charming descriptions of heavenly education in the writings of Swedenborg. Children, we are informed, are taught by a beautiful and perfect system of object lessons. Everything about them is representative, and they are instructed in the meaning of what they see.

> When they see any objects, it is as if every single thing they see were alive. (*Arcana Cœlestia,* No. 2298.)

> Children are more especially instructed by representatives suited to their character and genius, and it is impossible for any one to conceive or believe how beautiful those representatives are, and at the same time how full of wisdom from what is within. (*Ibid.,* No. 2299.)

Even their games and pleasures are made delightful means of instruction.

> On a time it was given me to see children, with their virgin governesses, in a paradisaical garden . . . and when the children entered . . . the beds of flowers, at the entrance, seemed to express joy by their increasing splendour; hence may appear what is the nature of their delights, and also that they are introduced, by what is thus pleasant and delightful, into the good things of innocence and charity, which are continually insinuated by the Lord into those delights and joys. (*Ibid.,* No. 2296.)

Children of maturer growth are also educated according to their nature and capacity. There are "museums, high-

175

schools, and colleges," also libraries, and "places where they have their literary sports." (*Conjugial Love,* No. 207.)

In the *Spiritual Diary,* Nos. 5660–5667, there is a charming picture of a place of training for maidens.

They are kept together, three, four or five; and each has her own room and therein her own bed; near it there is a tiny little room for their clothes, etc.; and there they store the things they prize, with which they are much delighted. They are always kept at their own work, which is embroidery . . . and the things they make are either for themselves, or to give to others. . . . They receive their garments gratis, not knowing how, which they put on daily, having better ones for festivals. They also have little gardens; and so long as they are maidens, there are only flowers there, and not fruits until they become wives. When they see spots on their garments, it is a sign that they have had evil thoughts, and that they have done something wrong; these spots cannot be washed out; when they have found out what they have thought and done . . . they see their blemishes and their evils, and if they then overcome them, the spots vanish from their garments of themselves. In like manner, when they see any of their garments missing from their little room, they at once know that they have done wrong . . . and if they themselves do not know what it is, a wife comes who tells them. If they see a new garment in their room, they feel an inmost joy, because they know that they have acted well. When they see the flowers becoming dull in their little gardens, or being changed into worse ones, they also take warning; but if they are changed into better and more beautiful ones, they are glad, because it is a sign that they have been thinking well. Silver and gold coins are also given them: these they store carefully, because they are tokens of diligence or of virtue. They have the Written Word and psalmodies and take them with them when they go to listen to the preacher. Also, they read them, and if they do not read, either some garment is taken away, or their little garden vanishes.

It will thus be seen that heaven is by no means a place or condition of languorous ease.

Eternal rest is not idleness; for idleness occasions a languor, listlessness, stupor, and drowsiness of the mind and thence of the whole body; and these things are death and not life, still less eternal life in which the angels of heaven are. (*Conjugial Love,* No. 207.)

A question that severely exercises many minds is that of the relation of the sexes in the other life. It is commonly thought that the spiritual existence will be sexless, because Jesus declared that in heaven there is neither marrying nor giving in marriage, but that all will be "as the angels of God." Swedenborg is able, from actual experience, to inform us that sex is persistent, because in its essence spiritual. There is the male soul and the female soul, and MAN is a conjunction of the two. Hence when married partners are truly united in this world, they will continue the same fellowship in the next; and if married life has not been entered upon here, or an unsuitable connection has been formed, congenial consorts will be found hereafter by all who so desire. With truly united pairs, the death of one does not effect even temporary separation, except as to conscious presence, for

the spirit of the deceased continually dwells together with the spirit of the survivor, and this even to the death of the latter, when they again meet and are reunited, and love each other more tenderly than before. (*Conjugial Love,* No. 321.)

All married partners meet in the other world and dwell

177

together for a time; but if their natures are discordant they ultimately part and know each other no more.

The nature of marriage love is discussed at length in Swedenborg's work entitled *Conjugial Love,* and reasons advanced why it is continued in heaven. We cannot enter into these reasons here, but must reserve the consideration of the subject for a special chapter.

In heaven, it is needless to say, there is no decreptitude. As men and women advance in life there, instead of becoming feeble and incapable, their powers increase and develop.

> Those who are in heaven are continually advancing to the springtime of life, and the more thousands of years they live, the more delightful and happy is the spring to which they attain; and this to eternity, with an increase according to the progressions and degrees of their love, charity, and faith. Women who have died old and worn out with age, and who had lived in faith in the Lord, in charity towards their neighbour, and in happy conjugial love with a husband, after a succession of years come more and more into the flower of youth and early womanhood, and into a beauty which exceeds all the conceptions of beauty which can be formed from that which the eye has seen. . . . In a word, *to grow old in heaven is to grow young. (Heaven and Hell,* No. 414.)

Another point upon which Swedenborg corrects prevailing impressions, is in regard to the nature of angels. It is commonly believed that they are a higher order of beings than men, and that they were created before the human race. Some of them are supposed to have rebelled against the Divine authority and to have been cast out of heaven in consequence. These are what are understood by "the devil and his angels." Such conceptions, Swedenborg tells us, are erroneous:

There is not a single angel in the universal heaven who was originally created such, nor any devil in hell who was created an angel of light and afterwards cast down thither; but all, both in heaven and in hell, are from the human race. (*Ibid.*, No. 311.)

Akin to the interest which is so universal in regard to the possibilities of the future life, though not of so absorbing a nature, is the curiosity to know whether the myriads of worlds that we see around us are inhabited, and what their inhabitants are like. Writers of fiction have speculated as to the character of the denizens of some of our nearest planetary neighbours; but no one except Swedenborg has ventured to make any positive statements on the subject. In a little work, *The Earths in the Universe,* first published in 1758, he describes the inhabitants of some of the principal planets, of the moon, and of some of the more distant stars. Interesting though the book is, the curious reader will probably not get much satisfaction from his descriptions, for he deals more with the spiritual characteristics of the people than with their mundane life. His main object in this work seems to have been to demonstrate that the other heavenly bodies, as well as our earth, exist for the sake of the human race, and that the One Lord reigns supreme in all. His information, he tells us, was gained from spirits who had come from the various earths, through whom, in some cases, he was enabled to learn facts in regard to the actual conditions of life in the worlds themselves.

It is not necessary to deal at length with the contents of this work, but the reader may be interested to learn something of its statements.

We have the fullest information in regard to the inhabitants of Mercury and of Jupiter. The former are said to be characterized by a consuming desire for knowledge, and the spirits from that planet love to wander throughout the next world in search of information. The knowledge which they seek, however, is not of outward things, but of the thoughts and characters of other people, and the essentials of the various matters discussed. When a spirit from another earth addressed some Mercurian spirits in a learned and rhetorical manner

> the only thing they attended to was, whether they heard from him anything which was not known to them before, rejecting thereby such things as obscured the subject, which are chiefly affectations of elegance in expression and in erudition; for these hide things themselves, and in their place substitute expressions, which are the material forms of things. (No. 23.)

Not only are the inhabitants of Mercury greedy for knowledge, but eager to communicate it to others. As, however, they are content to rest in knowledge, and do not regard practical ends, they are lacking in judgment, and are conceited in their supposed wisdom.

The inhabitants of Jupiter are of a much higher order; akin, we are told, to the men of the "golden age" of our own Earth. They are simple in their lives and value practical wisdom rather than human learning.

> Of the sciences, such as exist on our Earth, they know nothing whatever, nor have they any desire to know. (No. 62.)

Whether you are doubtful or not about giving credence to Swedenborg's statements, it must be admitted that his description of the inhabitants of Jupiter presents us with a beautiful ideal of human life. Their earth, he tells us, is densely populated, but as it is extremely fertile, and the people desire no more than suffices for the necessities of existence, there is no scarcity. The duration of life, moreover, is much less than on this Earth, on the average about thirty of our years; the population, therefore, does not increase unduly.

Life on this planet is patriarchal. The people are associated in clans, families, and households, and their habitual intercourse is confined to their own kindred.

> No one ever covets another's goods; nor does it ever enter the mind of any one to desire the possessions of another, much less to obtain them by artifice, and still less to attack and plunder them. (No. 49.)

Their faces, we are told, "are like the faces of the men of our Earth, fair and beautiful; sincerity and modesty shone forth from them." (No. 52.) So expressive are they, that facial movements form the principal means of the communication of thought; verbal speech being only accessory. In this, again, they are like the primitive inhabitants of our Earth, of whom we read:

> In the Most Ancient or primeval times sincerity prevailed, and no one cherished or wished to cherish a thought which he was not willing should shine forth from his face. . . . So long as sincerity and rectitude prevailed among men, such speech continued but as soon as the mind began to think one thing and speak another, which was the case when man began to love himself and not his neighbour, verbal speech began to increase, the face being either inexpressive or deceitful. (No. 54.)

All the inhabitants of Jupiter are not of this exalted character. There are some who are puffed up with insane pride, and who claim Divine honours for themselves: they worship the sun, and wish to be regarded by others as mediatory deities.

The inhabitants of Mars are of even higher character than those of Jupiter, "the best of all the spirits who come from the earths of this solar system" belonging to that planet. In general disposition they seem to be much like the Jovians.

Space will not permit me to enter into particulars regarding the inhabitants of Saturn, Venus, the Moon, and various more distant orbs, of whom Swedenborg speaks. It may be mentioned, however, that he describes the dwellers in the Moon as being dwarfs, but possessing thunderous voices, owing to the fact that they "do not, like the inhabitants of other earths, speak from the lungs, but from the abdomen, and thus from some collection of air therein; the reason of which is, that the Moon is not surrounded with an atmosphere of the same kind as that of other earths." (No. 111.) It is held by most that the Moon cannot be inhabited on account of the peculiar physical conditions which prevail there. Swedenborg says, however, that

it is known to spirits and angels, that there are inhabitants even in the Moon, and likewise in the moons or satellites which are about the earth Jupiter and the earth Saturn. Even those who have not seen spirits who are from them, and spoken with them, entertain no doubt that there are human beings upon them, for they, too, are earths, and where there is an earth, there is man; for man is the end for the sake of which an earth exists, and nothing has been made by the Supreme Creator without an end. (No. 112.)

It must be understood, however, that when Swedenborg describes the appearance and external circumstances of various stellar inhabitants, he does not speak from personal observation, but from information conveyed by spirits from these earths. Some of these descriptions should perhaps be regarded as representative, also. Although Swedenborg tells us that he was permitted to visit other heavenly bodies, it was in spirit and not in the body; the "things heard and seen," then, were heard and seen with his spiritual senses.

CHAPTER XII

MARRIAGE, ON EARTH AND IN HEAVEN

IF THEOLOGY in Swedenborg's day stood in need of revival, morals equally called for reform. We know how loose in his day were the principles of the upper classes, and how gross the lives of the lower: in nothing was the moral deficiency more manifest than in the relations of the sexes. With large numbers in all ranks of life the marriage tie was lightly regarded, and debauchery was open and shameless.

Swedenborg sets forth a most exalted and inspiring view. Instead of marriage being, at best, a happy earthly association, he teaches that, in its perfect realization, it is a spiritual union, not "till death do us part" only, but "eternal in the heavens." Here he at once runs counter to common interpretation of the passage that "in the resurrection they neither marry, nor are given in marriage, but are as the angels of God in heaven" (Matt. xxii. 30.) It is assumed that the latter, if they are not actually sexless, are at least without human passions. Swedenborg not only relates his experience of the fact in the next world, but advances weighty reasons for the nearest and dearest of earthly ties being continued in the higher life. The poets have felt that this must be so, but Swedenborg has demonstrated its truth.

Swedenborg's teachings, if we were to regard them as his own, would seem amazingly bold. Not only does he tell us that the married state is continued in the other life, but he explains that sex is a spiritual as well as a physical distinction, and that marriage love is the sweetest, holiest, and purest of all affections; that, indeed, it sums up all human happiness, as being the fundamental love of all celestial and spiritual loves, and hence of all natural loves. He denies the virtue of celibacy, and declares that "the state of marriage is to be preferred to the state of celibacy." He explains that the term "chaste" cannot be truly applied to anything except a perfect marriage relationship.

The following is a summary of his argument. He observes,

> That there are marriages in the heavens cannot enter into the faith of those who believe that a man after death is a soul or spirit, and who conceive of a soul or spirit as of thin ether or a breath of air: who believe also that a man will not live as a man till after the day of the Last Judgment; and, in general, of those who know nothing about the spiritual world, in which angels and spirits are, consequently, in which the heavens and hells are: and because that world has been heretofore unknown, and it has been altogether unknown that the angels of heaven are men in perfect form, and in like manner the spirits of hell, but in imperfect form, therefore it was impossible for anything to be revealed concerning marriages in that world; for they would have said, "How can a soul be conjoined with a soul, or a breath of air with a breath of air, as one married partner with another on earth?" besides many other things, which, the instant they were said, would take away and dispel all faith concerning marriages in the other world. But now, since many things have been revealed concerning that world, and its quality has also been described in the work *Heaven and Hell,* and also in the *Apocalypse Revealed,* the fact that marriages take place there, can be confirmed, even to the reason. (*Conjugial Love,* No. 27.)

He then proceeds to show that death takes nothing from man except the purely physical "covering," that in fact "a man lives as a man after death," possessed of all his faculties and organs, though these, now, are able to function in the spiritual world. Full capacity and identity being thus maintained, it follows that a man rises into the spiritual world as a man, and a woman as a woman, each with their own contrasting and complementary natures; for sex is not a mere accident or temporary endowment, nor is it a bodily distinction only.

The masculine in the male is masculine in every part of his body, even the smallest part, and also in every idea of his thought, and in every spark of his affection; so, likewise, is the feminine in the female; and since thus the one cannot be changed into the other, it follows, that after death the male is a male, and the female a female. (*Ibid.,* No. 33.)

The most essential part of a person's nature is his ruling love. It is this that shapes the whole character, and constitutes, in fact, the individuality. All else is subsidiary: knowledge in the memory is a store for the use of his love; his deeds are but the outward expression of his heart's affection. The love of a man thus forming his essential nature, it is carried with him into the spiritual world.

Every one has his own love, or a love distinct from the love of another, and every one's own love remains with him after death. (*Ibid.,* Nos. 34, 35.)

The love of the sex, especially, remains; . . . for the male and female man were so created that from two they may become as one human being, or one flesh; and when they become one, then taken together they are a human being in his fulness; but without this conjunction they are two, and each is, as it were, a divided or half human being. Since then this disposition to conjunction is latent, *inmostly, in the least things* of the male, and *in the least things* of the female, and there inheres the capability and desire in their least things for conjunction into one, it follows that the mutual and reciprocal love of the sex remains with human beings after death. (*Conjugial Love,* No. 37.)

The essence and origin of true marriage is the union of love and wisdom, and from this union all created things exist and are sustained. With mankind these elements are unequally distributed, love being predominant in the woman, and wisdom in the man, and it requires that the sexes should be united in order to achieve the full development of human possibilities. Human marriage is thus the union of love and wisdom in a finite degree. This principle must exist not only between the sexes, but in every individual. Indeed, the true spiritual marriage between the sexes cannot be entered into until each of the partners has realized the spiritual union of good and truth individually. The Kingdom of Heaven is compared by our Lord to a wedding, because none can be received into it but those in whom love and faith, or goodness and truth, are united. This is the heavenly marriage in its essence, and it is Divine in origin; for

> from the marriage of Divine Good and Truth, and of Divine Truth and Good in the Lord, comes all conjugial love, and thereby all love celestial and spiritual. (*Arcana Cœlestia,* No. 2618.)
>
> *A Universal Marriage Sphere* proceeds from the Lord, and pervades the universe from its primes to its ultimates, thus from angels even to worms. (*Conjugial Love,* No. 92.)

When we come to recognize that conjugial love in its essence is the union of the good and the true, we are able to understand some other statements of Swedenborg in regard to it. He tells us as we have just read, that conjugial love is the origin of all celestial and spiritual loves, for the union of the good and the true is the essence of all worthy love. Love without wisdom is passion or folly; wisdom without love, cold and forbidding. The spiritual marriage enters into all loves.

186

The chaste love of marriage is the fundamental love of all celestial and divine loves . . . in proportion as man is in the chaste love of marriage, in the same proportion he is in every good love, if not in act, yet in endeavour. (*Apocalypse Explained,* No. 981.)

The love of marriage is a fire enkindled from the love of good and truth, and from the delight of well-doing, thus from love to the Lord and from love towards the neighbour. (*Ibid.,* No. 992.)

No one can be in it unless he is principled in the good of truth, and in the truth of good from the Lord; . . . heavenly blessedness and happiness are in that love, and they who are in it, all come into heaven, or into the heavenly marriage. (*Arcana Cœlestia,* No. 2729.)

Conjugial love, being the central and fundamental love of man's life, is also the source of his fullest joy.

All delights whatsoever that are felt by man are of his love. . . . Now, since conjugial love is the fundamental love of all good loves, and since it is inscribed on the very least things of man, it follows that the delights of that love exceed the delights of all other loves; . . . for it expands the innermost parts of the mind, and at the same time the innermost parts of the body, as the delicious current of its fountain flows through and opens them. The reason why all delights from primes to ultimates are collected into this love, is on account of the surpassing excellence of its use: its use is the propagation of the human race, and hence of the angelic heaven; and as this use was the end of ends of creation, it follows that all the blessednesses, blissfulnesses, delights, joys, and pleasures, which could possibly be conferred upon man by the Lord the Creator, are collected into this his love. (*Conjugial Love,* No. 68.)

The states of this love are innocence, peace, tranquility, inmost friendship, full confidence, and a desire of the disposition and of the heart to make all good mutual to each other; and the states arising from all these are blessedness, blissfulness, delight, and pleasure; and from the eternal enjoyment of these is heavenly felicity. (*Ibid.*, No. 180.)

All these various delights proceed, and flow in, solely from His [the Lord's] Divine love through His Divine wisdom, together with life; consequently, into those who are in truly conjugial love, for these alone are recipients. (*Ibid.*, No. 180.)

We need not question the eternity of a love like this, for it is endued with essential life, and will ever grow in perfection and power.

Love truly conjugial conjoins two more and more into one man . . .; and as truly conjugial love lasts to eternity, it follows that the wife becomes more and more a wife, and the husband more and more a husband. The true reason of this is, that in a marriage of truly conjugial love, each married partner becomes continually a more interior man. For that love opens the interiors of their minds; and in the proportion in which these are opened the man becomes more and more a man. (*Ibid.*, No. 200.)

Not only is marriage love the source of the very highest of human delights, it is

holy, pure, and clean, above every other love which is from the Lord with the angels of heaven and with the men of the church. . . . If there be in the man's will a desire and effort towards it, that love becomes perpetually cleaner and purer from day to day; (*Ibid.*, No. 64.)

for

love truly conjugial is chastity itself. (*Ibid.*, No. 143.)

188

and

innocence itself. (*Arcana Cœlestia,* No. 3081.)

The chastity of marriage also makes one with religion. (*Apocalypse Explained,* No. 981.)

It should, however, be known, that altogether chaste and pure conjugial love does not exist either with men or with angels: there is still something not chaste and not pure which adjoins or subjoins itself to it; but this is of a different nature from that which gives rise to what is unchaste. . . . No love with either men or angels is altogether pure, or can become so; but the end, purpose, or intention of the will is primarily regarded by the Lord, and therefore so far as a man is in the end, purpose, or intention, and perseveres therein, so far he is initiated into purity, and so far he progressively approaches towards purity. (*Conjugial Love,* No. 146.)

With married partners whose relations are truly conjugial in character, the union is necessarily continued in the future life; for

with those who are in truly conjugial love, conjunction is effected more and more thoroughly to eternity. (*Ibid.,* No. 162.)

But the number of such is at present comparatively small. There are many happy marriages in this world, based upon pleasant external relations; but unless these outward amenities are accompanied by a similar love of goodness on both sides, they will not persist beyond the present stage of existence.

Two married partners most generally meet after death, recognize each other, consociate, and for a time live together: this takes place in the first state, thus while they are in externals as in the world. (*Ibid.,* No. 47 (*b*).)

189

When, however, they enter into their second state, in which the true inward nature is made known, they only continue together if there has been a true spiritual union. If their feeling towards one another is

concordant and sympathetic, they continue their conjugial life; but if it is discordant and antipathetic, they dissolve it. (*Conjugial Love,* No. 47 (*b*).)

The separation by death of two truly united married partners is more apparent than real.

Two such married partners are nevertheless not separated by the death of one of them, since the spirit of the deceased continually dwells together with the spirit of the survivor, and this even to the death of the latter, when they again meet and are reunited, and love each other more tenderly than before. (*Ibid.,* No. 321.)

We are told that

truly conjugial love at the present day is so rare that it is not known what its quality is, and scarcely that it exists; (*Ibid.,* No. 58.)

It follows therefore that comparatively few of the marriages which are made in this world prove to be permanent unions, and that some reassortment must take place in the other life. Swedenborg goes so far as to say that marriages interiorly conjunctive

can scarcely be entered into on earth, because the choice of internal likenesses cannot be provided by the Lord there as in the heavens; for the choice is limited in many ways, as to equals in state and condition, within the country, city, and village where they live; and there, again, the future consorts are bound together for the most part by externals, and thus not by internals; which internals do not come forth till some time after marriage, and are only known when they put themselves forth in the externals. (*Ibid.*, No. 320.)

When marriages are unhappy, or sympathy is imperfect, it does not necessarily follow that either of the partners is to blame: nor are we to think that such marriages are without benefit to the individuals concerned. It may be that the trials incident to an ill-assorted marriage are sometimes an important means of strengthening and refining the character; but, all the same, such associations cannot be permanent, and the mis-mated pair will find other partners, in the spiritual world, if they are desirous, and capable, of entering into the joys of the heavenly marriage. With the evil there is no such desire, or capacity; therefore conjugial love has no place in hell.

The Divine providence of the Lord is most particular and most universal in relation to marriages and in marriages, because all the delights of heaven flow from the delights of conjugial love, as sweet waters from the fountain head; and on this account it is provided that conjugial pairs be born; and that they be continually educated for their marriages under the Lord's auspices, neither the boy nor the girl knowing anything of the matter; and after a stated time when she has become a marriageable maiden, and he a young man fitted for marriage, they meet somewhere as by fate, and see each other, and they instantly know, as by a kind of instinct, that they are consorts, and by a kind of dictate they think inwardly in themselves, the young man that she is his, and the maiden that he is hers; and when this thought has been seated some time in the minds of both, they deliberately accost each other, and betroth themselves. It is said, as by fate, by instinct, and by dictate; though the meaning is, by Divine providence, because, while the Divine providence is unknown, it has such an appearance; for the Lord opens internal likenesses, so that they may see themselves. (*Conjugial Love,* No. 229.)

If there were no marriage in heaven, all those who have died in infancy or childhood, and all, a vast number, who have lived unmated on earth, would be doomed to forego the highest form of human happiness, and pass their eternal lives in lonely imperfection. But this is not so. Swedenborg tells us that infants do not remain infants in the other life, but are carefully nurtured and tended till grown to man's estate, when they enter into marriage relationship with some kindred soul, with whom they become spiritually one. The same happens with those who have not entered the marriage state on earth; in due time they meet with suitable partners and become united to them.

Marriage love, being the highest of all loves, and the source of the greatest bliss, is also the cause of the perfection of beauty in the female angels and of manly grace in the males. In a "Memorable Relation," Swedenborg describes the beauty of a married pair from the highest heaven.

> The husband appeared of age intermediate between youth and young manhood: from his eyes darted forth sparkling light by reason of the wisdom of love, from which light his face was as it were inmostly radiant; and in consequence of the radiance the surface of his skin as it were shone: hence his whole face was one resplendent beauty. (*Conjugial Love,* No. 42.)

Of the wife, we are told:

> Her face was seen by me, and it was not seen; it was seen as beauty itself, and it was not seen because this beauty was inexpressible, for in her face there was a splendour of flaming light, such as the angels in the third heaven have, and this light dimmed my sight; wherefore

I was simply lost in astonishment. (*Conjugial Love,* No. 42.)

The ancients believed in a fountain of perpetual youth. In heaven this dream is realized, for those who leave this world old, decrepit, diseased in body, or deformed, renew their youth, and maintain their lives in the full vigour of early manhood or womanhood.

All who come into heaven, return into their vernal youth, and into the powers of that age, and remain so to eternity. (*Conjugial Love,* No. 44.)

Conjugial love, as "the fundamental love of all loves," is the true fountain of perpetual youth.

They who . . . have lived in the chaste love of marriage, are above all others in the order and form of heaven, and hence in all beauty, and in the flower of their youth for ever. (*Heaven and Hell,* No. 489.)

CHAPTER XIII

SIGNS OF SEERSHIP

HAD Swedenborg possessed the nature of a charlatan, he might have made both wealth and fame by the exhibition of his extraordinary powers; but far from making a public show of these, he seldom referred to them unless occasion called for it, and refused to confirm his mission by such means. Prelate Œtinger wrote: "That Swedenborg has knowledge of hidden occurrences has been proved by a few well-attested instances, but he is indisposed to avail himself of them to procure assent and credibility to his writings." Even when appealed to by anxious persons for information about their deceased friends,—though the persons concerned might be members of Royal houses,—he kindly but firmly declined to satisfy them, unless there was some special reason for his doing so. The Rev. Nicholas Collin begged him, as a great favour, to procure him an interview with his brother, who had died a few months before; "he answered," Collin tells us, "that God having for wise and good purposes separated the world of spirits from ours, a communication is never granted without cogent reasons; and asked what my motives were. I confessed that I had none besides gratifying brotherly affection, and an ardent wish to explore scenes so sublime and interesting to a serious mind. He replied, that my motives were good, but not sufficient; that if any important spiritual or temporal concern of mine had been the case, he would then have solicited permission from those angels who regulate such matters." With reference to the last sentence, Mr. Collin must have misunderstood Swedenborg, as the latter teaches that such matters are under the control of the Lord alone, and not of any angel or spirit.

Notwithstanding this reticence on his part, there are many well-authenticated records of remarkable revelations made to different persons in the course of his life. Marvellous as they appear, he did not regard them as in any way miraculous, but simply as proofs of the reality of his intercourse with the spiritual world. "These must by no means," he wrote to Venator, "be regarded as miracles; for they are simply testimonies that I have been introduced by the Lord into the spiritual world, and have intercourse and converse there with angels and spirits; in order that the church, which has hitherto remained in ignorance concerning that world, may know that heaven and hell really exist, and that man lives after death a man, as before; and that thus no more doubts may flow into his mind in respect to his immortality." In affirming the truth of two of these occurrences to Cuno, "he did not dwell long upon them, observing that there were hundreds of similar stories; but he did not think it worth while to waste many words upon them; saying that all these things were trifles placing in the shade the great object of his mission."

For us to dwell unduly upon these extraordinary occurrences would be to show small respect to our author's own wishes; nevertheless, as genuine testimonies to his seership, we must allow the following due weight.

Jung-Stilling asserts that "three proofs that he had actual intercourse with spirits are generally known concerning him." These are the stories of his disclosing to the Queen of Sweden the nature of a secret that had existed between her deceased brother, the Crown Prince Augustus William of Prussia, and herself; his description of a destructive fire in Stockholm, while he himself was at Gothenburg; and his revealing to the widow of M. de Marteville, formerly Dutch Ambassador at Stockholm, the hiding-place of a missing receipt for money paid by her late husband. The stories have been related by different witnesses, with some variations, as was to be expected, but of their substantial accuracy there can be no question. The story of Queen Louisa Ulrica naturally excited most notice, and for that reason, perhaps, presents most variants. We are told that it "was much talked of in Stockholm and abroad, and every man dressed it up to suit himself." This is Count Höpken's account:

"Swedenborg was one day at a court reception. Her Majesty asked him about different things in the other life, and lastly whether he had seen, or had talked with, her brother, the Prince Royal of Prussia. He answered, No. Her Majesty then requested him to ask after him, and to give him her greeting, which Swedenborg promised to do. I doubt whether the Queen meant anything serious by it. At the next reception Swedenborg again appeared at court; and while the Queen was in the so-called white room, surrounded by her ladies of honour, he came boldly in, and approached Her Majesty, who no longer remembered the commission she had given him a week before. Swedenborg not only greeted her from her brother, but also gave her his [her brother's] apologies for not having answered her last letter; he also wished to do so now through Swedenborg; which he accordingly did. The Queen was greatly overcome, and said, 'No one, except God, knows this secret.'

"The reason why she never adverted to this before was that she did not wish any one in Sweden to believe that during a war with Prussia she had carried on a correspondence in the enemy's country."

Another account says that the Queen nearly fainted, and that Count von Schwerin, seeing her distress, bitterly reproached Swedenborg for his conduct, at the same time endeavouring to elicit from him the nature of his secret. The incident soon became known, and many were anxious to know the truth of the matter. "The wife of Swedenborg's gardener," says C. F. Nordensköld, "related to us that for days following the occurrence carriages stopped

before the door of her master, from which the first gentlemen of the kingdom alighted, who desired to know the
secret of which the Queen was so much frightened, but
her master, faithful to his promise, refused to tell it."
Jung-Stilling writes: "This occurrence has been questioned
in the public papers, but a distinguished Swede, who was
by no means an admirer of Swedenborg, has assured me
that it is the pure truth, and cannot be called in question.
He furnished me with some additional proofs, but which
I hesitate to make known, because, as is usually the case
with stories that deal with the realms of spirits, some are
thereby compromised who ought to be spared." In Stockholm, we are told the story was "universally believed."

The most particular account of the Stockholm fire is
contained in a letter of Immanuel Kant's to Charlotte von
Knobloch, dated Königsberg, August 10, 1758.* He
writes:

"The following occurrence appears to me to have the
greatest weight of proof, and to place the assertion respecting Swedenborg's extraordinary gift beyond all possibility
of doubt. In the year 1759, towards the end of September,† on Saturday, at four o'clock P.M., Swedenborg arrived
at Gothenburg from England, when Mr. William Castel
invited him to his house, together with a party of fifteen
persons. About six o'clock, Swedenborg went out, and
returned to the company quite pale and alarmed. He said
that a dangerous fire had just broken out in Stockholm, at
the Södermalm [Gothenburg is about 50 German miles—
about 300 English—from Stockholm], and that it was
spreading very fast. He was restless and went out often.
He said that the house of one of his friends, whom he
named, was already in ashes, and that his own was in dan-

---

* Dr. Tafel has shown conclusively that the date of this letter is incorrect. It could not possibly have been written in 1758 (see *Documents*,
vol. II, p. 616 *et seq.*). The correct date of the conflagration is July 19,
1759. See also Kant's other letter, p. 231.

† This date must also be incorrect.

ger. At eight o'clock, after he had been out again, he joyfully exclaimed, 'Thank God! the fire is extinguished, the third door from my house.' The news occasioned great commotion throughout the whole city, but particularly amongst the company in which he was. It was announced to the governor the same evening. On Sunday morning, Swedenborg was summoned to the governor, who questioned him concerning the disaster. Swedenborg described the fire precisely, how it had begun, and in what manner it had ceased, and how long it had continued. On the same day the news spread through the city, and as the governor had thought it worthy of attention, the consternation was considerably increased; because many were in trouble on account of their friends and property, which might have been involved in the disaster. On Monday evening a messenger arrived at Gothenburg, who was despatched by the Board of Trade during the time of the fire. In the letters brought by him, the fire was described precisely in the manner stated by Swedenborg. On Tuesday morning the royal courier arrived at the governor's with the melancholy intelligence of the fire, of the loss which it had occasioned, and of the houses it had damaged and ruined, not in the least differing from that which Swedenborg had given at the very time when it happened; for the fire was extinguished at eight o'clock."

Of the many versions of the Marteville incident given by Dr. R. L. Tafel in the *Documents,* I select again Kant's account as narrated by him to Charlotte von Knobloch, from information received from a friend whom, as we shall see presently, he commissioned to investigate the matter on the spot.

"Madame Harteville [Marteville], the widow of the Dutch ambassador in Stockholm, some time after the death of her husband, was called upon by Croon, a goldsmith, to pay for a silver service which her husband had purchased from him. The widow was convinced that her late husband had been much too precise and orderly not to have paid this debt, yet she was unable to find the receipt. In her sorrow, and because the amount was considerable, she requested Mr. Swedenborg to call at her house. After apologizing to him for troubling him, she said that if, as all people say, he possessed the extraordinary gift of conversing with the souls of the departed, he would perhaps have the kindness to ask her husband how it was about the silver service. Swedenborg did not at all object to comply with her request. Three days afterwards the said lady had company at her house for coffee. Swedenborg called, and in his cool way informed her that he had conversed with her husband. The debt had been paid seven months before his decease, and the receipt was in a bureau in the room upstairs. The lady replied that the bureau had been quite cleared out, and that the receipt was not found among all the papers. Swedenborg said that her husband had described to him, how after pulling out the left-hand drawer a board would appear, which required to be drawn out, when a secret compartment would be disclosed, containing his private Dutch correspondence, as well as the receipt. Upon hearing this description the whole company rose and accompanied the lady into the room upstairs. The bureau was opened; they did as they were directed; the compartment was found, of which no one had ever known before; and, to the great astonishment of all, the papers were discovered there, in accordance with his description."

Kant's interest in these stories arose through his friendship with Frau von Knobloch, who appealed to his judgment in the matter of Swedenborg's seership. To oblige his friend, he instituted searching inquiries into the alleged occurrences, the result of which he communicated in the letter referred to above. This letter appears in the original in Borowsky's *Life of Kant,* published at Königsberg in 1804; and an English translation is embodied in Dr. R. L. Tafel's *Documents,* vol. ii, pp. 625–636.

In fully confirming the truth of these stories, Kant is careful to guard himself against the charge of credulity. "I am not aware," he says, "that anybody has ever perceived in me an inclination to the marvellous, or a weakness tending to credulity. So much is certain, notwithstanding all the narrations of apparitions and visions concerning the spiritual world, of which a great number of the most probable are known to me, I have always considered it to be most in agreement with the rule of sound reason to incline to the negative side. . . . This is the position in which my mind stood for a long time, until the report concerning Swedenborg came to my notice.

"This account I received from a Danish officer, who was formerly my friend, and attended my lectures; and who, at the table of the Austrian ambassador, Dietrichstein, at Copenhagen, together with several other guests, read a letter which the ambassador about that time had received from Baron de Lutzow, the Mecklenburg ambassador in Stockholm; in which he says that he, in company with the Dutch ambassador, was present, at the Queen of Sweden's residence, at the extraordinary transaction respecting Swedenborg, of which your ladyship will undoubtedly have heard. The authenticity thus given to the account surprised me. For it can scarcely be believed that one ambassador should communicate to another for public use a piece of information, which related to the Queen at the Court where he resided, and which he himself, together with a distinguished company, had the opportunity of witnessing, if it were not true. Now in order not to reject blindfold the prejudice against apparitions and visions by a new prejudice, I found it desirable to inform myself as to the particulars of this surprising transaction. I accordingly wrote to the officer I have mentioned, at Copenhagen, and made various inquiries respecting it. He answered that he had again had an interview concerning it with Count Dietrichstein; that the affair had really taken place in the manner described; and that Professor Schlegel, also, had declared to him that it could by no means be doubted."

Not satisfied with this, Kant wrote to Swedenborg himself, and, failing to receive an answer, commissioned an English friend, who was going to Stockholm, to make full inquiries. This friend did not succeed in seeing Swedenborg for some time, but he wrote: "The most respectable people in Stockholm declare that the singular transaction alluded to [the message to the Queen] happened in the manner you have heard described by me." When, at length, he had made the acquaintance of Swedenborg, "his succeeding letters were quite of a different purport. [He had previously expressed his own incredulity in regard to the alleged facts.] He had not only spoken with Swedenborg himself, but had also visited him at his house; and he is now in the greatest astonishment respecting such a remarkable case. Swedenborg is a reasonable, polite, and openhearted man: he also is a man of learning. . . . He told this gentleman, without reserve, that God had accorded to him the remarkable gift of communicating with departed souls at his pleasure. In proof of this, he appealed to certain well-known facts."

After some further observations, Kant narrates the stories of the fire and the lost receipt, as given above, and concludes: "What can be brought forward against the authenticity of this occurrence [the conflagration in Stockholm]? My friend who wrote this to me has examined all, not only in Stockholm, but also, about two months ago, in Gothenburg, where he is well acquainted with the most respectable houses, and where he could obtain the most authentic and complete information; for, as only a very short time has elapsed since 1759, most of the inhabitants are still alive who were eye-witnesses of this occurrence."

We may take it that the authenticity of these three stories is established beyond the possibility of doubt. There are numerous similar ones, not so widely known and testified to, some of which, however, are of sufficient interest to be quoted here. One of the most remarkable relates to John Wesley, and is given in most detail in a letter from Mr. John Isaac Hawkins, a well-known engineer and inventor, to the Rev. Samuel Noble. An extract from this letter, which is dated February 6, 1826, is given below.

"In answer to your inquiries, I am able to state that I have a clear recollection of having repeatedly heard the Rev. Samuel Smith [one of Wesley's preachers] say, about the year 1787 or 1788, that in the latter end of February, 1772, he, with some other preachers, was in attendance upon the Rev. John Wesley, taking instructions and assisting him in the preparations for his great circuit, which Mr. Wesley was about to commence; that while thus in attendance, a letter came to Mr. Wesley, which he perused with evident astonishment; that, after a pause, he read the letter to the company; and that it was couched in nearly the following words:

" 'Great Bath Street,
Coldbath Fields,
Feb. —, 1772.

" 'Sir,—I have been informed in the world of spirits that you have a strong desire to converse with me; I shall be happy to see you if you will favour me with a visit.

" 'I am, sir, your humble servant,

" 'Eman. Swedenborg.'

"Mr. Wesley frankly acknowledged to the company that he had been very strongly impressed with a desire to see and converse with Swedenborg, and that he had never mentioned that desire to any one.

"Mr. Wesley wrote for answer that he was then closely occupied in preparing for a six months' journey, but would do himself the pleasure of waiting upon Mr. Swedenborg soon after his return to London.

"Mr. Smith further informed me that he afterwards learned that Swedenborg wrote in reply that the visit proposed by Mr. Wesley would be too late, as he, Swedenborg, should enter the world of spirits on the 29th day of the next month, never more to return."

Dr. Tafel, in his *Documents Concerning Swedenborg,* adduces confirmatory evidence of the truth of this story from several other witnesses.

Wesley was not the only person to whom Swedenborg announced the date of his death. The people with whom he lived, Mr. and Mrs. Shearsmith, both testified that he foretold the day he would leave this world some time before the end came. He also predicted the deaths of others, if we accept some of the stories that have come down to us. Here is one which is attributed to Dr. Scherer, professor of French and English at Tübingen in the early part of last century.

"Swedenborg was one morning in company in Stockholm, when, after his information about the world of spirits had been heard with the greatest attention, they put him to the proof as to the credibility of his extraordinary spiritual communications. The test was this: 'He should state which of the company would die first.' Swedenborg did not refuse to answer this question, but after some time, in which he appeared to be in profound and silent meditation, he quite openly replied,—'Olof Olofsohn will die to-morrow morning at forty-five minutes past four o'clock.' By this predictive declaration, which was pronounced by Swedenborg with all confidence, the company were placed in anxious expectation, and a gentleman who was a friend of Olof Olofsohn, resolved to go on the following morning, at the time mentioned by Swedenborg, to the house of Olofsohn, to see whether Swedenborg's prediction was fulfilled. On the way thither he met the well-known servant of Olofsohn, who told him that his master had just died; a fit of apoplexy had seized him, and had suddenly put an end to his life.

203

Upon which the gentleman through the evidence of the death which really occurred [according to the prediction] was convinced. At the same time this particular circumstance also attracted attention;—the clock in Olofsohn's dwelling apartment stopped at the very minute in which he had expired, and the hand pointed to the time."

In his memorandum-book for 1809 Jung-Stilling records the following story, on the testimony of a "certain beloved friend."

"In the year 1762, on the very day when the Emperor Peter III of Russia died, Swedenborg was present with me at a party in Amsterdam. In the middle of the conversation, his physiognomy became changed, and it was evident that his soul was no longer present in him, and that something was taking place with him. As soon as he recovered, he was asked what had happened? At first he would not speak out, but after being repeatedly urged, he said, 'Now, at this very hour the Emperor Peter III has died in prison,' explaining the nature of his death. 'Gentlemen, will you please to make note of this day, in order that you may compare it with the announcement of his death, which will appear in the newspapers?' The papers soon after announced the death of the Emperor, which had taken place on the very same day.

"Such is the account of my friend. If any one doubts this statement, it is a proof that he has no sense of what is called historical faith and its grounds; and that he believes only what he himself sees and hears."

The same witness relates another anecdote, "for the truth of which," he says, "I can vouch with the greatest certainty."

"About the year 1770, there was a merchant in Elberfeld, with whom, during seven years of my residence there, I lived in close intimacy. . . . He would not have dared, for all the world, knowingly to have told a falsehood. This friend of mine, who has long ago left this world for a better, related to me the following anecdote:

"His business required him to take a journey to Amsterdam, where Swedenborg at that time resided; and having heard and read much of this singular man, he formed the intention of visiting him, and becoming better acquainted with him. He therefore called upon him, and found a very venerable-looking friendly old man, who received him politely, and requested him to be seated; on which the following conversation began:

"*Merchant*. 'Having been called hither by business, I could not deny myself the honour, sir, of paying my respects to you: your writings have caused me to regard you as a very remarkable man.'

"*Swedenborg*. 'May I ask where you are from?'

"*M*. 'I am from Elberfeld, in the duchy of Berg. Your writings contain so much that is beautiful and edifying, that they have made a deep impression upon me; but the source from whence you derive them is so extraordinary, so strange and uncommon, that you will perhaps not take it amiss of a sincere friend of truth, if he desire incontestable proofs that you really have intercourse with the spiritual world.'

"*S*. 'It would be very unreasonable if I took it amiss; but I think I have given sufficient proofs, which cannot be contradicted.'

"*M*. 'Are these the well-known ones, respecting the Queen, the fire in Stockholm, and the receipt?'

"*S*. 'Yes, those are they, and they are true.'

"*M*. 'And yet many objections are brought against them. Might I venture to propose that you give me a similar proof?'

"*S*. 'Why not? Most willingly!'

"*M*. 'I formerly had a friend, who studied divinity at Duisberg, where he fell into consumption, of which he died. I visited this friend a short time before his decease; we

205

conversed together on an important topic; could you learn from him what was the subject of our discourse?'

"*S*. 'We will see. What was the name of your friend?'

"The merchant told him his name.

"*S*. 'How long do you remain here?'

"*M*. 'About eight or ten days.'

"*S*. 'Call upon me again in a few days. I will see if I can find your friend.'

"The merchant took his leave and despatched his business. Some days afterwards, he went again to Swedenborg full of expectation. The old gentleman met him with a smile, and said, 'I have spoken with your friend; the subject of your discourse was the *restitution of all things*.' He then related to the merchant, with the greatest precision, what he, and what his deceased friend had maintained. My friend turned pale; for the proof was powerful and invincible. He inquired further, 'How fares it with my friend? Is he in a state of blessedness?' Swedenborg answered, 'No, he is not yet in heaven; he is still in Hades, and torments himself continually with the idea of the restitution of all things.' This answer caused my friend the greatest astonishment. He exclaimed, 'My God! what, in the other world?' Swedenborg replied, 'Certainly; a man takes with him his favourite inclinations and opinions; and it is very difficult to be divested of them. We ought, therefore, to lay them aside here.' My friend took his leave of this remarkable man, perfectly convinced, and returned back to Elberfeld.

"What says highly enlightened infidelity to this? It says 'Swedenborg was cunning and employed a secret spy to get the matter out of my friend.' To this I reply in kindness, that Swedenborg was of too noble a mind, and had too much of the fear of God; and my friend was too discreet [for the matter to admit of such an explanation]. Such-like evasions may be classed in the same category as the 'transfiguration of the Redeemer by means of moonshine!'

"That Swedenborg for many years had frequent intercourse with the inhabitants of the spiritual world, is not subject to any doubt, but is a settled fact."

Many others have testified to the truth of the messages Swedenborg brought from their deceased friends. An important witness of this class is Christopher Springer, a man of much political influence in his time. He wrote to the Abbé Pernety in 1782, ten years after Swedenborg's decease: "All that he had told me of my deceased friends and enemies, and of the secrets I had with them, is almost past belief. He even explained to me in what manner peace was concluded between Sweden and the King of Prussia; and he praised my conduct on that occasion. He even specified the three high personages whose services I made use of at that time [Springer was employed by the English Government to arrange the peace]; which was, nevertheless, a profound secret between us."

The story of the Stockholm fire is paralleled by a somewhat similar one related by Dr. R. L. Tafel in the *Documents* (vol. ii., p. 724). He writes:

"Madame A. A. De Frese, wife of the late Captain Carl Georg De Frese, and granddaughter of the manufacturer Bolander of Gothenburg, mentioned in the following account, told the editor of these documents during his stay in Stockholm in 1869, the following anecdote:

"In a large company assembled in Gothenburg about 1770 in honour of Swedenborg, there was present the manufacturer Bolander, who was the owner of very extensive cloth mills. During dinner Swedenborg suddenly turned to Mr. Bolander, and said to him sharply: 'Sir, you had better go to your mills!' Mr. Bolander was very much surprised at the tone of voice in which Swedenborg spoke to him, and thought it anything but polite; but he rose nevertheless from the table, and went to his mills. On arriving there he found that a large piece of cloth had fallen down near the furnace, and had commenced burning. If he had delayed but a little longer, he would have found his property in ashes. After removing the danger, Mr. Bolander returned to the company and expressed his thanks to Swedenborg, telling him what had happened. Swedenborg smiled, and said that he had seen the danger, and also that there was no time to be lost, wherefore he had addressed him thus abruptly."

We have already remarked upon the good fortune, as regards weather, which Swedenborg enjoyed in his many voyages, and the almost superstitious delight with which the masters of the vessels he sailed in received him as a passenger. When he returned to Stockholm from England in September, 1766, he sailed with a Captain Dixon, of which voyage Springer gives this account in a letter to Abbé Pernety:

"When the captain of the vessel called for Swedenborg, I took leave of him, and wished him a happy journey; having then asked the captain if he had a good supply of provisions on board, he answered me that he had as much as would be required. Swedenborg then observed, 'My friend, we have not need of a large quantity; for this day week we shall, by the aid of God, enter into the port of Stockholm, at two o'clock.' On Captain Dixon's return, he related to me that this happened exactly as Swedenborg had foretold."

Of this voyage, Swedenborg wrote to Dr. Beyer, September 25, 1766: "I arrived here in Stockholm as early as September 8. The trip from England was made in eight days; a favourable wind increasing to a perfect storm carried the ship along in this style." The captain himself is said to have remarked that never in all his life had he experienced such a favourable wind as on that occasion, and that it followed him at every turn he made.

Now, what are we to say to these stories? Some may be explained as coincidences; some may have been exaggerated or coloured by their narrators; but they are too numerous and too well attested for all to be explained in this way. Unless all evidence is worthless, they indicate that Swedenborg's condition was distinctly supernormal, and that he was *en rapport* with spiritual beings to an unexampled degree. This, of course, does not prove the truth of his teachings, but it justifies the claim that he made to the possession of means of spiritual knowledge denied to the generality of men. Swedenborg in his last unpublished MS. says:

The manifestation of the Lord, and intromission into the spiritual world surpass all miracles. This has not been granted to any one since the creation as it has been to me. The men of the Golden Age, indeed, conversed with the angels; but it was not granted them to be in any other than natural light; but to me it is granted to be in spiritual and in natural light at the same time. By this means it was granted to me to see the wonderful things of heaven, to be together with the angels like one of them, and at the same time to imbibe truths in light, and thus to perceive and teach them; consequently to be led by the Lord. (*Invitation,* No. 52.)

CHAPTER XIV

RECEPTION OF TEACHINGS

In the *Spiritual Diary*, under date August 27, 1748, that is, before Swedenborg had published any of his theological works, we find an interesting entry, regarding their probable reception.

Evil spirits sometimes infused [the idea into me] that no one would comprehend these things, but that every one would reject them. Now, while in the street and talking with spirits, it was given me to perceive that there are five kinds of reception.

First, there are those who wholly reject; who are in another persuasion, and who are enemies of the faith. These reject; for they cannot receive it, as it cannot penetrate into their minds.

There is a second class who receive these things as matters of knowledge, and are delighted with them as such and as curious things.

There is a third class which receives intellectually, so that they receive with sufficient readiness, but still remain in respect to their life as before.

A fourth class receives persuasively, so that it penetrates to the amendment of their lives; they recur to these (truths) in certain states, and make use of them.

There is a fifth class, who receive with joy and are confirmed in them.

Swedenborg's anticipations were entirely fulfilled. His writings met with an extraordinary variety of reception. Some, like Dean Ekebom, of Gothenburg, condemned them without examination, pronouncing them "corrupting, heretical, injurious, and in the highest degree objectionable." The Bishop of Gothenburg regarded Swedenborg's teachings as tinged with Mohammedanism, and described them as spreading like a cancer. Bishop Filenius speaks of "this abominable infection which is not grounded in sound reason, and still less in God's Holy Word, but consists of untruthful visions and dreams . . . most infamous and untruthful nonsense." Dr. Beyer speaks of the "intense hatred with which even mere vague reports respecting Assessor Swedenborg's doctrinal views are regarded."

The hatred and opposition were chiefly from those who did not trouble themselves to examine his teachings. "Those who were able to read his books," said Carl Robsahm, "judged of him then, as they do now, quite differently from those who are unable to read them; and, what is remarkable, most of those who do read his books become in a greater or less degree his adherents; although . . . and on account of many and perhaps just causes, they do not openly profess their sentiments." "It is singular," wrote the Abbé Pernety, "or at least very remarkable, that almost all those who have read the writings of Swedenborg for the purpose of refuting them, have finished by adopting his views."

To receptive minds Swedenborg's teachings were, as they are now, a source of satisfaction and delight. C. F. Nordensköld, an early Swedish disciple, declared his acquaintance with them to be "the greatest good fortune that had happened to him during his whole life." General Tuxen wrote: "For my part, I thank our Lord, the God of Heaven, that I have been acquainted with this great man and his writings. I esteem this as the greatest blessing I have ever experienced in my life, and I hope I shall profit by them in working out my salvation." The Rev. Thomas Hartley, one of the earliest English disciples and translators of Swedenborg, wrote to him thus: "May I be permitted to tell you from a heart full of gratitude, that

I consider myself thrice blessed that your writings, by the Divine Providence, have fallen into my hands? For from them, as from a living fountain, I have drawn so many things, as well for instruction and edification as for my great delight, and I have been freed by them from so many fears, and from so many errors, doubts, and opinions, which held my mind in perplexity and bondage, that I seem to myself sometimes, as if transferred among the angels."

"It was remarkable," says Robsahm, "that Swedenborg, unlike sectarian persons, never tried to make proselytes, or to force his explanations upon any one"; and the Abbé Pernety testifies to the same effect: "He was not governed by that species of egotism usually noticed in those who start new ideas on matters of doctrine, neither did he desire to make proselytes, nor to communicate his views to any, except such as he considered single-minded, disposed to listen peaceably, capable of understanding him, and lovers of the truth." Robsahm once asked him how his teachings would be received in Christendom, and was answered: "About that I can say nothing; but I suppose that in their proper time they will be received; for otherwise the Lord would not have disclosed what has heretofore lain concealed." He was a great believer in the power of the press, and sent his books forth quietly into the world, hoping that their intrinsic reasonableness would prove convincing. He presented copies to the principal Universities in his own and foreign countries; also to the Bishops of Sweden, England, Holland, and Germany, and to other persons of note. His expectation was that some of the learned would accept his teachings, and then spread them through the world; but this did not happen. Instead of the bishops and clergy being his chief supporters, with a few notable exceptions, they either treated his writings with contempt, or became his persecutors. John Christian Cuno, who knew him well in Amsterdam remarks that "his books have been for years before the public, without a single theologian taking any notice of them."

"I wish very much," he writes in another place, "that upright men, whom God has placed as watchmen upon the walls of Zion, had occupied themselves with this man some time ago. I have read his writings and proved them impartially; but in my opinion dogmas are taught there which deserve to be examined more thoroughly by upright theologians, and there are others which ought to have been refuted at the very beginning." But no! "they are all dumb dogs, they cannot bark." In appealing to Swedenborg to make a more public declaration of his mission, Cuno reminds him that he had "sent copies of his works to all the bishops in England; yet not a single one has made a reply. . . . Your last work," he adds, "you have distributed among the clergy of every denomination in this city [Amsterdam] not only among the Reformed, but also among the Roman Catholics. You have also made it known in other towns, and in the universities of Holland. Almost a whole month has since elapsed, and I do not hear of a single person who is rising up against you." Swedenborg himself confessed that he had sent his works "to all the archbishops, and the chief men of this kingdom [England]; and, nevertheless, not a single voice was heard." He told Christopher Springer, one of the leading Swedish residents in London, and a close personal friend of his, that he had presented them to the bishops of Sweden also, but without result; they had received them with the same indifference as the bishops of England. It was not merely indifference he met with from the Swedish bishops, however; some of them were his active opponents during his life; and, after his death, two, who were his heirs, proposed to throw his manuscripts into the fire.

Swedenborg must have had a strong conviction of the necessity of his labours to the world, to go on writing in the face of such indifference and opposition. That he was disappointed in the way his first works were received, we know from his own confession, but he never allowed his disappointment to lead to discouragement. Only four copies of the first volume of his *Arcana Cœlestia* were sold in two months. In later years, when his name became known as the author of these works, he met with more encouragement, and some of his books had a large sale. In a letter, written from Amsterdam in 1771, to the Landgrave of Hesse-Darmstadt, he states that the *Arcana Cœlestia* "can not longer be obtained either here in Holland, or in England, as all the copies are sold," and offers to try and obtain a copy for him from a friend in Sweden. *Conjugial Love,* which was interdicted in his own country, was "very much in demand in Paris, and in many places in Germany," in 1769; the *Brief Exposition of the Doctrines of the New Church,* we are told, "has been spread throughout the whole of Christendom, Sweden excepted"; the *Intercourse Between the Soul and the Body* "has been very well received abroad in all places, as well as by many intelligent persons in Stockholm"; the librarian of the Royal Library at Stockholm informs us that Swedenborg's works "have been favourably received everywhere"; and the Rev. Thomas Hartley, writing a few years after Swedenborg's death, says: "It is a matter of great satisfaction to find that the small part of his works which has already been translated into English, has met with more success than might be expected in so short a time; and by the accounts received of the favourable reception of them in foreign countries, we have good reason to hope that this highly gifted ministry will in due time more fully appear, as a light shining in a dark world, to check the progress of infidelity, to diffuse the right understanding of the Sacred Scriptures, and to turn many to the knowledge of the Lord."

Though Swedenborg's works were widely circulated, it does not appear that he made many converts during his lifetime. He told General Tuxen that he did not know more than about fifty persons who favoured his doctrine. A small number of these were to be found in his own country, though he tells us "there are few in Sweden who penetrate with their understandings into any matter belonging to theology." The most prominent of his Swedish disciples were Count Anders J. von Höpken, at one time Prime Minister of Sweden, Dr. Gabriel Beyer, Professor of Greek in Gothenburg University, and Dr. John Rosén, Professor of Eloquence and Poetry in the same seat of learning. The two latter were subjected to bitter persecution on account of their acceptance of Swedenborg's doctrines. For almost a year their case was before the Consistory of Gothenburg; and though their enemies did not, as they desired, succeed in getting them deprived of office, or made to recant, the two professors received the royal censure, and were restricted in their duties afterwards. A full history of this heresy hunt will be found in Dr. R. L. Tafel's *Documents,* vol. ii. pp. 282–386.

Beyer's and Rosén's first introduction to Swedenborg and his teaching came about in this way: "In the year 1766, Swedenborg arrived at Gothenburg for the purpose of continuing his journey thence to England. Immediately after his arrival he engaged a berth in a ship, which was to sail for London in a few days. During his stay at Gothenburg, Beyer happened by chance to make his acquaintance, and as he did not know Swedenborg personally, but only by hearsay, and as he shared the prejudices of those times with regard to his religious views, he was very much astonished when he found Swedenborg discoursing in a most sensible manner, and without the least indication of any confusion in his imagination and thoughts, of which he had been suspected. The next day he invited Swedenborg to dine in company with Dr. Rosén. After dinner Beyer expressed a desire to hear in the presence of Rosén a brief statement of Swedenborg's religious system. The latter, therefore, gave him a sketch of his views with the ardour of inspiration and with logical clearness in all his arguments, so that both his hearers were very much astonished." After further study of his works, both became convinced and Beyer especially exerted himself to facilitate their study. Besides several explanatory treatises, he prepared a voluminous index to Swedenborg's works, which was published in Amsterdam in 1779, after its compiler had spent thirteen years in its preparation.

Other Swedes who took a prominent part in the dissemination of Swedenborg's teachings were the brothers Nordensköld, sons of Colonel Nordensköld of Finland; Johan Tybeck, a Lutheran minister, who was prosecuted for heresy and deprived of his ministerial office in his sixty-fifth year, only to make him more vigorous in his advocacy of the new doctrines; Major Gyllenhaal; C. L. Shön-herr, Councillor of Commerce; Christopher Springer, and C. B. Wadström, the two last named residing in London. Arvid Ferelius, pastor of the Swedish Church in London, was also favourable to Swedenborg's teachings, but not openly.

Wadström's name is well known in connection with the anti-slavery movement; he was one of the very first in Europe to attack the iniquities of the traffic. On his return from Africa in 1780, he published his *Observations on the Slave Trade,* which attracted much attention in this country. William Pitt, who was Prime Minister at the time, discussed the subject with him, and invited him to appear before the Privy Council. He (Wadström) co-operated with Wilberforce and others in the anti-slavery agitation, and was a distinguished member of "The African Association." His most important publication was his *Essay on Colonisation,* which appeared in 1794, in two parts, illustrated with plates. I happened upon one of the plates, representing a mutiny on a slave-ship, in the collection of historical pictures in the Liverpool Exhibition of

216

1907. Wadström died in poverty in Paris, on April 5, 1799, having exhausted his resources in his philanthropic labours. A more particular account of him will be found in Dr. R. L. Tafel's *Documents concerning Swedenborg,* vol. i., p. 644.

Outside of Sweden there were many prominent persons who wholly, or in part, accepted Swedenborg's claims. The Danish General Tuxen, already mentioned, was an ardent disciple; F. C. Œtinger, prelate of Murrhard, was the first to translate some of Swedenborg's works into German, and had to endure persecution therefor; the celebrated Lavater has been described as "an apt student of his writings," and several of his letters to Swedenborg attest his interest; Pastor Oberlin is said to have remarked respecting Swedenborg's *Heaven and Hell*: "I know from my own experience that everything in this book is true." The Marquis de Thomé translated some of the works into French, and exerted himself in many ways to promote their circulation; and the Abbé Pernety was also an open advocate of Swedenborg's teachings, but one who allowed his prejudices to influence him to the extent of mistranslating, abridging, and in some cases, falsifying the author's statements.

It was in England, however, that Swedenborg found most acceptance. One of the first to recognize the deep spirituality of Swedenborg's doctrine was the Rev. John Clowes, for sixty-two years Rector of St. John's Church, Manchester, a man of much learning and exemplary life. Thomas de Quincey, in his *Autobiographical Sketches,* described him as "Holiest of men whom it has been my lot to meet! Yes," he says, "I repeat; thirty-five years have passed, and I have yet seen few men approaching to this venerable clergyman in paternal benignity, none certainly in childlike purity, apostolic holiness, or in perfect alienation of heart from the spirit of the fleshly world." He is not forgotten; "his memory is still green in Manchester," remarked Bishop Fraser, and incidentally, a new edition of his Life, by Theodore Compton, was issued in 1898. Clowes translated almost the whole of the theological works into English—a stupendous task,—and openly advocated the views contained in them.

Clowes' introduction to the study of Swedenborg was somewhat remarkable, and apparently accidental. It was in his early life, in 1773, when he was only 30 years old and he had only been Rector of St. John's Church for four years. A friend persuaded him to procure *The True Christian Religion,* then lately published; but he was so little interested that he allowed it to lie for many months on his library table without opening it. One day, however, as he was about to set out upon a visit to a friend in the country, he casually opened the volume, and his eye caught the words *Divinum Humanum,* a phrase of Swedenborg's relating to the fundamental doctrine of all his writing, the "Divine Humanity" of the Lord Jesus Christ. "He merely thought it was an odd sort of phrase —closed the book—and rode off to his friends. He awoke next morning with a most brilliant appearance before his eyes, surpassing the light of the sun; and in the midst of the glory were the words *Divinum Humanum.* He did not then recollect having ever seen those words before: he thought the whole an illusion, rubbed his eyes, got up, and made every effort to get rid of it; but in vain. Wherever he went, or whatever he did, all day, the glorious appearance was still before him; though he spoke of it to no one. He retired to rest at night, and fell asleep. When he awoke the morning following, the words, *Divinum Humanum,* encircled by a blaze of light still more glorious than before, immediately flashed upon his sight. He then recollected that those were the words which he had seen in the book on his table at home. He got up, made an apology to his friend, and took an abrupt leave; and, in his own words, no lover galloped off to see his mistress with half the eagerness that he galloped home to read about *Divinum Humanum*. He speedily perused the whole book; but his feelings and convictions on reading it are best described in his own words. In a paper left behind him he says, 'The delight produced in my mind by the first perusal of the work entitled *Vera Christiana Religio*, no language could fully express. . . . It seemed as if a continual blaze of new and recreating light had been poured forth on my delighted understanding, opening it to the contemplation of the sublimest mysteries of wisdom, in a manner and degree, and with a force of satisfactory evidence, which I had never known before.' "

Clowes found a coadjutor in the work of translation, in fact a predecessor by several years, in the person of the Rev. Thomas Hartley, M.A., Rector of Winwick, Northamptonshire, mentioned above, a learned and saintly man like himself, who had the privilege, enjoyed by few Englishmen, of personal intercourse with Swedenborg.

Another Englishman who knew Swedenborg personally, and fully accepted his teachings, was William Cookworthy, a minister of the Society of Friends, a prominent citizen of Plymouth, and the discoverer of the Cornish china-clay. Several memoirs of him have been published. "On his first opening one of Swedenborg's works," we are told, "the book was soon thrown down in a fit of disgust. From some cause or other, not now remembered, he was induced to make another trial; and from that time forward he became gradually more and more convinced of the soundness of the views which Swedenborg had taken of Scriptural truths. So convinced indeed did he become of the truth and utility of his works, that . . . he, in part, translated from the original Latin, the treatise *Heaven and Hell* and, under the revision of the Rev. T. Hartley, had it printed in 1779, in a quarto volume, by the Friends' bookseller, James Phillips, of George Yard, Lombard Street, London, at his own expense."

Dr. Messiter, a London physician of some eminence, was an intimate friend of Swedenborg's, and was also acquainted with Mr. Hartley. In a letter of the latter's to Swedenborg, he communicates an offer from himself and Dr. Messiter, to provide a home for the aged theologian in England, in case persecution should make it uncomfortable for him to remain in his own country. Swedenborg declined the offer, as he did not share his friends' fear.

Another medical man among the early receivers of Swedenborg's doctrines in England was Dr. William Spence. He assisted in publishing the MS. of *Apocalypsis Explicata* (*Apocalypse Explained*) in Latin, and was one of the small party that first met together, in the year 1783, for the study of the author's writings.

Other early disciples in England were Benedict Chastanier, a French physician, who translated some of the works into French; Henry Peckitt, a retired physician and apothecary, possessed of considerable wealth and wide culture, who, as already stated, bore the whole expense of publishing *Apocalypsis Explicata*; Peter Provo, another medical man, and the translator of several of the smaller works (the doctors at this time seemed to have been especially receptive), Henry Servanté, who edited the first magazine devoted to the advocacy of Swedenborg's teachings; John Augustus Tulk, a man of independent means, which he employed freely in the dissemination of the new doctrines; and last, but not least, Robert Hindmarsh, Printer Extraordinary to the Prince of Wales, who did more than most, by preaching, writing, translating, publishing, and expending his not too abundant worldly wealth, to bring them before the world.

Generally speaking, the early receivers of Swedenborg's teachings found themselves isolated and misunderstood. They naturally, therefore, longed for the sympathy of kindred spirits; and this led to the formation of societies for the study of their revered author and for mutual edification. In Sweden, C. F. Nordensköld founded the "Exegetic-Philanthropic Society" which numbered among its members many well-known persons. After Swedenborg's death, indeed, considerable interest seems to have been taken in his teaching, in his native land. We are told (*Rise and Progress of the New Church in England, America, and other Parts,* by Robert Hindmarsh, (Ed. 1861), pp. 113, 114) that "this Society successively increased, till their number, in 1790, amounted to more than two hundred persons, the greatest part of whom were men holding respectable offices in the State, and of distinguished learning. Many of them were clergymen, not to mention two of the first princes in Europe, who took upon themselves the patronage of the Society. . . . The members assemble generally once a week; and they have opened a correspondence, on an enlarged scale, with other professors of the same doctrines in different parts of the kingdom. In one single bishopric, it is said, no less than forty-six respectable and profoundly learned clergymen have cordially embraced the Writings, and have frequently been exposed to severe persecutions on that account. . . . It appears that, at the colleges for education, no less than a hundred manuscript copies of the doctrinals of the New Church are in circulation among the young students."

This early zeal of Swedenborg's fellow-countrymen does not seem to have been maintained for long. Dissensions arose in the Exegetic-Philanthropic Society, owing to some of the members attempting to introduce mesmerism and other extraneous matters into its proceedings. It was ultimately dissolved, and was succeeded by the "Societas pro Fide et Charitate," which continued in existence until about 1835.

To return to our own country, Robert Hindmarsh's acquaintance with Swedenborg's writings began in 1782. "From that time," he says (*Rise and Progress of the New*

221

Church, p. 11), "I began to search out other readers of the same Writings in London, in order to form a Society for the purpose of spreading the knowledge of the great truths contained in them. I expected at first, that almost every person of sound judgment, or even of common sense, would receive them with the same facility as I did myself, and would rejoice with me, that so great a treasure had at length been found in the Church. But I was mistaken: and such was the prejudice in the minds of men of apparent candour in other respects, that so far from congratulating me, and their own good fortune, on the acquisition of such spiritual information, I was absolutely laughed at, and set down by them as a mere simpleton, an infatuated youth, and little better than a madman, led away by the reveries of an old enthusiast and impostor." "In one whole year after my reception of the Writings, I found only three or four individuals in London, with whom I could maintain a friendly intercourse on the subjects contained in them." (*Ibid.,* p. 14.)

In order to discover what amount of general interest there was in their study, an advertisement was issued inviting all sympathizers to meet at the London Coffee-House, Ludgate Hill, on the evening of December 5, 1783. A drawing of Ludgate Hill, showing the London Coffee-House, can be found in the Print Room of the British Museum. The Coffee-House was a well-known place of entertainment for more than a century, having been first opened in May, 1731. It was a favourite meeting-place of Clubs and Masonic Lodges, and greatly frequented by visitors to the Exeter Hall May meetings. It was closed in 1867. In response to Hindmarsh's invitation five persons presented themselves, whose names may be recorded here, as four, at least, of them took a very active part later on in the translation, publication, and circulation of our author's works. The five persons were, John Augustus Tulk, Peter Provo, William Spence, William Bonington, and

Robert Hindmarsh. After they were assembled, it was found that a private room could not be obtained at the Coffee-House; so the meeting was adjourned to the Queen's Arms Tavern, in St. Paul's Churchyard, "were we had a room to ourselves, and drank tea together." This change of place prevented a sixth person from participating in this first gathering of receivers of the doctrines, as Henry Peckitt arrived at the rendezvous after the adjournment had taken place, and failed to discover the new place of meeting.

The enthusiasm of these early disciples was great. They gave their time, talents, and means ungrudgingly, to the cause they had so much at heart, and did not hesitate to express openly their delight and thankfulness for their privileges.

The outcome of this private gathering was the establishment of a weekly meeting, first held in the Inner Temple, afterwards in New Court, Middle Temple, for the study of Swedenborg's doctrines, which developed in 1784 into "The Theosophical Society, instituted for the purpose of promoting the Heavenly Doctrines of the New Jerusalem, by translating, printing, and publishing the Theological Writings of Emanuel Swedenborg." Hindmarsh gives the names of thirty early members and sympathizers among which are several of note. No less than six are artists, sculptors, or engravers, including John Flaxman, R.A., P. J. Loutherbourg, and William Sharp, the engraver. There was one eminent musician, F. H. Barthelemon; three medical men, Spence, Peckitt, and Chastanier, above mentioned; a Proctor of Doctors' Commons; a barrister; Lieut-General Rainsford, afterwards Governor of Gibraltar, and several other army officers; and various merchants, tradesmen, and others. Several clergymen, also, are said to have attended the meetings.

In Lancashire, great interest was aroused in the study of Swedenborg through the energy of the Rev. John

Clowes, and reading circles were formed in many of the towns and villages, which he visited from time to time. To his labours is due the fact that Lancashire is at the present day the great stronghold of Swedenborg's followers.

It was Clowes who organized the first of the several societies that have undertaken the printing and publishing of Swedenborg's works, but this was of a semi-private character, among his own friends. In 1810 was established the London "Society for Printing and Publishing the Writings of Emanuel Swedenborg," generally known as the "Swedenborg Society." It is a catholic body embracing in its membership many who are not included in the organization of the New Church. One of its most devoted supporters was the late Rev. Augustus Clissold, M.A., who, among other benefactions, presented to the Society the lease of No. 1 Bloomsbury Street, where the Society remained till 1925, when it transferred to the present beautiful premises at No. 20 Hart Street, London, W.C. 1. The Society's publications are issued at nominal prices; many volumes, also, are presented to clergymen and ministers of different denominations, and to public libraries. In this manner, many thousands of volumes have been circulated in recent years. The Society's efforts have been chiefly confined to keeping the theological writings before the public, but attention is also paid to the scientific and philosophical treatises.

Among its recent publications is a Bibliography of the published and unpublished works of Swedenborg,* which will give the reader some idea of the vast extent of his labours, and the activity of the various agencies which have been engaged in translating and publishing his works during the past century and a half. The Bibliography is a bulky volume of some 760 pages, and contains 3,500

*A Bibliography of the Works of Emanuel Swedenborg, original and translated, by the Rev. James Hyde.—Swedenborg Society, London, 1906.

separate entries. Another important work of reference for the student is *The Swedenborg Concordance* (published 1888–1902), the outcome of the amazing industry of the Rev. John Faulkner Potts, B.A., who was engaged for twenty-seven years in its compilation. It contains more than 5,500 pages comprised in six quarto volumes.

Of the organization known as the "New Church," or "New Jerusalem Church," there is no need to say much here. The spread of new doctrines naturally leads to association, and the New Church has thus arisen among those who have discovered in Swedenborg's teachings, a new, constructive system of theology, and whose convictions make it difficult for them to worship in harmony with the members of other communions, whose beliefs they find so insufficient. It is not a sect in the sense of being a division, or offshoot, of some other body; it is a gathering together, from within and without the Churches of men who have found a new faith.

Among the early receivers of Swedenborg's doctrines, there was considerable difference of opinion as to the desirability or otherwise of forming a special organization for ecclesiastical purposes, and, it may be remarked, there are still many non-separatist Swedenborgians. The Rev. John Clowes, who did so much to make Swedenborg's teachings known, was strongly opposed to any secession from the established Church. When he heard that there was a movement on foot in London to establish public worship on New Church lines, he made a special journey to the metropolis in order to remonstrate with the friends there. "He thought it probable, that sooner or later the bishops and other dignitaries of the Church of England would be disposed to revise their Liturgy, and make it conformable to the truths of the new dispensation." (Hindmarsh's *Rise and Progress of the New Church*, p. 54, *et seq.*) Time has shown how unfounded were his anticipations, and has justified the adoption of a special organization for the New

Church. The first regular meeting of the newly constituted body was held on May 7, 1787.

In point of numbers the New Church is still small, counting less than several thousand registered members in the United Kingdom, with a somewhat larger number in the United States, and a small contingent in the principal British colonies and European countries. Many small centres have sprung up throughout the world since the Great War, specially among non-European peoples. But if small in numbers, New Church people are strong in their faith, and have ample evidence that their doctrines have very largely influenced current modes of religious thought. In the disintegration of the old orthodoxy, which has been visibly taking place for many decades, they see the preparation for a wider and fuller reception of the new light.

CHAPTER XV

SWEDENBORG'S SCIENCE

It will be our task in this chapter to examine the evidence as to Swedenborg's right to be regarded as an original discoverer; and we are confident that the result will be to the satisfaction, and possibly the astonishment, of the reader.

That our author anticipated many modern discoveries and theories is a well-established fact as the following testimonies show. Mr. Thomas French, in the University of Cincinnati, U.S.A., says that the following doctrines of modern science are more or less definitely stated in Swedenborg's *Principia,* published in 1734: "The atomic theory; the solar origin of the earth and her sister planets; the undulatory theory of light; the nebular hypothesis [In regard to this, an article by Professor Holden, formerly of the United States Naval Observatory, in *The North American Review,* October, 1880, forcibly testifies to the validity of Swedenborg's claims]; that heat is a mode of motion; that magnetism and electricity are closely connected; that electricity is a form of ethereal motion; and that molecular forces are due to the action of an ethereal medium."

Mr. J. D. Morrell says of Swedenborg's scientific studies: "The results of these studies exist to the present day in the form of volumes and tracts, which travel over almost the whole surface of natural history and science, and in which, it is only just to say, are found, more or less obscurely, many of the germs of recent and brilliant discoveries.*

Professor Anders Retzius, again, in an address deliv-

*An Historical and Critical View of the Speculative Philosophy of Europe in the Nineteenth Century, 2nd Edition, vol. i, p. 315.

ered before the Swedish Royal Academy of Sciences, in the year 1845, said: "Swedenborg had first distinguished himself as a mathematician, physicist, chemist, mineralogist, and geologist. Besides being in possession of an immeasurable learning in all the sciences, he wished to employ this information to seek for knowledge concerning the human soul and still further concerning the highest regions of thought. His *Regnum Animale* has now come forward as a wonder-book. Ideas belonging to the most recent times are found there—a compass, induction, and tendency which can only be compared to that of Aristotle. One may suppose that a decennary or two will still be required for rightly valuing the merits of this work."

Baron Berzelius, in a paper read before the Scandinavian Scientific Association in 1842, says:

"Emanuel Swedenborg, who became famous in many respects, was the first who called attention in a printed work to a rise of the Swedish coast. In 1719 he published a little work entitled: *Respecting the great Depth of Water and the Strong Tides in the Primeval World; Proofs from Sweden.* In a dedication to the Queen, he congratulated her on ruling over a land which is constantly enlarged at the expense of the sea. Among the proofs that a sea in a state of great commotion at one time swept over Sweden, he quotes the ridges of our mountains whose general direction from north to south he had correctly observed; and likewise the fact that all the stones occurring therein are rolled, worn off, and rounded, even those which weigh from five to ten *skeppund*. He was acquainted with Snäcklagren on the Kappelback, near Uddevalla, and several other places of a similar kind on the western coast of Sweden. He makes a report of the skeleton of a whale which during his stay at Upsala was discovered in West Gothland, ten Swedish miles inland, and which was left in the care of Professor Roberg, that it might be deposited by him in the anatomical museum of the University. He describes also the remnants of a wrecked ship which were excavated far up on the land, as well as some gigantic pots which he examined and found to have been hollowed out by other loose stones which were agitated to and fro by water in a state of great commotion." After mentioning some other writers on the same subject, Berzelius declares that "none of these writers, with the exception of Swedenborg, had made genuine geological examinations, and they all treated their subjects from a historico-geographical point of view."*

Part I of Swedenborg's *Miscellaneous Observations,* it may be mentioned, is almost entirely devoted to geological questions: the third volume of the *Opera Philosophica et Mineralia* also has several plates of fossils, etc.

A recent popular scientific writer, the Rev. H. N. Hutchinson, B.A., F.G.S., remarks: "Emanuel Swedenborg, who in his earlier days was Assessor in the School of Mines in Sweden, was probably the first to describe the erratics so conspicuous in that country, and to endeavour to explain them. He put forward the theory that they had been deposited there by a great marine deluge; and thus he also accounts for some of the other phenomena, such as the peculiar ridges of sand and gravel known as Äsar (in Scotland as Kames."†

The latest testimony to Swedenborg's claim to be considered one of the pioneers of modern geology is that of Professor A. G. Nathorst, Professor of Palæontology and Geology, who supplies an Introduction to the first volume of Swedenborg's scientific works published by the Swedish Royal Academy of Sciences. He says: "Swedenborg's contributions in the field of geology are of such significance and value that they alone would have been sufficient to have secured him a respected scientific name." "One im-

Documents, vol. ii, pp. 896 and 897.
†*Prehistoric Man and Beast* (Smith, Elder & Co., 1896), p. 92.

mediately notices," he continues, "in studying Swedenborg's geological writings, that an investigating nature of
the highest rank is in question, which on a solid foundation and with sharp power of observation noticed everything, even what was apparently insignificant in order to
draw conclusions from it. The wealth of observation which
he collected from various parts of Europe is astonishing,
and he did this at a comparatively early age." He observes further: "What Anders Retzius said concerning
Swedenborg's *Regnum Animale* . . . seems, after the
experience now attained, to be capable of application to
practically the whole of his scientific activity. He was a
mighty spirit, of which our country has the more reason
to be proud, because it was united with a personality in
every respect noble and unassuming."

Of the practical value of Swedenborg's geological and
metallurgical labours, we have abundant evidence. "We
should never be able to finish," says Professor Schleiden,
"if we should attempt to enumerate all the improvements
which Swedenborg introduced in the working of the mines
of his native country, and it would be impossible to say
how great were his merits in promoting the industry and
the arts of Sweden."*

As we have already mentioned Swedenborg's treatise on
iron in his *Opera Philosophica et Mineralia* was translated into French by M. Bouchu, and embodied in the
magnificent *Description des Arts et Métiers,* issued by the
Royal Academy of Sciences, "because this work was found
to be the best on this subject."†

In connection with his metallurgical studies, Swedenborg made careful investigations into the nature of fire, and
the construction of furnaces and stoves. The air-tight stove
described in his *New Observations and Discoveries respect-*

---

*Quoted by M. Matter in his *Vie de Swedenborg,* p. 40.

†*Swedenborg, as a Philosopher and Man of Science,* by R. L. Tafel,
Ph.D., p. 209.

ing Iron and Fire, published in 1721, is said to be the same in principle as one patented in recent years in Washington.‡

Swedenborg theorized much on the origin and constitution of matter; and, though some of his theories may seem to us too simply mechanical, the essence of his conclusions is a wonderful anticipation of the very latest conceptions of matter.

M. Dumas distinctly ascribes to Swedenborg the origin of the modern science of crystallography. He says, "It is then to him we are indebted for the first idea of making cubes, tetrahedrons, pyramids, and the different crystalline forms, by grouping the spheres; and it is an idea which has since been renewed by several distinguished men, Wollaston in particular."* Professor F. C. Calvert also asserted in a public lecture that "Swedenborg was the first to discover that atoms were spheres, and that with them cubes, octahedrons, etc., could be formed."

Though he gave so much attention to scientific theories, he always had an eye for putting them to some practical use. In his *Dædalus,* to which we have referred before, there is a description of a new ear trumpet for the deaf, designed in accordance with the laws which regulate the reflection of sound waves from hard substances. The article is accompanied by drawings and a mathematical discussion of the theory on which it is based. In the same work there is a description of a simple form of air-pump which depends on the fact that the pressure of the air can only sustain a column of water about thirty feet high. Even the idea of a "flying machine" exercised his inventive powers. In papers found after his death, and since reproduced by photo-lithography, there is a drawing of such a machine and a description of it. To Swedenborg also is due the first conception of a tank in which to test models of ships; a plan now adopted by our Admiralty,

‡*Swedenborg, as a Philosopher,* etc., p. 204.
*Swedenborg as a Philosopher, etc., p. 245.

and in a still more elaborate way by the Navy Department of the United States.

In his monograph on Mercurial Air-Pumps, Professor S. P. Thompson, Principal of the Technical College, Finsbury, gives to Swedenborg the credit of inventing the first mercurial air-pump. He quotes his description of it in the original Latin, and adds that, fitted with the valves that were usual in those days, it would be effective.

While Swedenborg's *Principia* deals mainly with the physical properties of matter, he has some very remarkable passages in the *Introduction* relating to what is now known as evolution. Herbert Spencer is usually credited with the conception that the motions of the ether had much to do with the production of the sense of sight. But in the clearest way Swedenborg propounds this theory. He says: "The ether seems to have formed in the eye a mechanism of its own by which its vibrations can be received." (*Principia,* part i, ch. i.) Still more remarkable is the statement with regard to the ear: "The undulating air flows into the ear, and occasions in its tympanum a motion imitative of itself, . . . ; so that [it] seems to have formed a mechanism of its own" (*Ibid*). In another place he says that "Man was constructed according to the motion of the elements" (*Ibid*), a saying that sums up Spencer's theory. The fact that Swedenborg afterwards modified this view, should not stand in the way of our giving him the credit of first propounding it.

In view of later scientific developments, many of Swedenborg's statements in regard to the nature and properties of the ether are most suggestive. He regarded it as composed of highly elastic particles, as most mobile, and as capable of penetrating other bodies. He attributes to this "element" the origin of light, heat, and electricity. Thus in the *Principia* (part iii., ch. v., § 21), he writes:

"The doctrine of ether, or of the phenomena caused by ether, may be reduced to the following compendious statement. Motion diffused from a given centre through a contiguous medium [*per contiguum*] or volume of particles of ether, produces light; for in consequence of this motion the ether is reflected from every entity it meets, and thus an idea of the object is presented to the eye. The central motion of the particles of ether causes not only a rigid expansion of every particle, but also heat; and if this motion be urged from the centre to the circumferences, it causes light together with heat. . . . There are corpuscles which resemble a species of effluvia, and which are so small as to be enabled to move only a volume of ether, but not a volume of air; and these, if spontaneously moved, excite light to a certain distance. If they are not spontaneously moved, but are put in motion by means of the tremulations of the parts of any hard body in which they reside, in this case also light is excited, and in like manner electricity, so long as the tremulation continues."

Magnetism absorbed much of Swedenborg's attention at different periods of his life, and he is credited with anticipating many modern discoveries. Professor Patterson, of Pennsylvania University, wrote to Dr. Atlee, in acknowledging a book of Swedenborg's which the latter had sent to him: "Many of the experiments and observations in magnetism, presented in this work, are believed to be of much more modern date, and are unjustly ascribed to much more recent writers."

"Fifty years after its publication [Swedenborg's *Opera Philosophica et Mineralia*], on the report of a commission to the unfortunate Louis XV., that there did not yet exist any theory of the magnet, the Marquis de Thomé responded indignantly and at length, declaring that the *Opera Philosophica* of Swedenborg was held in high esteem in all Europe, and that the most celebrated men had 'not disdained to draw materials from it to assist them in their labours'; that 'the theory of the Swedish author is a true theory of the magnet, and of all magnetism'; and

233

that M. Camus, who performed such surprising things with the magnet before their eyes, admitted that he had 'derived from this author all the knowledge he exhibited on the subject.' To this we may add," says Mr. Worcester, "that some practical electricians of the present day are finding in this theory explanations of results which they do not find explained by any other." (*The Life and Mission of Emanuel Swedenborg*, by Benjamin Worcester, p. 98.)

It is in his contributions to astronomical knowledge, however, that Swedenborg's anticipations of modern discovery are the most remarkable. It can scarcely be questioned that the nebular theory of the formation of planetary systems originated with him; he also first conceived the idea of a harmonious relation of the different systems, and assigned its position in the galaxy to our own; he announced the translatory motion of the stars along the Milky Way, and propounded the doctrine of a cyclic return in the movements of the planets.

Respecting his right to be regarded as the originator of the nebular theory, generally attributed to Laplace and Kant, the evidence is strong and most interesting. Professor E. S. Holden, of Lick Observatory, wrote thus, in 1880, in *The North American Review*:

"It has long been known to students of the philosophical writings of Emanuel Swedenborg that he was the author of an elaborate theory of the origin of the solar and stellar systems, which was the prototype of those now received. The facts in the case are that in his *Principia,* published in 1734, a complete system of cosmogony was proposed, in which the genesis of the planets and satellites from a primitive nebulous mass was maintained. The details of the imagined process are given and are illustrated with drawings in the fullest manner."

"Bohn, the publisher, had in his possession a copy of Swedenborg's *Principia,* containing Buffon's autograph and bearing marks of use. There is no doubt, when the essential points of the three systems are considered, that the suggestion of the system of Swedenborg (published fifteen years before Buffon's) influenced him largely, and that the ideas of Buffon, with the reflections on the construction of the heavens by the later Herschel, led Laplace to the final form of his nebular hypothesis."

Both Kant and Buffon had some acquaintance with Swedenborg, and the former jealously remarked upon the similarity of some of our author's theories to his own. Laplace owns that Buffon first suggested to him the idea of the derivation of planets and their moons from their suns.

Dr. Magnus Nyrén, Astronomer at the Observatory of Pulkowa, Russia, published an article, in 1879, on *Swedenborg and the Nebular Hypothesis,* in which he gave full credit to Swedenborg as the originator of the theory. "It cannot be disputed," he says, "that the real germ of the nebular hypothesis, namely, that the entire solar system has formed itself out of a single chaotic mass which rolled itself at first into a colossal sphere and afterwards threw off a ring which then through continued rotation at length broke into parts, these finally contracting into balls, planets —that to this idea Swedenborg was the first to give utterance. Kant's work on the same subject, *Allgemeine Naturgeschichte und Theorie des Himmels,* appeared, for example, in 1755, thus twenty-one years later; Laplace published his hypothesis sixty-two years later. And here we must remark that Swedenborg, in all probability, has given the more correct form to his theory, in so far as—and this Laplace has admitted—the planets have arisen from the shattered rings (according to the vortical theory, Swedenborg found only one such necessary), and not, as Kant supposed, through a conglomeration formed immediately out of the original vapour mass." (*Vierteljahrschrift der Astronomischen Gesellschaft,* p. 81.)

Swedenborg's theory is different from that of Laplace, in that he regarded the planets as being projected from the body of the sun, or rather from a nebulous ring that surrounded it, and as gradually receding to their present orbits; whereas Laplace assumed that the atmosphere of the sun once extended far beyond the orbit of the most distant of the planets, which were formed successively by its condensation into nebulous rings as the central mass contracted. Swedenborg's theory also postulated a central vortical area which first gave rotation to the sun, and incidentally to its progeny, the planets; while Laplace's theory was based upon the law of gravitation. Mr. Beswick contends that Swedenborg's theory explains more of the phenomena of the solar system than Laplace's and holds that it is destined yet to supersede it. One point that he insists upon is that, if the planets were formed at the successive confines of the solar atmosphere, the speed of rotation would decrease with those that approached nearer to the sun; whereas the contrary is the fact, as we should expect to find if the planets were thrown out from the central orb.

The folowing is a brief statement of Swedenborg's theory of the solar system. The sun he assumed to be a mass of matter in a state of incandescence, revolving by inherent vortical force. From this body were thrown off vapours, which gathered into a nebulous ring in the plane of the equator. By condensation this ring became more and more solid, and at length broke and scattered into space the masses which subsequently formed the planets and satellites of the solar system. The nebulous ring, whirling with the rapid rotation of the central body, gave to the chaotic masses thus detached a rotatory movement of their own. This was naturally greatest when they were near to the sun, otherwise they would have fallen back into his body; but by degrees they receded to their present orbits and attained their present rate of motion.

There was a time, he says, when the rotation of the earth on its axis only occupied about two hours, and its annual journey was accomplished in no more than a month of our time. This, he concludes, was a time of perpetual spring, the rapid changes preventing any extremes of climate. By degrees, as the days and the years lengthened, the heat and cold were intensified, and our years and days, with the changes of climate they give rise to, became as they are now.

Swedenborg stated that "the common axis of the sphere, or sidereal heavens, seems to be the Milky Way, where there is the largest gathering of stars" (*Principia,* part iii., chap. i., No. 8) as to which statement Dr. Nyrén remarks: "If there is no other meaning to be given to it than that the Milky Way is the equatorial section [zodiac] of our whole visible firmaments, then the priority of the suggestion of the galactic stellar system belongs also to Swedenborg."

As regards the position of our solar system in space, Swedenborg says: "Our solar vortex or system is not in the axis of the sphere, but is near the axis where there is a considerable incurvation or inflection." (*Principia,* part iii., chap. i., No. 7.) Sir J. Herschel remarks: "Our system is placed eccentrically, so as to be much nearer to the parts about the cross, than to that diametrically opposed to it." "This confirms," says Mr. Beswick, "the wonderful exactness of Swedenborg's statement." "In the year 1789," again he says, "Herschel directs his monster telescope to the sides and surfaces of the galaxy, and without knowing of Swedenborg's announcement of the sun's position therein, conjectures the identical spot, seeks for evidence of its truth by a species of star gauging and a few efforts reward his labours with the most abundant confirmation of the reality of his conjecture. Certainly, never did a more bold assertion receive a more striking confirmation."

237

There is little space to speak of Swedenborg's anatomical studies, which were lifelong and profound. The value of his work was rather in his suggestive conclusions on facts ascertained by others, than in original investigations, though Count Höpken says that "he made singular discoveries which are preserved somewhere in the *Acta Literaria*."

Many of Swedenborg's conclusions are now being reached by leading anatomists. In his address as president of the International Congress of Anatomists, which met at Heidelberg in May, 1903, Professor Gustaf Retzius drew attention to some of Swedenborg's extraordinary anticipations of modern science. There were more than a hundred of the leading anatomists of Europe present, including many of the greatest living authorities, who were astonished at the facts placed before them. They were unaware that Swedenborg was the discoverer of the localization of the functions of the brain. Dr. Retzius created a sensation by stating that, in his work on "The Brain," Swedenborg was more than a century ahead of modern anatomists. His own eyes had been opened to the fact by Dr. Max Neuburger, of Vienna. This learned physician had two years previously delivered an address before the assembly of German Naturalists and Physicists, on "Swedenborg's Reference to the Physiology of the Brain," in which he pointed out many of Swedenborg's discoveries. Of one of these, he said: "He leaped a whole century ahead of his age by the announcement of another discovery, for he was the first one to show that the cortical substance of the brain is the exclusive seat of the higher physical activity, the point of attack of the soul." In concluding his address, he remarked that "this man, during the scientific period of his life, exhibited a penetration in various fields of research that is nothing less than magnificent."

Dr. Neuburger's interest in the matter was so earnest, that he had addressed a communication to the Swedish

Royal Academy of Sciences, in which he had expressed his regret that Swedenborg's extensive manuscript on the brain, which is in the possession of the Academy, had not yet been published. This led to the appointment of a committee to investigate the matter, of which committee Professor Retzius was appointed chairman. He made a study of Swedenborg's physiological treatises, with the result that we have seen. The outcome of the committee's deliberations was a recommendation that the Academy should undertake the publication of Swedenborg's scientific and philosophical works, Dr. Retzius offering to bear the cost of the first three volumes himself, which were duly published. Volume I embraces Swedenborg's contributions to geology and palæontology, and a mass of his correspondence on scientific subjects. The other two are on chemistry, physics, mechanics, and cosmology. Thus, tardy justice is being accorded to his genius in his own country.

Dr. J. J. Garth Wilkinson says of Swedenborg's anatomical and physiological works:

"Swedenborg's physiological doctrines are so new, deep, and comprehensive, that when presented to even a candid mind, full of ordinary notions, and breathing the gross atmosphere of modern science, they will probably appear to be little more than a confused mass of assumptions. Such is my experience of their first effect on my own mind. Now, however, I am every day becoming more penetrated with the truth and consequent importance of these works. . . . They are the result of rigid physical induction. And it is both curious and satisfactory to observe that medical authors have been for ages approximating, in the way of effects and details, to some of the principles elicited by Swedenborg. To instance one of these cases—the influence of the respiratory movements on, and their propagation to, the viscera and to the whole body. The law that the body in general and in particular, respires with

239

the lungs—that the perpetuation of all the functions, and, in a word, of corporeal life, depends on the universality of this action, as a law—is peculiar to Swedenborg. And yet, for centuries, the fragments of this truth have flitted across the mental vision of physiologists. *Glisson* has declared it of the liver—*Blumenbach* of the spleen—*Barry,* and many others, of the heart—*Bell,* of the neck—*Schlichting,* of the blood in the brain—*Fortat,* of the circulation in the spinal cord: and I could easily add many other names and instances to this list. Another principle discovered by Swedenborg is the permeability of membranes, and the circulation of fluids through them in determinate channels; some of the details of which are now grouped under the names 'Endosmosis' and 'Exosmosis,'—two phenomena which are thought discoveries of the present day. With regard to the lymphatic system, Swedenborg has thoroughly anticipated the beautiful theory of *Dr. Prout, etc.* And although it is as a discoverer of principles that Swedenborg is undoubtedly most valuable, yet his subordinate, theoretical details, are also far superior to those of other authors, because they refer themselves to a head, and derive from it a universalizing vital essence."

Jacob Berzelius, "the father of modern chemistry," wrote to Dr. Wilkinson, of Swedenborg's *Animal Kingdom*: "I have gone through some parts of *The Animal Kingdom,* which have interested me especially; and I have been surprised to find how the mind of Swedenborg *has preceded* the present state of knowledge, writing his work at the time he did. I hope the anatomists and physiologists of our day will profit by this work, both for the sake of extending their ideas, and of rendering justice to the genius of Swedenborg." In another letter he says, "I am surprised at the great knowledge displayed by Swedenborg in a subject that a professed metallurgist would not have been supposed to have made an object of study, *and in which,*

as in all that he undertook, he was in advance of his age."
He was not only in advance of his age in science, but in the use he made of his knowledge; for his physiological studies were only undertaken as a basis for his profound psychological speculations. Coventry Patmore truly observes: "We have had only one psychologist and human physiologist, at least only one who has published his knowledge, for at least a thousand years, namely, Swedenborg."

The great scheme of *The Animal Kingdom* was never completed, as we have already mentioned. Among the material intended to be incorporated were voluminous manuscripts on *The Brain,* already mentioned, two volumes of which were translated into English and published in 1882 and 1887. It is an encyclopædic work, and its value has now been acknowledged in many quarters. Its editor, Dr. R. L. Tafel, asserts that it contains many important discoveries and suggestions, some of which have been credited to more recent investigators. Dr. Rabagliati, reviewing these two volumes in *Brain,* vol. vi., describes it as "one of the most remarkable books we have ever seen."

The modern student is at a loss to form a just estimate of Swedenborg's scientific position from the fact that the philosophical works which have been translated and published are to be found in few libraries, and have, most of them, been for some little while out of print. The Swedenborg Society, however, is always at work, and aims not only at keeping in print those previously issued, but at bringing out all the scientific and philosophical works still lying in manuscript, to remedy this deficiency.

CHAPTER XVI

ANOTHER proof of the many-sidedness of Swedenborg's genius, and of the absolute sanity of his mind, is furnished by the brief records that exist of his political activity. From the time he first took his seat in the House of Nobles, in 1719, to the year 1761, he appears to have shown a warm interest in the public affairs of his native land; and, when at home, to have taken an active part in the proceedings of the Diet. A fellow-countryman writes of him: "Up to the time of his extreme old age he interested himself in the financial, administrative, and political affairs of his country, as well between, as during, the sessions of the Swedish Diet. A considerable number of papers on these subjects, partly preserved to the present day, bear witness to his activity as the head of his family, and show how great an interest he had in the debates that took place in the House of Nobles. . . . As a member of the House of Nobles, Swedenborg belonged neither to the party of the 'hats,' nor to that of the 'caps' in those times, but he was an independent member, supporting whatever he saw to be worthy of his own position, and to be right and generally useful, without allowing himself to be influenced either by the right or the left side. He, like every true friend of liberty, was opposed alike to despotism and to anarchy. As the son of a distinguished and universally beloved bishop, he was ennobled by Queen Ulrica Eleonora in 1719, together with his brothers and sisters. His entrance into the House of Nobles was consequently contemporaneous with the establishment of freedom in Sweden. During his childhood and youth he had witnessed the misfortunes, into which an unlimited monarchy had precipitated his country. He himself had seen the misery and distress, which a war of eighteen years' duration, with dearly bought victories and bloody defeats, with decimated armies and bankrupt finances, attended by pestilence and famine, had entailed on his oppressed country. . . . Need we wonder, then, that Swedenborg was in favour of a constitution, which set bounds to the arbitrary power and whims of a hitherto unlimited monarchy; which prevented the dissolution of the country, and gradually changed discontent into satisfaction, at least, among the majority of its citizens." (*Nya Kyrkan och dess inflytande på Theologiens Studium i Sverige,* part ii, p. 48.)

Another Swedish writer says: "He conversed much on scientific and political subjects, and was especially much interested in the proceedings of the Diet of his country, even after he had ceased to take any part in them, and his judgment in these matters was always sure, quick, and to the point."

Financial questions especially interested him, and he presented various memorials on currency, exchange, etc., between the years 1723 and 1761. Count von Höpken states that: "The most solid and best-written memorials at the Diet of 1761, on matters of finance, were presented by Swedenborg."

No biography of Swedenborg could be regarded as complete without some notice of his political career. We shall therefore review briefly the various memorials of his that have been preserved. Of his speeches we have no record, though he has been described as one of the sharpest and severest speakers in the House. This can scarcely be true, however, for two reasons: severity was not characteristic of the man, though he could be firm on occasion; and a slight impediment in his speech made public utterance a difficulty to him.

The earliest memorial that we have is dated February 5, 1723, and relates to the finances of the country. In it,

Swedenborg deplores the decay of Swedish commerce, which had thrown the balance of trade from the credit to the debit side and so impoverished the State. The causes of the decline he attributes to the loss of many Swedish provinces in the wars, the absorption of capital by war expenditure, and the consequent dilapidation of Swedish ships "during the weary years of war." The remedies he proposes are the development of the internal resources of the country, especially the iron and copper industries; and the improvement of native manufactures that it might not be necessary to import so many articles of daily use.

Several memorials relate to the encouragement of iron manufactures in Sweden, but his efforts in this direction were not seconded by his colleagues at the Board of Mines —to whom some of the memorials were referred—and therefore came to nothing. An important memorandum advocating the establishment of rolling mills in Sweden to deal with the crude product, which was accompanied by drawings of suitable machinery, was filed for future reference on September 1, 1726, and may still be seen in the Archives of the Board. In this paper he draws attention to the fact that—"Many thousand tons of Swedish pig-iron are annually shipped, with great expense in freight and custom-house duties, to Holland, whence it is re-shipped inland to Sauerland and Liège, where it is broken up, rolled, and converted into four, six, ten to twelve iron rods or bars, or converted into sheet-iron. Afterwards it is carried back to Holland, and conveyed thence to many places in Europe, where it is sold with great profit; so that our Swedish iron must in this manner be ennobled in Brabant, and yield them a handsome income, which we, with small expense and industry, might keep at home."

He shows that the establishment of such mills would give encouragement to various small manufactures in

Sweden, and that the surplus production over and above home requirements might become an important item in the national exports. "The greater part of the rolled iron," he says, "which is sent out of Liège, consists of the iron of Liège and Brabant, which many nations are compelled to use for want of a better iron, although it is cold, short, and brittle. But if Sweden would furnish the same sort of iron rods and sheeting, the inferior iron would be scorned and sink in price, while the better would rise."

In the year 1734 a war fever arose among the "hat" party in Sweden, who advocated an alliance with France against Russia, and the attempted re-conquest of the Baltic provinces. Against this mad scheme Swedenborg strenuously protested by a lengthy memorial, in which he summed up in a masterly way the possible advantages and disadvantages of such a war and such an alliance. He pointed out the contracted means of Sweden for the carrying on of a great war, and the small number of men available for service, compared with former years; and emphasized the need of developing the material resources of the country, which would be of more importance to her than recovered territory. The possession of Dantzic by Russia threatened the trade of the Baltic, but he had the prescience to see that "naval and other powers in time will so arrange it, that Russia will not enjoy its possession perpetually." He was not opposed to a war of self-defence, but "putting oneself into training and commencing a war, simply for the purpose of showing that one is not afraid, even when this is feasible, is no proof or argument in the case of a nation that need not fear in any case to be attacked by its neighbours, and which is well known to be able to defend itself against those by whom it may be attacked." So he advocated neutrality as Sweden's proper attitude, and had the satisfaction of seeing his views adopted by the Diet.

The financial embarrassment of the country exercised

245

his mind again in 1755, and in connection with it the question of intemperance, which was adding to the impoverishment of the people. Intemperance, which prevailed in an alarming degree among his countrymen, he regarded as one of the worst internal foes of Sweden, preventing her from becoming a great manufacturing and agricultural nation. He was so much convinced of this, that he wrote on the flyleaf of one of his theological manuscripts: "The immoderate use of spirituous liquors will be the downfall of the Swedish people."

Among the remedies he proposed was that "all public-houses in town should be like baker's shops, with an opening in the window, through which those who desired might purchase whisky and brandy, without being allowed to enter the house, and lounge about in the tap-room." Another proposition, which was subsequently adopted by the Diet, was to limit the distillation of whisky, and to raise it in price by farming out the right of making it. "If the distilling of whisky," he said, "were farmed out in all judicial districts, and also in towns, to the highest bidder, a considerable revenue might be obtained for the country, and the consumption of grain might also be reduced: that is, if the consumption of whisky cannot be done away with altogether, which would be more desirable for the country's welfare and for morality than all the income which could be realized from so pernicious a drink." In this project we have the germ of the Gothenburg system.

Another cause of the decreasing wealth of the country he found to be the facilities for raising loans on all fixed and movable property, whereby large numbers of all classes were deeply indebted to the bank. In order to ease the financial situation, therefore, he proposed, in addition to the farming out of the distillation of whisky, to call in the banknotes advanced on mortgaged property, and to restore specie payments.

Five years later he returned to these subjects, and presented a lengthy memorial which displayed a confident knowledge of sound financial principles. He pointed out that the rise in exchange, which in twenty years had resulted in the value of the rix-daler jumping from thirty-five marks to sixty-six marks, was ruining the country, and suggested various remedies. He showed that the main cause of the rise was the displacement of a metallic currency by paper money, issued by the bank in immense quantity against the mortgages spoken of above, and exceeding very much the deposits of coined money possessed by the bank. The high rate of exchange was rapidly denuding the country of the ordinary currency, since "as soon as exchange rises above sixty marks . . . the copper contained in it is of more intrinsic value than the value represented by our paper currency"; and so it went to the melting pot, or was sent abroad.

He argued strenuously for an honest currency as a cure for the evil; for, he said, "coin alone regulates exchange." "The currency in a country is like the blood in the body, upon which depends its life, health, strength, and defence." His proposals were "that the general loans upon all fixed and movable property do cease, and that henceforth no other loan be negotiated at any banking office, except for the purposes of the State, and upon gold and silver as was formerly the custom"; that the present mortgages should gradually be redeemed by the payment of a part of the loan annually in addition to the interest, and that thereafter "certificates of indebtedness" should cease to be legal tender; that the bank should increase its stock of "coin plates," which stood for bullion, and that, in the meantime, the exportation of either "plates" or crude copper should be forbidden; that the number of bank officials should be gradually reduced; and, finally (I have omitted some less important suggestions), that the distillation of whisky should be farmed out by the Government.

247

This memorial goes to the root of the matter, and evinces a remarkable grasp of a difficult question; the more remarkable when we remember that its author was at this time (1760), and had been since 1747, deeply engaged in spiritual studies, and that he was the subject of much remark on account of his wonderful supernatural experiences which had only lately become publicly known. The so-called mystic would have made an excellent chancellor of the exchequer, if Sweden had happened to want one just then.

Swedenborg followed up this weighty document with an "Appeal to the Houses of the Diet in favour of the Restoration of a Metallic Currency," some "Additional Considerations" on the Exchange rate, and a "Memorial to the King" on the subject of the exportation of copper. In the first of these papers he urges, that, "unless the various Houses of the Diet at the present session take steps to secure the return of the paper currency to the bank, and the issue of coin possessing an intrinsic value in its place, there is danger that the dearness of everything will continue to increase more and more, until the country at last will become utterly exhausted and ready to perish; which it assuredly will, unless another remedy for its restoration be found than a general bankruptcy on all the paper currency. This bankruptcy, however, stares every man willing to reflect upon this subject in the face, when he considers that six dalers in paper are now equivalent to three dalers in "plates" in our foreign commerce, and two dalers in plates in our inland traffic." He concludes his appeal with these words of sober wisdom: "In coined specie itself lies the real value of exchange, and consequently that of all merchandise. If any country could exist by means of a paper currency, which is in the place of money, but which is not money, it would be a country without a parallel."

Swedenborg was offered a seat on the "Private Commission on Exchange," and would have been an invaluable member, but he declined to serve as he was not satisfied with its constitution. His suggestions, however, carried weight with the Commissioners, and it was resolved, in January, 1762, that no more money should be advanced on movable property. The following session a law was enacted limiting the circulation of paper money to the amount of bullion held by the bank.

The condition of Sweden at this time gave much concern to her responsible statesmen. The Councillor of Commerce, Anders Nordencrantz, issued a bulky work dealing with the financial difficulty, in which "he sounded a fearful alarm about the condition of the country, and made charges in general against judges, senators, and civil officers, and also proposed several radical changes which seemed necessary to him in the form of the government." To moderate the effect of this alarmist production, Swedenborg wrote a brief reply in the shape of a memorial to the Houses of the Diet; a statesman-like document well calculated to effect its purpose. In it he defends the Swedish form of government, as, together with that of England and Holland, the best in Europe, "as every inhabitant, notwithstanding all the shortcomings which happen there, is safe in his life and property, and no one is a slave, but they are all free men." He admits imperfections, "yet it is impossible," he says, "to escape all distortions of right, and all wrong interpretations of law, since most men are subject to human weaknesses, and hence are inclined to one of two parties either by friendship, relationship, hope of promotion, or of presents, and this malpractice cannot be uprooted under any government, however excellent it may be."

One of Nordencrantz's proposals was that "all state offices, high as well as low, except the ecclesiastical and military, should be changed every second or third year"; to which Swedenborg advanced several weighty objections. "What an amount of gifts and bribes," he remarks, "would have to be given and taken, in order that they might secure a livelihood for future time! From this the full absurdity of the proposal may be seen; yea, it appears almost at first sight from this consideration only, that it militates directly against an institution which has been established in Sweden from time immemorial, and which is likewise one of the pillars for the preservation of our freedom, inasmuch as every one finds himself secure in his office during his lifetime, but insecure under an arbitrary government, and still more so in case such a proposal should be enacted."

Nordencrantz complained of corrupt practices among politicians. "In free governments," said Swedenborg, "it is impossible to prevent corrupt practices, and power being exercised by cliques on the ground of such practices"; but "corrupt practices in free governments are like small ripples, compared with large waves in absolute monarchies; in absolute or arbitrary monarchies, favourites and the favourites of favourites, yea, the unlimited monarch himself, are corrupted by men studying and appealing to their passions. . . . One absolute or arbitrary monarch is able to do more mischief in one year, than a clique or combination of many at a session of the Diet could accomplish in a hundred years; inasmuch as in the various Houses of the Diet their influence is counterbalanced generally and individually; while in an absolute monarchy there is no such counterweight."

Nordencrantz resented Swedenborg's criticism of his book and a somewhat acrimonious correspondence ensued; —acrimonious on the worthy Councillor's part, that is to say, for Swedenborg was courteous and dignified, as usual. This led to a breach between them, which was healed, however, by the intervention of the President of the Board of Commerce, Niklas von Oelreich, who wrote to Swedenborg on the last day of 1761:

"Herr Nordencrantz, Councillor of Commerce, invites the Herr Assessor and myself to come to church to-morrow morning at ten o'clock, and afterwards to dine with him. He will send his carriage, and at the above-named time I shall call for the Herr Assessor with the carriage. I am very anxious that you two should become good friends."

The last political document that we have bearing Swedenborg's signature is an address to the Diet, presented between March and July, 1761, in favour of the re-instatement of three senators who had been compelled to resign on account of the part they had taken in the disastrous war against Frederick the Great. The memorial bears the title: "Frank Views concerning the Maintenance of the Country and the Preservation of its Freedom," and raises a warning voice against the revival of an absolute monarchy, which a party in the state was working to bring about, and which these senators had opposed. He was no believer in the Divine right of kings, as his father had been; "no one," he said, "has the right to leave his life and property in the absolute power of any individual; for of these God alone is master, and we are merely His stewards in this world." He had again the satisfaction of seeing his views carried out, as two at least of the senators were restored to their places.

Thus ends the record of Swedenborg's political acts. All the documents referred to, and some others of less consequence, display clear judgment, commonsense, and a sincere desire for the good of his native land. Their importance to us now is the evidence they afford of his mental condition at a time when he was supposed by many to be the subject of hallucinations.

CHAPTER XVII

LONDON HAUNTS AND HABITATIONS

It is a pleasing sentiment that causes men to seek out, and set a mark upon the homes and haunts of famous men. To those who believe in Swedenborg's claims, the places associated with his various sojourns in England, are naturally of great interest, though little has been done in the past to explore and describe them. Some information, then, in regard to these localities, may be acceptable to the reader.

In all, Swedenborg probably passed five or six years in this country, but there is no precise record of his comings and goings. In his student days, he spent about two years in London and Oxford, and he came to England on various occasions afterwards during the following sixty years. The last time was in 1771, and from this visit he never returned to his own country, as he died at his London lodgings on March 29, 1772.

We have no information as to where Swedenborg resided during his first sojourn here, but he states, as already mentioned, that he changed his lodgings frequently, that he might learn something of useful trades from his hosts; with this intent, he seems to have purposely chosen the houses of artificers.

It is a pity that we have such scanty records of his impressions during this visit. London, at this time, must have been a most interesting city, a new city in fact, just arisen from the ashes of the great fire; but the young student tells us little about the place, in the few letters of this period that have been preserved. In the earliest of these, he says: "Whatever is worthy of being seen in the town, I have already examined"; but he only mentions particularly St. Paul's Cathedral and Westminster Abbey.

We know more of Swedenborg's movements in London during his later visits. He lodged at various times in the Minories, in Fetter Lane, in Wellclose Square, and in the neighbourhood of Cold Bath Square, Clerkenwell.

Before we attempt to follow his footsteps, let us try to realize what the London that met his eyes was like. The closely inhabited portion lay alongside the river, and did not extend far to north or south. "From any part of London it was possible to get into the country in a quarter of an hour." "Queen's Square, Bloomsbury, had its north side left purposely open in order that the residents might enjoy the view of the Highgate and Hampstead Hills."* Where now are crowded and squalid streets, were open fields and villages. Bow, Bromley, Stepney, and Mile End, were but clusters of roadside cottages, and Bethnal Green only a small hamlet. Islington is described as "a beautiful village"; a view published in 1789, shows fields on all sides. "Clerkenwell was a suburban place, with Coppice Row, Field Lane, a Green and a Well, whither the law "clerken" used to resort from the Inns of Court."†

The population of London at the beginning of the eighteenth century has been estimated at three-quarters of a million, but it had increased to a million before the century closed. The whole of the West End from the Strand to Hyde Park, was built during this period, the fashion of country families spending a portion of the year in London having become thoroughly established, thus creating a demand for town houses. Beyond Hyde Park, again, were only villages and family mansions.

Though London in the eighteenth century was more rural than most great cities of the present day, it was by no means an idyllic place. The streets were badly made and ill-kept, and unsafe for pedestrians after dark, as they were miserably lighted, and there was no effective police force.

---

*London in the Eighteenth Century, by Sir Walter Besant, p. 78.
†Extract of Letter from Theodore Compton, Esq., to the author.

Lord Tyrconnel complained of the filthy condition of London, in a speech delivered in the House of Lords, in 1741; and in Gwynn's *Essay on Improvements,* published a few years later, the author enumerates fourteen crying nuisances which required to be abated. One of these was "the deluge of profanity in the streets." (*London in the Eighteenth Century,* pp. 90, 91.)

Dirt and disorder also reigned in the semi-rural suburbs. The roads were bad; rubbish was deposited indiscriminately on waste land, there were dirty and untidy farms, and numerous brickfields sending forth sulphurous fumes.

The following lines, from an old poem, describing the purlieus of London, give a somewhat depressing picture:

> Where'er around I cast my wand'ring eyes,
> Long burning rows of fetid brick arise,
> And nauseous dunghills swell in mould'ring heaps,
> While the fat sow beneath their covert sleeps.

This, then, was the London in which Swedenborg passed some years of his life. We proceed now to consider some of his special haunts more particularly.

Fetter Lane seems to have been the first place at which he stayed on his visit in 1744. We have some information in regard to this period from Magister Aaron Mathesius, who was pastor of the Swedish Church from 1772 till 1784.

"Some time in the year 1743,* a Moravian Brother, by name Senniff, on his return to London from Holland, where he had been visiting his children, became acquainted with Baron Emanuel de Swedenborg, who desired to be recommended to a family in London, where he could live retired." In his *Diary,* May 5–6, 1744, Swedenborg speaks of "a pious shoemaker, who had been with me on the journey, and with whom I was then lodging." Dr. Tafel suggests that this may have been Senniff. Mr. Senniff introduced him to Mr. Brockmer, who was very easily prevailed upon to take him under his roof.

---

*This date is incorrect as Swedenborg only arrived in England in May 1744.

Fetter Lane, in which Brockmer lived, is a thoroughfare running from Fleet Street to Holborn, near Chancery Lane. It has many interesting associations; Praise-God Barebone, who gave his name to the Puritan Parliament of 1653, was a leather-seller in Fetter Lane; it was the abiding place of Hobbes the philosopher, and the poets Dryden, Otway, and Flatman; here, also, Charles Lamb went to school. So, in coming to Fetter Lane, Swedenborg came to a famous neighbourhood. It was also, at that time, a pleasant residential locality: at the back of Fetter Lane and north of the Strand there were still gardens. (See *London in the Eighteenth Century*, p. 79.) Although it is not generally known, there are still gardens attached to some of the houses in Nevill's Court, between Fetter Lane and Great New Street.

Mathesius tells us that, "while residing here, Swedenborg went every Sunday to the chapel of the Moravians in Fetter Lane. Though he lived very recluse, he nevertheless would often converse with Mr. Brockmer, and was pleased with hearing the Gospel in London. So he went on for several months, continually approving of what he heard. At last he came to Mr. Brockmer and told him that he rejoiced that the Gospel was preached to the poor; but lamented over the learned and the rich, who he said must all go to hell."

Confirmation of Mathesius' statement that Swedenborg attended the Moravian Chapel at this time is found in his journal for the year 1744.

Under date of May 19–20 we read:

"By various circumstances I was led into the church belonging to the Moravian Brethren, who maintain that they are the true Lutherans, and, that they feel the influx of the Holy Spirit, as they tell each other; further, that they have respect only to God's grace, to Christ's blood and merit, and that they go about in simplicity. On this subject I shall speak more fully some other time; for as yet I am

255

not allowed to join their brotherhood." In another place, he says: "I am with them and yet not accepted by them."

At this time Swedenborg was very unsettled in religious matters, as his diary shows. He seems to have been drawn towards the Moravians, but did not find satisfaction in their communion. In later years he spoke of them severely as secretly denying the Divinity of Christ, maintaining the doctrine of faith alone, and disparaging the Old Testament; also, for their exclusiveness, lack of charity and other unchristian qualities.

The Moravian Chapel, which at present stands at the rear of No. 32 Fetter Lane, is not identical with the one that Swedenborg attended. The existing building dates from the year 1748, when the chapel was rebuilt on the foundations of a former one; but the internal arrangements are probably very similar to those of the earlier structure.

Swedenborg did not remain long in Fetter Lane. He left, we learn, "because the persons he lodged with used to meddle with his papers." Possibly his Moravian landlord was curious as to his lodger's views, thinking that he was likely to associate himself with the fraternity. Another account says that "he (Brockmer) and his maid were continually interrupting him in his studies, and wanted him to conform to their manner of living."

From a statement made by Shearsmith (see page 259) to Mr. Provo, it seems that when Swedenborg left Brockmer's lodgings, he went to reside with a Mrs. Carr, at No. 4 Great Warner Street, Cold Bath Fields, next door to the Red Lion Inn. The house is still standing unchanged. It is now No. 26 Warner Street, as the distinction between Great and Little Warner Street has been abolished.

Swedenborg's third visit to London was at the latter end of the year 1748, and it must have extended to some considerable length, as he took lodgings for six months on November 23rd. The object of his stay on this occasion was to publish the first volume of his *Arcana Cœlestia*. This was issued, as already mentioned, by John Lewis, of No. 1 Paternoster Row: the printer was John Hart, of Poppin's Court, Fleet Street, with whom Swedenborg was on friendly terms. We have no intimation as to the locality of his lodgings on this occasion, nor of the place where he resided during his sojourn in London in the spring of 1766. We learn, on the information of Eric Bergström, landlord of the King's Arms Tavern in Wellclose Square, that our author once stayed for ten weeks in that hostelry, and it seems probable that this was on the last mentioned visit. Possibly he lodged in the neighbourhood on other occasions, as it was a sort of Scandinavian colony; speaking of the Swedish Church in Prince's Square, and the Dane's Church in Wellclose Square, the Rev. David Lysons, in his *Environs of London* (published in 1795), says, "The Swedes, as well as the Danes, are very numerous in this parish" (vol. ii., p. 427). Bergström states that Swedenborg frequently called upon him.

Although so centrally situated, being in close proximity to the Docks, Wellclose Square was quite a newly developed district in Swedenborg's time, and was, in fact, almost in the country. It abutted upon the famous Ratcliffe Highway, but there were fields close by, and "garden grounds" are shown on the old maps between that thoroughfare and the river. Wellclose Square took its name from Goodman's Fields' Well, which was near at hand: "it was originally called Marine Square, from its being a favourite residence of naval officers." (*Curiosities of London,* by John Timbs, F.S.A., p. 753.)

It is needless to remark that this locality is greatly changed at the present day, Wellclose Square being in the heart of a densely populated district; but even in its present "reduced circumstances" it still presents some features of interest. Many of the houses are old, and have remained unchanged since the time Swedenborg lived there. Down a passage behind these houses there is an old wooden house with an interesting doorway. The centre of the square is occupied by a range of rambling buildings forming the schools of St. Paul's Church for Seamen; but in Swedenborg's time it was the site of a handsome church belonging to the Danish community. This was built in the year 1696, by Caius Gabriel Cibber, father of the celebrated Colley Cibber, at the expense of Christian V, King of Denmark. In the Guildhall Library there are two excellent prints,* showing the exterior and the interior of the church, the latter being especially fine. The building was taken down in 1845.

This neighbourhood is as closely associated with the memory of Swedenborg as that of Cold Bath Fields; for not only did he reside here for a time, but he sometimes attended the Swedish Church in Prince's Square (a short distance from Wellclose Square), and was buried within its walls.

The records of the Church refer to his presence on various occasions, and mention the fact that he sometimes dined with the minister afterwards. There is one reference in his diary (May 19-20, 1744) to his attendance at this church: he says—"On the twentieth I was to go to the Lord's Supper in the Swedish Church."

The Swedish Church was built in the year 1728, and remained until a few years ago, when it was demolished, in all essential features, as it appeared to Swedenborg. The exterior was not beautiful, but the interior was interesting, there being an imposing altar-piece, and a richly carved pulpit. On the south wall there was a tablet to the memory of Swedenborg, erected by an admirer in the year 1857. In the Sacristy at the rear of the church were a number of portraits of former ministers and notable persons connected with the Swedish community: amongst others, of Baron

---

Plans and Prints of Southwark, etc. (Shadwell section).

von Nolcken, who was Swedish Ambassador at the Court of St. James' from 1763 till 1794, and with whom Swedenborg was acquainted; and of Arvid Ferelius, Pastor from 1761 till 1772, whom our author knew intimately, and who performed the last offices of the Church for him.

When Swedenborg came to London in 1769, he returned to the neighbourhood of Cold Bath Fields. He went to the place where he had stayed twenty-five years before (presumably Mrs. Carr's in Great Warner Street), but found that the people had moved; so he settled at the house of Richard Shearsmith, a peruke maker, who lived at 26 Great Bath Street. "Before he came to their house, he was offered another lodging in the neighbourhood, but he told the mistress there was no harmony in the house; which she acknowledged, and recommended him to Mr. Shearsmith's." Here he resided for seven months, and to the same lodgings he returned in the summer of 1771, remaining there until his death. During his first visit "numbers of people came to see him . . . but not so many at his second coming." For his accommodation at Shearsmith's he paid the modest sum of five shillings a week, but this need not be taken to suggest that the lodgings were mean; we are told, in fact, that they were "decently furnished," and had been occupied previously by a clergyman.

The neighbourhood of Cold Bath Square has greatly changed during the past hundred years or so, though many old houses still remain, which must have been familiar to Swedenborg's sight. In his day, it was quite a country district, and much frequented by the well-to-do classes as a health resort. Maps of the time show nothing but fields beyond Cold Bath Square. It was a new neighbourhood, which owed its development to the discovery of a particularly cold spring in the year 1697. Its discoverer, one Walter Baynes, built a bath-house, and took up his residence on the premises, that he might personally superintend operations. The bath-house was situated in a large garden, enclosed by a brick wall, with a summer house, resembling a little tower, at each angle.

Around the bath arose many new houses, for the accommodation of the numerous visitors, who were attracted by its virtues; for the water soon gained a reputation. An advertisement, which appeared in the year 1752, states that "the price of bathing at the 'Cold Bath' has for many years, on account of its superior qualities, been at double the price of all other baths in London." It also announces that there are "very superior lodgings to be lett." Great Bath Street, in which Swedenborg resided, was built in 1725.

There were other attractions besides the Bath, in the vicinity of Cold Bath Fields. Mount Pleasant, which is not a very charming locality now, deserved its name then, for it was an open hill-side with a stream, the Fleet River, running at its foot; the London Spa, Sadler's Wells, New Tunbridge Wells, and Bagnigge Wells, were not far away; and there were numerous hostelries, with pleasure grounds, close at hand. The "Lord Cobham" in Cold Bath Square was one of the most famous of these: it had a large garden attached to it, in which was "a very handsome grove of trees, with gravel walks, and finely illuminated." Altogether, it was an attractive neighbourhood, and full of life; except in the latter respect, a striking contrast to its present condition. Now it is a resort of Italian organgrinders, and ice-cream vendors, bird-fanciers, costermongers, *et hoc genus omne.*

A visit to the locality will hardly enable the reader to realize the aspect of the place once so well known to Swedenborg, and to the residents of which his face and figure were also familiar. The houses are still standing, though the famous chestnut tree, which grew at the corner of Cold Bath Square, has gone. Sir John Oldcastle's house, which was situated at the corner of Farringdon Road, opposite to Cobham Row, has also disappeared, its site having been absorbed by Clerkenwell Prison (Middlesex House of Correction), which in its turn has had to make way for the parcel post department of the General Post Office. The side of the square nearest to Farringdon Road remains unaltered, though now somewhat dilapidated. The doorways are interesting, and as many of the doors stand open, you may see that the oak panelling of the halls has been preserved.

The geography of this locality has, however, been transformed in recent years by the construction of Rosebery Avenue. About half of the area of Cold Bath Square was cut off by this new thoroughfare, so that the present appearance of things gives little idea of what the square was like in Swedenborg's time, especially as the garden ground, in which he used to walk, is now occupied by artisans' dwellings many stories high. In olden times the area of the square was about 210 feet long by 90 feet broad, without including the surrounding streets. At the time that the Avenue was made, the whole space was occupied by houses: the bath, however, still existed, and was approached by a vaulted passage from the northeast side of the square. It was filled up during subsequent improvements.

CHAPTER XVIII

PERSONAL CHARACTERISTICS

HAVING followed Swedenborg through his long and varied career, and briefly reviewed his principal works, let us now try to get a look at the man himself. Portraits, unfortunately, do not help us much, none of the existing ones being of high artistic merit. The best, perhaps, is the one that forms the frontispiece of the *Opera Philosophica et Mineralia,* representing him at the age of forty-five. The face is pleasing and not unhandsome, alert with intelligence and full of conscious power; but somewhat prim and self-satisfied-looking. Cuno declares that this portrait, "although finished forty years ago by the skilful engraver Bernigroth is still perfectly like him, especially in respect to the eyes, which have retained their beauty, even in his old age.

These eyes were undoubtedly the most striking features of his countenance. Cuno says again: "When he gazed upon me with his smiling blue eyes, which he always did in conversing with me, it was as if truth itself was speaking from them." They had a magnetic power, even with unsympathetic subjects; the same witness writes: "I often noticed with surprise how scoffers, who had made their way into large societies where I had taken him, and whose purpose it had been to make fun of the old gentleman, forgot all their laughter and their intended scoffing, and how they stood agape and listened to the most singular things which he like an open-hearted child told about the spiritual world without reserve and with full confidence. It almost seemed as if his eyes possessed the faculty of imposing silence on every one."

On his taking leave of Cuno in 1769, the conversation turned upon the improbability of their meeting again.

Swedenborg spoke with eager anticipation of the last great change which he knew must come to him before long; and, as he spoke, "he looked so innocent and so joyful out of his eyes, as I had never seen him look before. I did not interrupt him," said Cuno, "and was, as it were, dumb with astonishment." Other witnesses speak of his seraphic look at times, and of the general serenity of his countenance. "An inward serenity and complacency of mind," says the Rev. Thomas Hartley, in a letter to the Rev. John Clowes, "were manifest in the sweetness of his looks and outward demeanour." Sometimes, when he had been in converse with spiritual beings, his eyes are said to have been filled with a wonderful light, which awed beholders; but under ordinary circumstances his appearance was placid and benignant.

In figure Swedenborg is described by most observers as tall, though it appears that he was not much above medium height. Some, indeed, have described him as small. Mr. Theodore Compton, when in his ninety-first year, wrote: "An old schoolmaster of my acquaintance when I was a child, told me he remembered seeing Emanuel Swedenborg at Clerkenwell—'a little man'—fond of the children, to whom he would give gingerbread nuts, when he met them in the street." In his old age, at any rate, he was of spare habit, which doubtless added to his apparent stature. His landlord Shearsmith said: "Formerly he must have been a corpulent man, but by being sedentary and studious he became thin and lean, and also pale in countenance." The Rev. Nicholas Collin, Rector of the Swedish Church in Philadelphia, who visited him in 1766, thus describes his personal appearance: "Being very old when I saw him, he was thin and pale; but still retained traces of beauty, and had something very pleasing in his physiognomy, and a dignity in his tall and erect stature." Carl C. Gjörwell, the Royal Librarian in Stockholm, who had occasion to call upon him officially two years earlier, tells us: "Although he is an old man, and grey hair protruded in every direction from under his wig, he walked briskly, was fond of talking, and spoke with a certain cheerfulness. His countenance was indeed thin and meagre, but cheerful and smiling."

Swedenborg's bodily activity in his later years was much remarked upon. Cuno wrote: "In respect to Mr. Swedenborg's external appearance, he is for his years a perfect wonder of health. He is of middle stature, and although he is more than twenty years older than I am, I should be afraid to run a race with him; for he is as quick on his legs as the youngest man. When I dined with him the last time at Mr. Odon's, he told me that a new set of teeth was growing in his mouth; and who has ever heard this of a man eighty-one years old?"

In the course of his last journey abroad, in 1770, Swedenborg was delayed by contrary winds at Elsinore, where resided an early disciple of his, General Christian Tuxen. The latter boarded the ship to offer the hospitality of his house, and found Swedenborg *en déshabille*. He proffered his invitation, to which "he [Swedenborg] immediately consented, pulling off his gown and slippers, putting on clean linen, and dressing himself as briskly and alertly as a young man of one and twenty."

"The dress that he generally wore, when he went out to visit, was a suit of black velvet, made after an old fashion; a pair of long ruffles; a curious-hilted sword; and a gold-headed cane." From a Swedish biography we learn that "according to the custom of his times, Swedenborg wore the customary wig on his head, yet it was not too long; the rest of his body was usually covered by a long light blue or greyish velvet coat, with an undergarment of black taffeta, and stockings and shoes with large buckles of gold." Another account says: "His dress in winter consisted of a fur coat of reindeer skin, and in summer, of a dressing-gown, both well worn, as became a philosopher's wardrobe. His wearing apparel was simple, but neat. Still, it happened sometimes, that when he prepared to go out, and his people did not call his attention to it, something would be forgotten or neglected in his dress; so that, for instance, he would put one buckle of gems and another of silver in his shoes; an instance of which absence of mind I myself saw at my father's house, where he was invited to dine; and which occurrence greatly amused several young girls, who took occasion to laugh at the old gentleman." His countryman, Eric Bergström, who kept the King's Arms Tavern, in Wellclose Square, London, and sometimes entertained Swedenborg, tells us that "he usually walked out after breakfast, generally dressed neatly in velvet, and made a good appearance." Shearsmith remarked to Mr. Provo: "His common garments were quite plain, and not worth much. . . . But sometimes when he went out, he wore a suit of black velvet lined with white, a silver-hilted sword, and white ruffles."

Swedenborg's manners in society were easy, polished and agreeable. He was equally at home with high and low, dining not infrequently with royalty in his own country, and living on friendly terms with his humble landlord in England. Cuno observes: "Mr. Swedenborg moves in the world with great tact, and knows how to address the high as well as the low." "He was not only," says Robsahm, "a learned man, but also a polished gentleman; for a man of such extensive learning, who by his books, his travels, and his knowledge of languages, had acquired distinction both at home and abroad, could not fail to possess the manners and everything else which, in those so-called serious or sober times, caused a man to be honoured, and made him agreeable in society. He was accordingly, even in his old age, cheerful, sprightly, and agreeable in company; yet, at the same time, his countenance presented those uncommon features, which are only seen in men of great genius."

Sandels tells us: "He was cheerful and pleasant in company, and as a recreation from his severe labours, he enjoyed intercourse with intelligent persons, by whom he was always well received and much respected. He could also properly meet, and playfully direct into another channel, the kind of curiosity which frequently desires to obtrude itself into the consideration of serious things."

Very important testimony as to Swedenborg's deportment in society is given by the Rev. Arvid Ferelius, Pastor of the Swedish Church in London from 1761 till 1772, who knew Swedenborg well, and ministered to him on his death-bed. In a letter to Professor Trätgård, Greifswalde, dated March 17, 1780, he wrote:

"Some one might think that Assessor Swedenborg was eccentric and whimsical; but the very reverse was the case. He was very easy and pleasant in company, talked on every subject that came up, accommodating himself to the ideas of the company; and he never spoke on his own views, unless he was asked about them. But if he noticed that any one asked him impertinent questions, intended to make sport of him, he immediately gave such an answer, that the questioner was obliged to keep silence, without being the wiser for it."

Owing to defective utterance, Swedenborg was not a brilliant conversationalist: nevertheless, "whenever he spoke, all other talk was hushed." "Ordinarily he pronounced very distinctly; but he stuttered a little when he tried to speak quickly. . . . He was unwilling to enter into any disputes on matters of religion; and, if obliged to defend himself, he did it with gentleness, and in few words." "When he was contradicted, he kept silence." "He was a kind and sensible man," testifies the Rev. Thomas Hartley, "and had something so loving and taking in his manner as highly delighted those he spoke with."

Swedenborg was fond of the society of ladies, and we have several charming pictures of his intercourse with them. On the occasion of his visit to General Tuxen, already referred to, the latter apologized that he had "no better company to amuse him than a sickly wife and her young girls. He replied, 'And is not this very good company? I was always partial to ladies' company.'" "He entertained them very politely and with much attention (this old man of eighty-two) on indifferent subjects," and seeing a harpsichord in the room, asked if they were fond of music. The daughter was persuaded to play, and Swedenborg listened appreciatively, beating time with his foot, and exclaiming when she ceased: 'Brava! you play very well. Do you not sing also?' Both mother and daughter sang some French and Italian airs and duets, to which also he beat time, afterwards complimenting Madame Tuxen on her tasteful singing and her fine voice, which she had preserved in spite of long illness."

Cuno once took Swedenborg to dine at a friend's house, where he met several highly educated ladies. "His deportment was exquisitely refined and gallant. When dinner was announced, I offered my hand to the hostess, and quickly our young man of eighty-one years had put on his gloves, and presented his hand to Mademoiselle Hoog, in doing which he looked uncommonly well. . . . Our old gentleman was seated between Madame Konauw and the elder Demoiselle Hoog, both of whom understood thoroughly well how to talk. . . . He seemed to enjoy very much to be so attentively served by the ladies."

Swedenborg, as we have said, was never married, "but," says Sandels, "this was not owing to any indifference to the sex; for he esteemed the company of a fine and intelligent woman as one of the purest sources of delight; but his profound studies required that in his house there should be perfect stillness both day and night. He, therefore, preferred being alone."

Though there was no prattle of children in his house, he often sought their company outside. Himself childlike in manner, he delighted in the society of the young and innocent. His landlady in Amsterdam remarked to Cuno: "My children will miss him most; for he never goes out without bringing them home sweets; the little rogues also dote upon the old gentleman so much that they prefer him to their own parents." As stated above, he used to carry sweetmeats in his pockets for the children he met in his walks.

A Mr. Hart of Poppin's Court, Fleet Street, was Swedenborg's printer for many years and often received the great man at his house. "He used to take particular notice of Mr. Hart's little girl," a child of about three years old at the time of his (Swedenborg's) death. "Heaven lies about us in our infancy," wrote Wordsworth; and Swedenborg had expressed the same thought many years before. Their heavenly associates doubtless drew him towards the young. He was childlike himself. "He seemed," said Shearsmith, "to lead a life like an infant, putting little value on money, and giving what people asked for their goods when he bought them."

A pretty story is told by Anders Fryxell, the Swedish historian, of a bit of pleasantry on the part of Swedenborg with a child of somewhat larger growth. "My grandmother, Sara Greta Askbom," he says, "who was married to Anders Ekman, councillor of commerce and burgomaster, had grown up in the neighbourhood of Björngårdsgatan in the Södermalm, where her father lived not far from Swedenborg, with whom he had frequent intercourse. The pretty maiden, only fifteen or sixteen years old, had often asked 'Uncle' Swedenborg to show her a spirit or an angel. At last he consented, and leading her to a summer-house in his garden, he placed her before a curtain that had been lowered, and then said, 'Now you shall see an angel'; and as he spoke, he drew up the curtain when the maiden beheld herself reflected in a mirror."

Of Swedenborg's personal habits we have many particulars. He was most temperate in eating and drinking, seldom touching flesh meat, and never taking more than two or three glasses of wine at a time, and this only in company. Shearsmith says: "As to diet, he never ate any meat, but only took milk and coffee for breakfast, and the same in the afternoon, with a few cakes, and ate no supper. . . . He was very fond of having much sugar in his milk and coffee, and of sweet cakes that had much sugar in them, saying the spirit of the sugar nourished him. . . . He was so temperate in living that he was never known to drink any wine, or beer, or spirituous liquors whatever whilst at my house. . . . He arose generally at 5 or 6 o'clock in the morning, wrote or studied until 8, when he drank about a pint of milk; afterwards, if he did not go out, he continued to study until 3 or 4 o'clock in the afternoon, when he had another pint of milk, or drank a basin of coffee for his dinner, and often went to bed at 6 or 7 in the evening, never eating any supper." "When not invited out," says Robsahm, "his dinner consisted of nothing but a roll soaked in boiled milk; and this was his meal always when he dined at home." He doubtless accommodated himself to circumstances when traveling, for Cuno tells us: "Chocolate and biscuits served in his own room usually constituted his dinner; and of this his landlord, his landlady, and the children generally received the greater part." If he had a better appetite he went into a neighbouring restaurant in the so-called "holy way." He told General Tuxen in 1770, that for twelve years past he had scarcely taken any other food than coffee and biscuits, as in his old age he was afflicted with a weak stomach. Of coffee he was very fond, and took it at all hours of the night and day, well sweetened with sugar. He was also much addicted to snuff. Hindmarsh remarks: "One advantage of his profuse snuff-taking appears to have been the preservation of his Manuscripts; for when printing his posthumous work, entitled *Apocalypsis Explicata,* I found everywhere between the leaves a sufficient quantity of snuff to prevent their being perforated and injured by those little active mites or insects, which are so destructive to old books and papers." (*Rise and Progress of the New Church,* note, p. 20.)

His habits seem to have been less regular in his own home than when in lodgings. His natural considerateness would no doubt make him conform, as far as possible, to such a mode of life as would give the least trouble to his entertainers, when abroad. But at home, Robsahm tells us: "He worked without much regard to the distinction of day and night, having no fixed time for labour or rest. 'When I am sleepy,' he said, 'I go to bed.'" Often he slept for as much as thirteen hours at a stretch, and when in a trance condition would sometimes lie in bed for several days without eating. Not long before his death, "he lay some weeks in a trance, without any sustenance; and came to himself again." At such times he desired to be left alone, telling his landlord not to be troubled, as all would be well.

The Abbé Pernety tells us that our author was "an indefatigable man who worked day and night"; and Cuno writes: "He labours in a most astonishing and superhuman manner at his new work. Sixteen sheets, in type twice as small as those used in his former works, are already printed. Only think! for every printed sheet he has to fill four sheets in manuscript. He has now two sheets printed every week. These he corrects himself; and consequently he has to write eight sheets every week." This was written on January 26, 1771, when Swedenborg was within three days of completing his eighty-third year! Counsellor Sandels exclaims: "I cannot help being filled with astonishment, in reflecting upon his extraordinary industry"; and when we remember that, in addition to nearly thirty considerable volumes and many smaller works that he published himself, he left an enormous quantity of unpublished manuscript behind him, probably equal in amount to what he had printed, we may well be astonished also, and can readily accept his brother-in-law's (Bishop Benzelius') statement that he was "most economical with his time."

With this enormous productiveness, Swedenborg's work was neither loose nor careless. Some of his more important works went through several drafts before they appeared in final form, and others were abandoned altogether because he was not satisfied with the result of his labours.

Several witnesses testify that in later years Swedenborg used no aids in his work beyond the Bible and his own carefully prepared indexes. "Although he was a learned man," says Robsahm, "no books were ever seen in his room, except his Hebrew and Greek Bible and his manuscript indexes to his own works, by which, in making quotations, he was saved the trouble of examining all that he had previously written or printed." He possessed four different editions of the Hebrew Bible, but the one from which he habitually worked, and which he took with him on his travels, was Sebastian Schmidius' with Latin translation, published at Leipzig, in 1740. This, which was underscored everywhere, he left, at his death, to the pastor of the Swedish church in London, the Rev. Arvid Ferelius, above mentioned, who also asserts that he had "no books, no, not so much as a Directory."

Swedenborg, for many years, published his theological works anonymously, and derived no benefit from their sale. His London publisher, John Lewis, of Paternoster Row, wrote, in the advertisement of the second volume of *Arcana Cœlestia,* "I do aver that this gentleman, with indefatigable pains and labour, spent one whole year in studying and writing the first volume of *Arcana Cœlestia,* was at the expense of two hundred pounds to print it, and also advanced two hundred pounds more for the printing of this second volume; and when he had done this, he gave express orders that all the money that should

271

arise in the sale of this large work should be given towards the charge of the propagation of the gospel. He is so far from desiring to make a gain of his labours, that he will not receive one farthing back of the four hundred pounds he has expended; and for that reason his works will come exceedingly cheap to the public."

According to Cuno, the public did not always get his works "exceedingly cheap," but this was not the author's fault. "He has published his manifold writings in England and in this country [Holland] entirely at his own expense; and has never gained a farthing from their sale. All these writings are printed on large and expensive paper; and yet he gives them all away. The booksellers to whom he gives them for sale charge as much for them as they can get. Indeed, they sell them dear enough, as I found out by my own experience; for I had to pay four florins and a half to the bookseller Schreuder in this town for a copy of his *Apocalypsis Revelata*. The bookseller himself, however, mentioned to me that the author never demands an account either from himself, or any other dealer."

Another little incident in connection with his publishing transactions is worth mentioning, as witnessing to his absolute truthfulness. He desired to publish his *True Christian Religion* in Paris, and submitted it to the Press Censor for his approval. Consent was given with the proviso that the title-page should declare, "as was usual," that the book was printed either in London or Amsterdam. This was not Swedenborg's way of doing things, however; so he took his MS. to Amsterdam and issued the book with an honest imprint. Most of his theological works were published in England or Holland, because in those countries "he had full liberty accorded to him to print whatever he liked; which liberty would never have been granted to him in his native town, and probably nowhere else in Christendom."

Something must be said about Swedenborg's home. It was situated in the Södermalm, the southern district of

Stockholm, and was a modest structure of wood built to suit his own convenience. Attached to it was a large garden (the whole property occupied nearly 6,000 square yards), in which were several other structures, summer-houses, an aviary, a maze, etc. One of the summer-houses was fitted up as a study, an inner room containing the owner's library; the others were furnished with movable screens, mirrors, etc., for the amusement of visitors. There was a flower garden, with curiously cut box-trees, in the Dutch manner; and an extensive kitchen garden containing choice fruit-trees, and some large and splendid limes. The whole produce of this garden, beyond his own modest requirements, Swedenborg made over to his gardener, who with his wife, composed his whole retinue.

In the flower garden Swedenborg took a personal interest, making its care a recreation from his serious labours. A Swedish biographer tells us that "with his pious child-like mind he especially attached himself to Flora's variegated and beautifully coloured children. I had occasion to see one of Swedenborg's almanacs for the year 1750, where with the same preciseness, as if it had been the beginning or close of some profound treatise, he marked down when he had planted an auricula or a pink, the time when they bloomed, how much seed he had gathered of them, and so forth." In his correspondence with Joachim Wretman of Amsterdam, we find several references to the purchase of rare plants and seeds, box-trees, etc. When Gjörwell, the Royal Librarian, called on him in 1764 to request copies of his lately published books, he found him in his garden, "where he was engaged in attending his plants, attired in a simple garment. . . . Without knowing me, or the nature of my errand, he said, smiling, 'Perhaps you would like to take a walk in the garden,'" thinking probably he was an ordinary visitor, as his garden was open to the public.

It would be impossible to imagine a more simple and unworldly man than Swedenborg. Though he had ample

273

means, he did not spend them on himself, but was content with the barest necessaries of life. He was so trustful of others that he would send his landlord to a drawer in which he kept money, to help himself to what he needed. At his death he left no will, and little property.

In his later years he always travelled alone. He told Cuno that he had no need of an attendant as his angel was always with him. Wherever he went he was beloved, and people said that he brought them good fortune. Even sea captains averred that they always had prosperous voyages when he was on board. One of them is stated to have said: "If Swedenborg chooses, he can always have a free passage with me; for during the whole of my experience at sea, I have never sailed better." Shearsmith, with whom Swedenborg lodged latterly in London, remarked that "everything went on prosperously with him, while Swedenborg lodged at his house"; and Mrs. Shearsmith told Mr. Peckitt that "he was a blessing to the house, for that they had harmony and good business while he was with them."

For some years Swedenborg seldom went to church, on which account his friends sometimes remonstrated with him, and his enemies reproached him. The reasons Robsahm assigned for his omission were that "he could not be edified by preaching which was so different from his own revelations, and partly because he suffered from the stone." Swedenborg told Ferelius that "he had no peace in the church on account of the spirits who contradicted what the minister said, especially when he treated of three persons in the Godhead, which is the same as three gods." Some Sabbatarian observed to Shearsmith that Swedenborg could not be considered a good Christian because he did not observe the Sabbath; "to which Mr. Shearsmith replied that 'to a good man like Swedenborg every day of his life was a Sabbath.'"

Swedenborg was peculiarly regardless of times and seasons. He turned night into day, and day into night, as we observed above, and did not trouble himself about the day of the week. On one occasion he called for his land-lord and asked him to have his carpet shaken, as it was covered with snuff. Shearsmith reminded him that it was Sunday, a fact of which he seemed quite oblivious; he replied to the remonstrance with "Dat be good," in his broken English, and allowed the matter to rest.

In order to throw contempt upon his theological teach-ings, unscrupulous persons have endeavoured to establish the idea that Swedenborg's mental capacity gave way in middle life. There is not a shred of evidence of either bodily or mental failure until within a few weeks of his death, except that once he suffered from fever, with the usual accompaniment of delirium. "He enjoyed," says Sandels, "a most excellent state of bodily health, having scarcely ever been indisposed." The records of the Board of Mines show that his attendance was regular when he was at home, except for occasional brief illnesses, probably colds, and such like. Even on his last journey, which he commenced in his eighty-third year, he travelled alone.

The closing scenes of Swedenborg's life are in keeping with its peaceful tenor throughout. He had no fear of death, but rather joyful anticipation. "If," he said to Cuno, "any one is conjoined with the Lord, he has a foretaste of the eternal life in this world; and if he has this, he no longer cares so much about his transitory life. Believe me, if I knew that the Lord would call me to Him-self to-morrow, I would summon the musicians to-day, in order to be once more really gay in this world." Some time before his death he foretold the date to his landlady and the maidservant who waited on him; and, the latter re-marked, he seemed as pleased at the prospect "as if he was going to have a holiday, to go to some merry-making." This was no affectation of prospective delight, nor was he weary of his natural life; for, "as he was always content with himself and with his circumstances, he spent a life which was, in every respect, happy, nay, which was happy in the very highest degree." In his *Spiritual Diary* (October 20, 1748) Swedenborg wrote: "Some think that they who are in the faith should remove from themselves all the delights of life, and all the pleasures of the body: but this I can assert, that delights and pleasures have never been denied to me; for I have been permitted to enjoy not only the pleasures of the body and the senses, like those who live (in the world), but I have also been permitted to enjoy such delights and felicities of life, as, I believe, no persons in the whole world ever before enjoyed, which were greater and more exquisite than any person could imagine and believe."

CHAPTER XIX

TESTIMONIES

IF men could only be induced to set aside their prejudices, and form an independent judgment of a writer from his own life and works, there would be little need to quote the opinions of others as to his personal character or literary merits. In the case of Swedenborg, as Dr. Beyer justly remarks in a letter to Prelate Œtinger, "the most Divine seal, and the one most suitable to the state of all men, is this, that his principles harmonize with sound reason, and that a lover of his writings will find his way cleared by their means from so many doubts and so many contradictions, and so many doctrines revolting to sound reason." But in regard to our author, prejudice is so strong that no apology is necessary for citing the testimony of his contemporaries to his high character, learning, and general reliability; and of contemporary and later witnesses to the value of the truths he taught.

First, as to character. Among all who knew him during life, whether friendly to his teachings or not, there is but one voice, that of unqualified praise. Even his most ungenerous critic is compelled to admit that "wherever Swedenborg *was known,* we find a gracious memory"; and that in him was "no vehemence, anger, nor hatred; no sarcasm, contempt, nor fretfulness. . . . Of envy he appears to have been utterly free; a malignant or a flippant sentence we shall in vain look for through all his books. If he desired fame he never left the path of good sense to look for it; and of any eccentricity, or any clap-trap for the sake of attention or admiration he was simply incapable." There are few public men of whom so much could be truthfully said.

Professor Scherer, who resided in Stockholm during Swedenborg's lifetime, testifies that "on account of his excellent character, he was universally held in high estimation"; and there are many who support his statement. Shortly after Swedenborg's death the general sentiment in regard to his character was expressed by Counsellor Sandels, in the eulogium he delivered in the House of Nobles, in the name of the Royal Academy of Sciences of Stockholm. Such a panegyric may be regarded as possibly overcharged; but, on the other hand, we must remember that Sandels was not favourable to Swedenborg's theological views, and had no interest to serve in unduly exalting the subject of his remarks. He described him as "a noble man, celebrated alike for his virtues and the depth of his knowledge, who was one of the oldest members of this Academy, and whom we all knew and loved." "The beautiful picture of his life," he said, "deserves to be carefully examined." Speaking of his appointment as a young man to the Assessorship of the Board of Mines, he remarked that "he was even then well known, both in his own country and abroad, by his acquisitions in general literature and in science and by his worthy demeanour." He refers to his "genuinely good disposition," and declares that "he deserves to be set up as a pattern of virtue and of reverence for his Maker; for in him there was no sort of double dealing." He says again, "We cannot discover in him any sign of arrogance, rashness, or intention to deceive."

The Abbé Pernety tells us: "Swedenborg was of a very gentle disposition; but he was straightforward, and would not betray the truth from respect to men, or for any other reason." "He always practised the morality he taught."

Count Höpken, writing to General Tuxen, May 21, 1773, remarks: "The late Swedenborg certainly was a pattern of sincerity, virtue, and piety, and at the same time, in my opinion, the most learned man in this kingdom"; and speaks of him elsewhere as "that honest old gentleman."

"I know," he writes in another letter, "that Swedenborg has related his *'memorabilia' bona fide.*"

John Christian Cuno, of Amsterdam, who knew Swedenborg intimately in his later years, is full of praise for his moral excellence, although he could never bring himself to accept his teachings. He speaks of him as "a righteous, just, and most learned man." He was convinced, he said, of his probity, and sincere love of the truth; and declared that he was "too honest a man deliberately to lie." He speaks of him affectionately as "dear, old, honest Mr. Swedenborg"; and says that he was irresistibly drawn towards him, notwithstanding his objections to his teachings.

Professor Atterbom, who also was sceptical in regard to Swedenborg's spiritual experiences, says that "in everything else he was a shining light of northern erudition, and a pattern of moral excellence." Kant bore similar testimony on the ground of information received from a personal friend who was acquainted with Swedenborg. "Swedenborg," he said, "is a reasonable, polite, and openhearted man: he also is a man of learning." The Rev. Nicholas Collin wrote to the Rev. John Hargrove, of Baltimore, U.S.A., the first minister of the New Church in America, under date March 16, 1801: "Swedenborg was universally esteemed for his various erudition in mathematics, mineralogy, etc., and for his probity, benevolence, and general virtue." Captain Stalhammar wrote to the *Berlinische Monatsschrift* (May 13, 1788) to correct some false statements respecting Swedenborg, which had appeared in that journal; and, while declaring that he was "far from being a follower of Swedenborg," testified thus: "The only weakness of this truly honest man was his belief in ghost-seeing; but I knew him for many years, and I can confidently affirm that he was as fully persuaded that he conversed with spirits, as I am that I am writing at this moment. As a citizen and as a friend, he was a man of the greatest integrity, abhorring imposture, and leading an exemplary life."

Sincerity and truthfulness were striking qualities in Swedenborg's character, as many who knew him have borne witness. Mrs. Hart, the wife of his London printer, told Mr. Provo that "he was of such a nature that he could impose on no one, that he always spoke the truth concerning every little matter, and that he would not have made an evasion though his life had been at stake"; and others speak to the same effect. Even his enemies could find no occasion against him in his mode of life; Bishop Filenius, inveighing against his theological teachings as "most infamous and untruthful nonsense," is compelled to admit that their author "has at all times been universally honoured, and has been distinguished for his learning in the sciences of mining and physics."

If enemies were thus subdued by the blameless and lovable character of our author, how must he have been regarded by sympathetic friends? The Rev. Thomas Hartley wrote to him (August 2, 1769): "I consider myself most highly favoured and I rejoice from my inmost heart in having had the honour, which you lately granted me, of conversing with you: and also in your having been so kind and friendly towards me who am quite unworthy of such a favour. But your charity towards the neighbour, the heavenly benignity shining from your countenance, and your childlike simplicity, devoid of all vain show and egotism, are so great, and the treasure of wisdom possessed by you is so sweetly tempered with gentleness, that it did not inspire in me a feeling of awe, but one of love, which refreshed me in my innermost heart."

Swedenborg's reply to these effusive sentiments is characteristically modest. "The friendship which you manifest in your letter," he says, "greatly pleases me; and I thank you sincerely for both, but especially for your friendship. The praises with which you overwhelm me, I receive simply as expressions of your love for the truths contained in my writings; and I refer them to the Lord, our Saviour, as their source, from Whom is everything true, because He is the Truth Itself."

In the preface to his translation of Swedenborg's *Intercourse between the Soul and the Body,* Mr. Hartley takes the opportunity of defending the character of the author. "That Mr. Swedenborg's life, qualifications, and high pretensions," he says, "have passed through a strict scrutiny in his own country, as to every part of his character, moral, civil, and divine, is not to be doubted; and that he maintains dignity, esteem, and friendship there with the great, the wise, the good, I am well informed by a gentleman of that nation, now residing in London." Speaking from his own knowledge, he says: "He has nothing of the precisian in his manner, nothing melancholy in his temper, and nothing in the least bordering upon the enthusiast in his conversation or writings, in the latter of which he delivers facts in the plain style of narrative, speaks of his converse with spirits and angels with the same coolness that he treats of earthly things, as being alike common to him; he proves all points of doctrine from Scripture testimony; always connects charity and *good life* with true faith, and is upon the whole as rational a divine as I have ever read.

"If these parts of character may be allowed to gain credit to his testimony, I think it may be pronounced concerning him, that he is the most extraordinary Messenger from God to man that has appeared on earth since the Apostolic age, and that he may properly be called the Living Apostle of these days."

Writing to the Rev. John Clowes, of Manchester, the same witness says: 'It may reasonably be supposed that I have weighed the character of our illustrious author in the scale of my best judgment, from the personal knowledge I had of him, from the best information I could procure concerning him, and from a diligent perusal of his

281

writings; and according thereto I have found him to be the sound divine, the good man, the deep philosopher, and universal scholar, and the polite gentleman; and I further believe that he had a high degree of illumination from the Spirit of God, was commissioned by Him as an extraordinary messenger to the world, and had communication with angels, and the spiritual world, beyond any since the time of the apostles."

Dr. Beyer, in defending himself before the Consistory of Gothenburg, remarked that "Swedenborg is generally known to be, as to his person and life, a God-fearing and virtuous, and also a quiet, peaceable, and well-reputed citizen; and in the public prints is declared to be a giant of learning in the various sciences; but especially is he known to have an unbounded reverence for the Divine Word. The thoughts of such a man on matters of religion," he justly observes, "ought surely not to be condemned rashly, and without a previous most thorough examination."

Dr. Messiter, writing (October 23, 1769) to the Professor of Divinity at Edinburgh University, says: "As I have had the honour of being frequently admitted to the author's company when he was in London, and to converse with him on various points of learning, I will venture to affirm that there are no parts of mathematical, philosophical, or medical knowledge, nay, I believe I might justly say, of human literature, to which he is in the least a stranger; yet so totally insensible is he of his own merit, that I am confident he does not know that he has any; and, as he himself somewhere says of the angels, he always turns his head away on the slightest encomium." To the Professor of Divinity at Glasgow, he wrote: "I can with great truth assert, that he is truly amiable in his morals, most learned, and humble in his discourse, and superlatively affable, humane, and courteous in his behaviour; and this joined with a solidity of understanding and penetration far above the level of an ordinary genius."

Thorild, the Swedish poet and metaphysician, described Swedenborg as a "man of vast and consummate learning, an honour and glory to his nation, who preserved the veneration for his genius by the truly apostolical simplicity and purity of his morals." "Dr. v. Baur, the founder of the so-called 'Tübingen School of Theology,' said to some of his students who visited him at his house, 'that Swedenborg was the greatest mortal that ever lived.' This statement," says Dr. R. L. Tafel, "was made to my father by my late uncle, Prof. Immanuel Tafel, of Tübingen, who likewise added that by the influence of Prof. v. Baur all the original editions of Swedenborg's works were bought for the University Library."

As to Swedenborg's intellectual capacity and attainments there is no dispute. Dr. Beyer remarks: "Swedenborg's works give evidence of an unexpected insight into all the so-called learned languages, as the Hebrew, Arabic, Greek, without mentioning the Latin, which knowledge with him is fully commensurate with the importance of the matters on which he treats; further, that he possesses in a remarkable degree a knowledge of various commendable and useful sciences, as, of philosophy in its most abstruse depths, of mathematics, architecture, natural history, chemistry, experimental philosophy, astronomy, history, and especially of anatomy, and others." Dr. Rosén speaks of his "most unusual learning in natural and spiritual things," and his "great and profound insight." "His works," says Count Höpken, 'everywhere sparkle with genius." Cuno writes: "No one will be able to deny that Swedenborg is a philosopher, and indeed, one of the first magnitude. . . . In the whole history of the world I have found no other scholar with whom I could compare him except the great physician and chemist Theophrastus Paracelsus." M. Matter, the author of a French life of Swedenborg, thus expresses himself: "In the whole of the last century, which produced so many eminent men, there is not one that was

283

more vigorously constituted as to body and mind than Swedenborg; and there is not one who was a more industrious, more learned, more ingenious, and more fertile writer and a more lucid teacher. Not one in the whole of that century in which Rousseau proclaimed himself to be as virtuous as any other man, was better than Swedenborg, nor more beloved, nor happier."

Of the prominent writers of the nineteenth century, many have acknowledged their indebtedness to Swedenborg; and many others, consciously or unconsciously, have adopted some of his characteristic ideas without acknowledgment.

Coleridge was very strongly drawn towards him, and spoke in the highest terms both of his philosophical and theological teachings. In a private letter, written in 1820, he said: "Of the too limited time which my ill health and the exigencies of the day leave in my power, I have given the larger portion to the works of Swedenborg, particularly to the 'Universal Theology of the New Church.' I find very few, and even those but *doubtful,* instances of tenets in which I am conscious of any substantial difference of opinion with the enlightened author." This letter may be seen in the library of the Swedenborg Society. It is a lengthy document, closely written, covering three sides of a quarto sheet. It was published at length in *The New-Church Magazine,* for March, 1897, at the time of its acquisition by the Society. Various theological subjects are discussed in it, *e.g.,* the Trinity, and the use of the word "Person" in relation to it; the Creeds, Faith, etc. To Swedenborg's teaching respecting Solifidianism, he says, "I subscribe with my whole heart and spirit." He describes this doctrine as "the Queen Bee in the Hive of Theological Error." There are several references to Swedenborg in Coleridge's *Literary Remains.* Of some parts of *The Economy of the Animal Kingdom,* he wrote: "I remember nothing in Lord Bacon superior, few passages equal, either in depth of thought, or of richness, dignity, and felicity of diction, to the weightiness of the truths contained in these articles." Speaking generally, he said: "I can venture to assert that as a moralist Swedenborg is above all praise; and that as a naturalist, psychologist, and theologian he has strong and varied claims on the gratitude and admiration of the professional and philosophical student." (Vol. iv., p. 423.)

Emerson's estimate of Swedenborg is so well known that it is hardly necessary to refer to it. Although he did not spare criticism, he was lavish in praise also. He described our author as 'one of the missouriums and mastodons of literature . . . not to be measured by whole colleges of ordinary scholars: a colossal soul, . . . [who] requires a long focal distance to be seen."

Another American writer who fell under the influence of Swedenborg was Henry James the elder. In his book, *Substance and Shadow,* he wrote: "I fully concede to Swedenborg what is usually denied him, namely, an extreme sobriety of mind displayed under all the exceptional circumstances of his career, and which ends by making us feel at last his very words to be almost insipid with veracity. . . . Such sincere books it seems to me were never before written." (P. 103.)

It was partly through Emerson, and partly through James, and partly through Dr. J. J. Garth Wilkinson, the translator into English of Swedenborg's philosophical works, that Carlyle made some acquaintance with Swedenborg's teachings. Although the fact is not generally recognized, *Sartor Resartus* is saturated with Swedenborg. On one occasion Emerson sent Carlyle a copy of *Observations on the Growth of the Mind,* by Sampson Reed, in acknowledging which the Chelsea philosopher wrote: "He is a faithful thinker, that Swedenborgian druggist of yours, with really deep ideas, which makes me, too, pause and think, were it only to consider what manner of man *he* must be, and

285

what manner of thing, after all, Swedenborgianism must be." (*Correspondence of Carlyle and Emerson,* vol. i., p. 19.) About the same time he wrote to Dr. Wilkinson "a beautiful letter," in which he said: "Hitherto I have known nearly nothing of Swedenborg; or indeed, I might say less than nothing, having been wont to picture him as an amiable but inane visionary, with affections quite out of proportion to his insight; from whom nothing at all was to be learned. It is so we judge of extraordinary men. But I have been rebuked already. A little book, by one Sampson Reed, of Boston, in New England, which some friend sent hither, taught me that a Swedenborgian might have thoughts of the calmest kind on the deepest things; that, in short, I did *not* know Swedenborg, and ought to be ready to know him."

Many years later, he wrote to a lady who drew his attention to his unfair classification of Swedenborgians with mesmerists, magicians, cabalists, etc., in his essay on Cagliostro (published in 1833, the year in which he first met Emerson) expressing regret for the libel, and explaining that he spoke in ignorance and "from mere common hearsay." "I have since," he said, "made some personal acquaintance with the man; read several of his books, what biographies of him could be heard of, and have reflected for myself on the singular appearance he makes in the world, and the notable message he was sent to deliver to his fellow-creatures in that epoch. A man of great and indisputable cultivation, strong mathematical intellect, and the most pious, seraphic turn of mind—a man beautiful, lovable, and tragical to me, with many thoughts in him, which, when I interpret them for myself, I find to belong to the high and perennial in human thought." In William Allingham's published *Diary,* there are several references to conversations with Carlyle about Swedenborg; also with Tennyson and Professor A. R. Wallace. The writer speaks more than once of his own studies of Swedenborg.

It would be impossible even to mention the names of all the recent writers who show the influence of Swedenborg in their works: Tennyson, the Brownings, and Coventry Patmore, of English poets, exhibit it most strongly, while the writings of Ruskin, George Macdonald, Henry Drummond, Oliver Wendell Holmes, Thoreau, Elizabeth Stuart Phelps, Goethe, Heine, and Balzac are all more or less tinctured with his ideas. Some of them have spoken in the highest terms of his teachings, and others have quoted striking passages from his works with approval.

Balzac's interest in Swedenborg is well known, and is manifested in several of his novels. He makes one of his characters say: "I have returned to Swedenborg after vast studies of all religions; after convincing myself, by all the books which patient Germany, England, and France have published during the last sixty years, of the profound truth of my youthful perceptions of the Bible. Beyond a doubt, Swedenborg gathers to himself all religions, or rather the young religions of humanity. . . . Though his books are diffuse and obscure, they hold the elements of a vast social conception. His theology is sublime; and his religion is the only one a superior mind can accept. He alone enables man to touch God; he creates a thirst for Him; he rescues the majesty of God from the swaddling-clothes in which other human faiths have muffled it."

The view that Swedenborg's books are "diffuse and obscure" is a common one, but is not shared by all who are acquainted with them. R. A. Vaughan, in his *Hours with the Mystics,* expresses an exactly contrary opinion. He says:

"The thoughts of Swedenborg have never to struggle for expression, like those of the half-educated Behmen. The mind of the Swedish seer was of the methodical and scientific cast. His style is calm and clear. . . . He describes with the minuteness of Defoe. Nothing is lost in cloud. . . . He is never amazed, he never exaggerates. He is unimpassioned, and wholly careless of effect. . . . Swedenborg never pants and strives,—has none of the tearful vehemence and glowing emotion which choke the utterance of Behmen. He is never familiar in this page, and rhapsodical in that. Always serene, this imperturbable philosopher is the Olympian Jove of mystics. He writes like a man who was sufficient to himself; who could afford to wait. . . . Strong and deep is the stream of this mysticism which carries no fleck of foam." (Vol. ii., p. 279 (Edition 1856).)

"He sets up no doctrine based on arbitrary or fantastical interpretations. His doctrinal system is drawn from the literal sense, and calmly . . . deduced, by citation, exegesis, and comparison of passages, without any mysticism whatever. Thus the balance between the letter and the spirit is maintained in his theology with a fairness almost unparalleled in the history of mysticism." (Vol. ii., p. 275.)

It is not generally known how greatly the Brownings, especially Mrs. Browning, were imbued with Swedenborg's ideas. *Aurora Leigh* is full of thoughts culled from his books. Mrs. Browning makes no secret of her indebtedness to our author: in her published *Letters* she frequently mentions him. We learn that the winter of 1852-3 was spent in meditation on Swedenborg's philosophy (vol. ii., p. 141) ; and, in October of the latter year, she wrote to Miss I. Blagden: "I shall get at Swedenborg in Rome, and get on with my readings. There are deep truths in him, I cannot doubt, though I can't receive *everything,* which may be my fault." It is evident that as her studies continued, her conviction of the truth of his teachings deepened; until in March, 1859, she uses the phrase "we Swedenborgians," thus including herself, and possibly her husband, in the category of his disciples.

Coventry Patmore is another poet who has made frank acknowledgment of his indebtedness to Swedenborg. Mr. Edmund Gosse, in his recently published *Life of Patmore,* quotes a remarkable letter of which the following is an extract: "I never tire of reading Swedenborg; he is unfathomably profound and yet simple. I came on a passage . . . which I don't know how to admire enough for its surpassing insight into truth. . . . You will think it all very odd at first, but after you have got used to the queerness, you will find that it abounds with perception of the truth to a degree unparalleled perhaps in uninspired writing." (P. 192.)

It will be evident that Swedenborg's influence is by no means to be measured by the number of his professed followers. His teachings are taking hold of men's minds, and directing the current of modern thought silently but surely. "Swedenborg," writes James Freeman Clarke, "became the organ of a spiritual philosophy, the power of which is hardly yet understood, but which seems likely to leaven all religious thought." Emerson also perceived this. "The most remarkable step in the religious history of recent ages," he said, "is that made by the genius of Swedenborg. . . . These truths passing out of his system into general circulation, are now met with every day, qualifying the views and creeds of all churches, and of men of no church." The reason of this is put succinctly in a phrase by Henry James, the elder, who says that Swedenborg "grasped with clear and intellectual vision the seminal principles of things."

While many recognize that Swedenborg's teachings form a powerful element in the development of modern thought, only those are able fully to appreciate them whose moral and spiritual natures as well as their mental faculties are appealed to by him. Such are irresistibly drawn to him. Thus Dr. Beyer, writing to Swedenborg himself, says: "I refrain from describing to you the joy I have often experienced, and how the glorious truths are beginning to shine before me"; while to Prelate Œtinger he wrote: "Surely mankind never received the revelation of heavenly and Divine Truths with greater marks of certainty than the present." General Tuxen thus expressed himself: "It appears to me that no system of divinity is more worthy of the dignity of God, or more consolatory to man; and by the Divine help I will always retain this thought in my mind, until I can be convinced that any part thereof is either contrary to the Word and Scriptures of God, or to sound reason."

Thus, on the testimony of the best informed and most reliable witnesses, Swedenborg was a man of extraordinary intellectual powers, of perfect sincerity and integrity, and of undoubted sanity, even to the very end of his life. His teachings, therefore, are entitled to the fullest consideration. This they would doubtless have received in a greater degree, had their author not put forward a claim to special enlightenment, and declared that he was the Divinely appointed teacher of truths for a new dispensation. This has been justly described as "an awful claim"; but its seeming presumption should not debar us from giving it a candid examination. We must ask ourselves if the state of the world in Swedenborg's time was such as to call for Divine intervention; and if the doctrines he propounded were so high and holy that their gift to the world may be regarded as constituting the descent of the New Jerusalem from God out of heaven; for thus, he tells us, the prophecy of the Apocalypse has been fulfilled.

When Swedenborg proclaimed that a new age was dawning upon the world, there were few signs of its approach. The moral condition of civilized society was very low, and the Church was sunk in formalism and apathy. Such efforts at betterment, as were made, came for the most part from outside the Church, and were often revolutionary in character. They were concerned with the reform of old abuses, the abolition of unjust privileges, and the assertion of the natural rights of man; thus touching only external evils. The intellectual forces at work were largely critical and disintegrating, and literature generally was lacking in motive and ideal. No one at the time could have foreseen the tremendous changes that have since taken place. These changes has been most noticeable on the material plane, but there have been great spiritual movements also, both moral and intellectual. The moral movements have been chiefly in the direction of a widening of human sympathy; the intellectual ones, often negative or rationalistic, although the philosophy of religion has been substantially advanced by various thinkers. At the present time, the Churches are in a condition of unrest: one by one the old doctrines, which used to be considered as the very essentials of the Christian religion have been overthrown by destructive criticism, and the cry is for a new theology to take their place.

Swedenborg alone offers a new constructive theology to the world, and gives satisfactory answers to the questions that every one is asking in regard to the fundamental doctrines of the Christian religion. His teachinges are exactly suited to meet the needs of the age. On all questions Swedenborg gives us definite teachings of the utmost value. He teaches a rational doctrine of the Incarnation of the one God; he shows us wherein the Divinity of the Word consists, and throws a revealing light upon its mysteries; in the doctrine of *use,* he provides a new impulse and inspiration for the regeneration of society; and in his revelation of the nature of life in the spiritual world, he gives all the knowledge that is so eagerly sought after, and the lack of which sends men and women to spirit mediums, and other illicit sources of information. The spiritual psychology of man, the creation of the world, the universality of Divine Providence receive in his works a new and comprehensive form. He does not propound these teachings as his own, but constantly avers that he wrote under the direction and guidance of the Lord, describing himself humbly as "Servant of the Lord Jesus Christ."

Swedenborg's influence is steadily growing, and is destined to become greater as the years go by, for mankind is hungering for the truth he offers, and must in the end come to him. "The fact is," as Dr. Wilkinson has so forcibly expressed it, "that an unbelieving age could see nothing in Swedenborg; that its successor, more trustful and truthful, sees more and more; and strong indications exist that in another five-and-twenty years the field occupied by this author must be visited by the leaders of opinion *en masse,* and whether they will or no; because it is not proselytism that will take them there, but the expansion and culmination of the truth, and the organic course of events." More than thrice twenty-five years have passed since these words were written; but, though the fulfilment of the prophecy has been delayed, it is being gradually realized in our own time.

INDEX

293

Brief Descriptions of
THE THEOLOGICAL WRITINGS
OF EMANUEL SWEDENBORG

These books may be ordered through your nearest bookshop or direct from—

SWEDENBORG FOUNDATION, INC.
139 East 23 Street
New York, N. Y.   10010

Complete catalogue and current price list sent free on request.

Apocalypse Explained, 3562 pages, 6 volumes.

This work is the largest of the author's expository writings except for the Arcana Coelestia. It sets forth the spiritual (symbolic) sense of the Book of Revelation up to chapter 19, verse 10, and in connection with that, the inner meaning of many other parts of the Scriptures, especially the Psalms, the Prophets and the Gospels. Towards its close, extensive and practical doctrinal discussions are introduced.

Apocalypse Revealed, 1105 pages, 2 volumes.

In contrast with the work just described, the Apocalypse Revealed, concentrates upon the exposition of the spiritual (symbolic) sense of the Book of Revelation, without the many excursions into other Scripture. It is the work, therefore, to which the reader would turn first for the profound meaning in this dramatic book of the New Testament. That meaning is as dramatic as all else in the book, and gives one a vision of the end of a first Christian age, of the conditions at that time in Christianity, of the falling of judgment upon these, and of the steps then taken by the Lord in pursuance of His promise to make all things new.

Arcana Coelestia (Heavenly Secrets), 7103 pages, 12 volumes.

Volume 1—An exposition of the spiritual sense of the first nine chapters of Genesis showing that the stories of Creation, Eden, the Flood and the Ark are symbolic renderings of everlasting truth and religious experience.

Volume 2–12—Continue the exposition of Genesis and also unfold the meaning of Exodus.

Conjugal Love, 612 pages.

Swedenborg's monumental work on marriage published in 1768 when he was eighty years of age. This book treats of the relation of the sexes and of the sex extending to the spirit, of the nature and origin of love truly conjugal (marital) and of its indissoluble nature, of the marriage of the Lord and the Church and its spiritual significance, of sexual irregularities and the avoidance of them.

Divine Love and Wisdom, 293 pages.

This book is an interpretation of the universe as a spiritual-natural or psychophysical world. It treats of the activity of God's love and wisdom in the creation of this world and of the human being, who is similarly constituted.

Divine Providence, 392 pages.

Another profound philosophical work, revealing the law abiding ways and merciful means by which God, in His immanence, cares for the individual and for mankind, enlisting man's choices and conscience to bring him to His goal, a heaven from the human race.

Earths in the Universe, 106 pages.

This little book recounts what Swedenborg learned from spirits in the other world about the inhabitants of other planets. This revelation was permitted to assure men that other earths are inhabited and to give them some idea of the infinite operation of the Divine Love and Wisdom. It also contains a chapter which gives the reasons why the Lord was born on this earth and not on another.

End of the Age, 90 pages.

It describes the end of the age as foretold in the Gospel of Matthew, and consists of extracts from the *Arcana Coelestia*.

Four Doctrines, 388 pages.

Swedenborg restates in this work four leading doctrines of the Christian religion: The Lord, The Sacred Scriptures, Life and Faith. These doctrines are drawn from, and substantiated by numerous passages from the divine Word, examined as a unified whole.

Intercourse of the Soul and the Body, 61 pages.

As indicated by the title, this work deals with the relationship between the soul and the body. Also discussed are the related subjects of the spiritual and natural suns, the influx and reception of life, how the spiritual clothes itself with the natural, and the distinction between men and animals.

Miscellaneous Theological Works, 634 pages.

Bound together in this volume are the following treatises: The New Jerusalem and Its Heavenly Doctrine; A Brief Exposition of the Doctrine of the New Church; The Nature of the Intercourse between the Soul and the Body; On the White Horse Mentioned in the Apocalypse; On the Earths in the Universe; The Last Judgment (on a first Christian era) ; and A Continuation Concerning The Last Judgment.

New Jerusalem and its Heavenly Doctrine, 221 pages.

This book consists of a brief exposition of the principal teachings of the Writings, especially the *Arcana Coelestia*, and is an excellent introductory work. It teaches from the Word how a man must live in order to be saved, showing that no one who believes in God and lives well, whatever his religion, is condemned.

Posthumous Theological Works, 634 pages, 2 volumes.

These two volumes include a number of the small posthumous works which had not previously been brought together in a form convenient for use. Included in the volumes are a number of extracts from Swedenborg's correspondence.

Spiritual Diary, 5 volumes.
Volume 1
New Translation.

Volume 2–5   Offset reprint of old edition.

The *Diary* is a storehouse of spiritual facts, phenomena and principles which Swedenborg wrote at the time of his other-world experiences.

The Spiritual Life, The Word of God, 160 pages.

This volume consists of some extracts from Swedenborg's *The Apocalypse Explained* and makes devotional reading on the spiritual or regenerating life, the significance of the Ten Commandments, our possible profanation of good and truth, and the power of God's Word.

True Christian Religion, 1098 pages, 2 volumes.

This is Swedenborg's crowning work giving a complete and connected exposition of the doctrines of the New Christian Era. A powerful and massive presentation dealing with a broad spectrum of modern Christian concerns. It draws upon more than nine hundred passages from all parts of the Bible.

OTHER TITLES

Gist of Swedenborg, by Julian K. Smyth & William F. Wunsch, 110 pages.

A compilation of excellently chosen and well arranged quotations from Swedenborg's Works, dealing with a broad spectrum of modern Christian concerns such as God, Man, Regeneration, Marriage, Charity and Faith, Divine Providence, Death and the Resurrection, Heaven, Hell, The Church.

Introduction to Swedenborg's Religious Thought, by John Howard Spalding, 235 pages.

A new edition, revised by Richard H. Tafel. A clear, comprehensive and forcefully reasoned presentation of Swedenborg's teachings by a British layman and scientist.

Marital Love, 760 pages.

The 1938 translation by William F. Wunsch of Swedenborg's *Conjugial Love* on the basis of a re-edited original Latin text. See page 2 for description of content.

My Religion, by Helen Keller, 208 pages.

The beautifully written and inspiring account of the help which the teachings of Swedenborg have been to Miss Keller from her early years onward.

The Swedenborg Epic, by Cyriel O. Sigstedt, 501 pages.

A thorough chronological biography of Swedenborg with interesting sidelights of his impact on contemporaries. Of general appeal to the reading public and a valuable student's source-book.

Swedenborg: Life and Teachings, by George Trobridge, 300 pages.

The most widely read biography of Emanuel Swedenborg, with summaries not only of his Theological Works but also of his Scientific and Philosophical Works.